SECRET CHURCH

KNOW HIS WORD. KNOW HIS PERSECUTED.

For millions of believers around the world, faith
in Christ and belief in the teachings of the Bible
are not only discouraged but actually dangerous.

KNOW HIS WORD.
KNOW HIS PERSECUTED.

Periodically, Secret Church gatherings are held
to engage in an intense six-hour Bible study as we
identify with and pray for our persecuted brothers
and sisters around the globe.

The objective of Secret Church is for you to pass
along what you learn in these gatherings to others
so that you can make disciples of Christ
in all nations for God's glory.

secretchurch.org

What Is Secret Church?

Secret Church began at The Church Brook Hills based on time Dr. Platt had spent with brothers and sisters in underground Asian house churches. In those contexts, they gather together at the risk of their lives for 8-12 hours at a time simply to pray, worship, and study the Word. It's simple, raw, dangerous, and satisfying … all at the same time.

The leaders at Brook Hills began asking if they could do the same thing and decided to try it. They set up a Friday evening where people could gather from 6 p.m. until midnight for two main purposes: to worship through intensive study of the Word, and to identify with our persecuted brothers and sisters by praying intentionally for them. Simply six hours of straight teaching and prayer.

At the first gathering there were about 1,000 people, and after that it began to grow. Secret Church now takes place with thousands of believers joined together in homes church buildings, and other locations all around the world. One of Dr. Platt's favorit sights as a pastor is to look out across a room packed with people at midnight with their Bibles open, just soaking in the Word of God.

Beyond These Walls

We're glad you've decided to attend tonight's Secret Church meeting. But even if no one showed up, it would still be worth the effort. Actually, this Bible study will hopefully benefit far more people than just those who were in attendance.

Here's how ...

Tonight we will record the teaching sessions, and in the coming months these sessions will be transcribed and translated into many different languages, including Spanish, Mandarin, Hindi, Arabic, and others. The foreign-language versions of Secret Church will be available online as translations are completed. But that is just the beginning.

Most Christ-followers around the world don't have access to seminaries or Bible colleges. In fact, Christ-followers in many parts of the world have no formal Christian teaching at all. Pastor David will lead additional Secret Church studies, creating numerous hours of Bible teaching on various biblical and theological issues. We will then be able to distribute those resources worldwide. The sessions together will compose a portable seminary, so to speak, with minicourses in biblical training accessible to anyone.

At each Secret Church gathering we collect an offering. All the proceeds will support persecuted Christians worldwide through ongoing ministry initiatives and provide Secret Church Bible-teaching materials in multiple languages. Imagine a house-church leader in Asia or the Middle East, now able to hear hours of Bible teaching as he listens to Secret Church in his own language. With your help, this can become a reality.

If you would like to make a donation to Secret Church or would like any of the Secret Church resources in another language, go to Radical.net.

Program

5:00 p.m.	Simulcast Begins
6:00 p.m.	Announcements
6:05 p.m.	Welcome from Pastor David
6:10 p.m.	Musical Worship
6:30 p.m.	Teaching Segment 1
7:30 p.m.	Break
7:45 p.m.	Teaching Segment 2
8:45 p.m.	Persecuted Church Highlight
9:00 p.m.	Prayer for the Persecuted Church
9:20 p.m.	Break
9:35 p.m.	Teaching Segment 3
10:35 p.m.	Giving Report/Offering*
10:45 p.m.	Break
11:05 p.m.	Teaching Segment 4
11:50 p.m.	Musical Worship
12:00 p.m.	Simulcast Concludes

(Times are approximate, and the schedule is subject to change.)

Program Notes:

Pastor David will be teaching tonight from the English Standard Version (ESV). Scriptures and references are included in the Study Guide.

So as not to distract from the study, please turn all cell phones to the "silent" or "off" mode during our time together.

* If you are attending a simulcast of Secret Church and your host site is taking up an offering we encourage you to participate with them in your giving. If you would like to give to the Secret Church Offering directly you can give online by going to Radical.net/Offering.

HEAVEN, HELL, AND THE END OF THE WORLD
Secret Church

Where We Need To Begin ...

- We need to __Pause__.
    - We are continually blinded by the temporal.
    - We are subtly numbed by the trivial.
    - We desperately need to contemplate the eternal.

"Let no one apologize for the powerful emphasis Christianity lays upon the doctrine of the world to come. Right there lies its immense superiority to everything else within the whole sphere of human thought or experience. When Christ arose from death and ascended into heaven He established forever three important facts; namely, that this world has been condemned to ultimate dissolution, that the human spirit persists beyond the grave and that there is indeed a world to come .... The church is constantly being tempted to accept this world as her home, and sometimes she has listened to the blandishments of those who would woo her away and use her for their own ends. But if she is wise she will consider that she stands in the valley between the mountain peaks of eternity past and eternity to come. The past is gone forever and the present is passing as swift as the shadow on the sundial of Ahaz. Even if the earth should continue a million years, not one of us could stay to enjoy it. We do well to think of the long tomorrow."
A.W. Tozer

We need to listen with __humility__.

> *Heaven and earth will pass away, but my words will not pass away.*
> *Matthew 24:35*

- Let's minimize the thoughts of man and magnify the truth of God.

> *Who has ascended to heaven and come down? ... Surely you know!*
> *Proverbs 30:4*

> *No one has ascended into heaven except he who descended from heaven, the Son of Man.*
> *John 3:13*

- Let's lay aside our traditions and submit to God's Word.

> *Then Pharisees and scribes came to Jesus from Jerusalem and said, "Why do your disciples break the tradition of the elders? For they do not wash their hands when they eat." He answered them, "And why do you break the commandment of God for the sake of your tradition? For God commanded, 'Honor your father and your mother,' and, 'Whoever reviles father or mother must surely die.' But you say, 'If anyone tells his father or his mother, "What*

you would have gained from me is given to God," he need not honor his father.'
So for the sake of your tradition you have made void the word of God."
Matthew 15:1-6

○ Let's leave room for disagreement over secondary (and tertiary) doctrines while celebrating agreement on primary doctrines.

I therefore, a prisoner for the Lord, urge you to walk in a manner worthy of the calling to which you have been called, with all humility and gentleness, with patience, bearing with one another in love, eager to maintain the unity of the Spirit in the bond of peace. There is one body and one Spirit—just as you were called to the one hope that belongs to your call—one Lord, one faith, one baptism, one God and Father of all, who is over all and through all and in all.
Ephesians 4:1-6

- Theological Triage …
  - Christians divide from non-Christians over primary doctrines, and Christians are willing to ___die___ for these doctrines.
  - Churches _____ themselves from one another over secondary doctrines, yet they partner together around primary doctrines.
  - Christians in the same church disagree with one another over tertiary doctrines, but it does not in any way _____ the intimacy of their fellowship with one another.
- Guiding Principle …
  - In essentials, unity.
  - In non-essentials, liberty.
- We need to live with ___eargencey___.

"Resolved, to endeavor to my utmost to act as I can think I should do, if I had already seen the happiness of heaven, and hell torments."
Jonathan Edwards

○ With a height of confidence that has no fear in the face of the future.

For to me to live is Christ, and to die is gain.
Philippians 1:21

○ With a breadth of ___Compassion___ that compels us to lay down our lives for the lost.

I am speaking the truth in Christ—I am not lying; my conscience bears me witness in the Holy Spirit—that I have great sorrow and unceasing anguish

in my heart. For I could wish that I myself were accursed and cut off from
Christ for the sake of my brothers, my kinsmen according to the flesh.
Romans 9:1-3

Therefore, since we are surrounded by so great a cloud of witnesses, let us also lay aside
every weight, and sin which clings so closely, and let us run with endurance the race
that is set before us, looking to Jesus, the founder and perfecter of our faith, who for
the joy that was set before him endured the cross, despising the shame, and is seated
at the right hand of the throne of God. Consider him who endured from sinners
such hostility against himself, so that you may not grow weary or fainthearted.
Hebrews 12:1-3

○ With a depth of courage that defies death in this world.

"'I know your tribulation and your poverty (but you are rich) and the slander
of those who say that they are Jews and are not, but are a synagogue of Satan.
Do not fear what you are about to suffer. Behold, the devil is about to throw
some of you into prison, that you may be tested, and for ten days you will have
tribulation. Be faithful unto death, and I will give you the crown of life.'"
Revelation 2:9-10

▪ May loyalty to God be more important to us than **life** itself.

And I heard a loud voice in heaven, saying, "Now the salvation and the power
and the kingdom of our God and the authority of his Christ have come, for the
accuser of our brothers has been thrown down, who accuses them day and night
before our God. And they have conquered him by the blood of the Lamb and by
the word of their testimony, for they loved not their lives even unto death."
Revelation 12:10-11

• Hear the testimony of Old Testament saints …

These all died in faith, not having received the things promised, but having seen them and
greeted them from afar, and having acknowledged that they were strangers and exiles on
the earth. For people who speak thus make it clear that they are seeking a homeland. If
they had been thinking of that land from which they had gone out, they would have had
opportunity to return. But as it is, they desire a better country, that is, a heavenly one.
Therefore God is not ashamed to be called their God, for he has prepared for them a city.
Hebrews 11:13-16

Some were tortured, refusing to accept release, so that they might rise again
to a better life. Others suffered mocking and flogging, and even chains and
imprisonment. They were stoned, they were sawn in two, they were killed with
the sword. They went about in skins of sheep and goats, destitute, afflicted,
mistreated—of whom the world was not worthy—wandering about in deserts and

mountains, and in dens and caves of the earth. And all these, though commended through their faith, did not receive what was promised, since God had provided something better for us, that apart from us they should not be made perfect.
Hebrews 11:35-40

• Hear the testimony of New Testament apostles …

But Peter and the apostles answered, "We must obey God rather than men."
Acts 5:29

… and when they had called in the apostles, they beat them and charged them not to speak in the name of Jesus, and let them go. Then they left the presence of the council, rejoicing that they were counted worthy to suffer dishonor for the name. And every day, in the temple and from house to house, they did not cease teaching and preaching that the Christ is Jesus.
Acts 5:40-42

But when the disciples gathered about him, he rose up and entered the city, and on the next day he went on with Barnabas to Derbe. When they had preached the gospel to that city and had made many disciples, they returned to Lystra and to Iconium and to Antioch, strengthening the souls of the disciples, encouraging them to continue in the faith, and saying that through many tribulations we must enter the kingdom of God.
Acts 14:20-22

"And now, behold, I am going to Jerusalem, constrained by the Spirit, not knowing what will happen to me there, except that the Holy Spirit testifies to me in every city that imprisonment and afflictions await me. But I do not account my life of any value nor as precious to myself, if only I may finish my course and the ministry that I received from the Lord Jesus, to testify to the gospel of the grace of God."
Acts 20:22-24

Then Paul answered, "What are you doing, weeping and breaking my heart? For I am ready not only to be imprisoned but even to die in Jerusalem for the name of the Lord Jesus."
Acts 21:13

Are they servants of Christ? I am a better one—I am talking like a madman—with far greater labors, far more imprisonments, with countless beatings, and often near death. Five times I received at the hands of the Jews the forty lashes less one. Three times I was beaten with rods. Once I was stoned. Three times I was shipwrecked; a night and a day I was adrift at sea; on frequent journeys, in danger from rivers, danger from robbers, danger from my own people, danger from Gentiles, danger in the city, danger in the wilderness, danger at sea, danger from false brothers; in toil and hardship, through many a sleepless night, in hunger and thirst, often without food, in cold and exposure.
2 Corinthians 11:23-27

- Hear the testimony of martyrs throughout history …

"Matthew suffered martyrdom by being slain with a sword at a distant city of Ethiopia. Mark expired at Alexandria, after being cruelly dragged through the streets of that city. Luke was hanged upon an olive tree in the classic land of Greece. John was put in a cauldron of boiling oil, but escaped death in a miraculous manner, and was afterward banished to Patmos. Peter was crucified at Rome with his head downward. James, the Greater, was beheaded at Jerusalem. James, the Less, was thrown from a lofty pinnacle of the temple, and then beaten to death with a fuller's club. Bartholomew was flayed alive. Andrew was bound to a cross, whence he preached to his persecutors until he died. Thomas was run through the body with a lance at Coromandel in the East Indies. Jude was shot to death with arrows. Matthias was first stoned and then beheaded. Barnabas of the Gentiles was stoned to death at Salonica. Paul, after various tortures and persecutions, was at length beheaded at Rome by the Emperor Nero."
Author Unknown

"No one makes us afraid or leads us into captivity as we have set our faith on Jesus. For though we are beheaded, and crucified, and exposed to beasts and chains and fire and all other forms of torture, it is plain that we do not forsake the confession of our faith, but the more things of this kind which happen to us the more are there others who become believers … through the name of Jesus."
Justin Martyr

"The blood of the martyrs is the seed of the Church."
Tertullian

"Never did the church so much prosper and so truly thrive as when she was baptized in the blood. The ship of the church never sails so gloriously along as when the bloody spray of her martyrs falls on her deck. We must suffer and we must die, if we are ever to conquer this world for Christ."
Charles Spurgeon

"We do not know the value of Christ, if we will not cleave to Him unto death!"
Robert Murray McCheyne

- Hear the words of Jesus …

"So have no fear of them, for nothing is covered that will not be revealed, or hidden that will not be known. What I tell you in the dark, say in the light, and what you hear whispered, proclaim on the housetops. And do not fear those who kill the body but cannot kill the soul. Rather fear him who can destroy both soul and body in hell."
Matthew 10:26-28

o _____ with an eternal perspective.

If then you have been raised with Christ, seek the things that are above, where Christ is, seated at the right hand of God. Set your minds on things that are above, not on things that are on earth. For you have died, and your life is hidden with Christ in God. When Christ who is your life appears, then you also will appear with him in glory.
Colossians 3:1-4

○ Speak with a holy boldness.

"But you will receive power when the Holy Spirit has come upon you, and you will be my witnesses in Jerusalem and in all Judea and Samaria, and to the end of the earth."
Acts 1:8

Therefore do not be ashamed of the testimony about our Lord, nor of me his prisoner, but share in suffering for the gospel by the power of God, who saved us and called us to a holy calling, not because of our works but because of his own purpose and grace, which he gave us in Christ Jesus before the ages began, and which now has been manifested through the appearing of our Savior Christ Jesus, who abolished death and brought life and immortality to light through the gospel, for which I was appointed a preacher and apostle and teacher, which is why I suffer as I do. But I am not ashamed, for I know whom I have believed, and I am convinced that he is able to guard until that Day what has been entrusted to me.
2 Timothy 1:8-12

○ _____ with reckless abandonment.

"And whoever does not take his cross and follow me is not worthy of me. Whoever finds his life will lose it, and whoever loses his life for my sake will find it."
Matthew 10:38-39

■ May mission in the world be more important to us than _____ in our churches.

And Jesus came and said to them, "All authority in heaven and on earth has been given to me. Go therefore and make disciples of all nations, baptizing them in the name of the Father and of the Son and of the Holy Spirit, teaching them to observe all that I have commanded you. And behold, I am with you always, to the end of the age."
Matthew 28:18-20

"Then they will deliver you up to tribulation and put you to death, and you will be hated by all nations for my name's sake. And then many will fall away and betray one another and hate one another. And many false prophets will arise and lead many astray. And because lawlessness will be increased, the love of many will grow cold. But the one who endures to the end will be saved. And this gospel of the kingdom will be proclaimed throughout the whole world as a testimony to all nations, and then the end will come."
Matthew 24:9-14

"When you know the truth about what happens to you after you die, and you believe it, and you are satisfied with all that God will be for you in the ages to come, that truth makes you free indeed. Free from the short, shallow, suicidal pleasures of sin, and free for the sacrifices of mission and ministry that cause people to give glory to our Father in heaven."
John Piper

• We need to pray.

> *When he saw the crowds, he had compassion for them, because they were harassed and helpless, like sheep without a shepherd. Then he said to his disciples, "The harvest is plentiful, but the laborers are few; therefore pray earnestly to the Lord of the harvest to send out laborers into his harvest."*
> *Matthew 9:36-38*

   o Our lives are at stake for eternity.
   o _____ lives are at stake forever.

> *Then I saw a great white throne and him who was seated on it. From his presence earth and sky fled away, and no place was found for them. And I saw the dead, great and small, standing before the throne, and books were opened. Then another book was opened, which is the book of life. And the dead were judged by what was written in the books, according to what they had done. And the sea gave up the dead who were in it, Death and Hades gave up the dead who were in them, and they were judged, each one of them, according to what they had done. Then Death and Hades were thrown into the lake of fire. This is the second death, the lake of fire. And if anyone's name was not found written in the book of life, he was thrown into the lake of fire.*
> *Revelation 20:11-15*

How We Plan To Proceed ...

• The Fragility of Life and the Finality of Death
• The Intermediate State
• The Return of Christ
• The Resurrection of the Dead
• The Final Judgment
• The Horror of Hell
• The Hope of Heaven
• Three Controversial Questions in Revelation
   o What does this book mean and why do we have it?
   o What is the millennium and when will it happen?
   o What is the tribulation and who will experience it?
• Seven Critical Conclusions from Revelation

THE FRAGILITY OF LIFE AND THE FINALITY OF DEATH

So teach us to number our days that we may get a heart of wisdom.
Psalm 90:12

Eight General Foundations ...

• Life is _precious_ .

Then God said, "Let us make man in our image, after our likeness. And let them have dominion over the fish of the sea and over the birds of the heavens and over the livestock and over all the earth and over every creeping thing that creeps on the earth." So God created man in his own image, in the image of God he created him; male and female he created them. And God blessed them. And God said to them, "Be fruitful and multiply and fill the earth and subdue it, and have dominion over the fish of the sea and over the birds of the heavens and over every living thing that moves on the earth." And God said, "Behold, I have given you every plant yielding seed that is on the face of all the earth, and every tree with seed in its fruit. You shall have them for food. And to every beast of the earth and to every bird of the heavens and to everything that creeps on the earth, everything that has the breath of life, I have given every green plant for food." And it was so. And God saw everything that he had made, and behold, it was very good. And there was evening and there was morning, the sixth day.
Genesis 1:26-31

... then the LORD God formed the man of dust from the ground and breathed into his nostrils the breath of life, and the man became a living creature. And the LORD God planted a garden in Eden, in the east, and there he put the man whom he had formed. And out of the ground the LORD God made to spring up every tree that is pleasant to the sight and good for food. The tree of life was in the midst of the garden, and the tree of the knowledge of good and evil.
Genesis 2:7-9

"You clothed me with skin and flesh, and knit me together with bones and sinews. You have granted me life and steadfast love, and your care has preserved my spirit."
Job 10:11-12

Yet you are he who took me from the womb; you made me trust you at my mother's breasts. On you was I cast from my birth, and from my mother's womb you have been my God.
Psalm 22:9-10

For you formed my inward parts; you knitted me together in my mother's womb. I praise you, for I am fearfully and wonderfully made. Wonderful are your works; my soul knows it very well. My frame was not hidden from you, when I was being made in secret, intricately woven in the depths of the earth.

Your eyes saw my unformed substance; in your book were written, every one of
them, the days that were formed for me, when as yet there was none of them.
Psalm 139:13-16

• Life is valuable.

When I look at your heavens, the work of your fingers, the moon and the stars, which you
have set in place, what is man that you are mindful of him, and the son of man that you
care for him? Yet you have made him a little lower than the heavenly beings and crowned
him with glory and honor. You have given him dominion over the works of your hands;
you have put all things under his feet, all sheep and oxen, and also the beasts of the field,
the birds of the heavens, and the fish of the sea, whatever passes along the paths of the seas.
Psalm 8:3-8

Listen to me, O coastlands, and give attention, you peoples from afar. The LORD
called me from the womb, from the body of my mother he named my name.
Isaiah 49:1

"Before I formed you in the womb I knew you, and before you were born
I consecrated you; I appointed you a prophet to the nations."
Jeremiah 1:5

But when he who had set me apart before I was born, and who called me by
his grace, was pleased to reveal his Son to me, in order that I might preach
him among the Gentiles, I did not immediately consult with anyone ...
Galatians 1:15-16

• Life is _____.

"O LORD, make me know my end and what is the measure of my days; let me know
how fleeting I am! Behold, you have made my days a few handbreadths, and my
lifetime is as nothing before you. Surely all mankind stands as a mere breath!"
Psalm 39:4-5

My days are like an evening shadow; I wither away like grass.
Psalm 102:11

As for man, his days are like grass; he flourishes like a flower of the field; for
the wind passes over it, and it is gone, and its place knows it no more.
Psalm 103:15-16

Come now, you who say, "Today or tomorrow we will go into such and such a town and
spend a year there and trade and make a profit"—yet you do not know what tomorrow will
bring. What is your life? For you are a mist that appears for a little time and then vanishes.
James 4:13-14

- Death is _____.

> "We must all die; we are like water spilled on the ground,
> which cannot be gathered up again."
> 2 Samuel 14:14a

> *The years of our life are seventy, or even by reason of strength eighty; yet*
> *their span is but toil and trouble; they are soon gone, and we fly away.*
> Psalm 90:10

> *It is the same for all, since the same event happens to the righteous and the wicked, to the*
> *good and the evil, to the clean and the unclean, to him who sacrifices and him who does not*
> *sacrifice. As the good one is, so is the sinner, and he who swears is as he who shuns an oath.*
> *This is an evil in all that is done under the sun, that the same event happens to all. Also,*
> *the hearts of the children of man are full of evil, and madness is in their hearts while they*
> *live, and after that they go to the dead. But he who is joined with all the living has hope,*
> *for a living dog is better than a dead lion. For the living know that they will die, but the*
> *dead know nothing, and they have no more reward, for the memory of them is forgotten.*
> Ecclesiastes 9:2-5

> "Resolved, to think much, on all occasions, of my own dying, and
> of the common circumstances which attend death."
> Jonathan Edwards

> "Whatever the church does, it should prepare its members to face death and meet God."
> D.A. Carson

- Death is often sudden.

> *There were some present at that very time who told him about the Galileans*
> *whose blood Pilate had mingled with their sacrifices. And he answered them, "Do*
> *you think that these Galileans were worse sinners than all the other Galileans,*
> *because they suffered in this way? No, I tell you; but unless you repent, you will*
> *all likewise perish. Or those eighteen on whom the tower in Siloam fell and killed*
> *them: do you think that they were worse offenders than all the others who lived in*
> *Jerusalem? No, I tell you; but unless you repent, you will all likewise perish."*
> Luke 13:1-5

- Death is often surprising.
- Death is inevitably sure.
  - The current death rate is 100 percent.
  - Over _____ people die every day in the world.

"One hundred [people] are dying [every] minute. If you could hear them all, you'd hear so many screams you'd go insane. Only God can hear them all and not go insane. God parcels out our awareness in small amounts lest we go under. How can you live in a world like that as a loving person and rejoice in the Lord?"
John Piper

• Death is _____.

The LORD God took the man and put him in the garden of Eden to work it and keep it. And the LORD God commanded the man, saying, "You may surely eat of every tree of the garden, but of the tree of the knowledge of good and evil you shall not eat, for in the day that you eat of it you shall surely die."
Genesis 2:15-17

Then the LORD God said, "Behold, the man has become like one of us in knowing good and evil. Now, lest he reach out his hand and take also of the tree of life and eat, and live forever—" therefore the LORD God sent him out from the garden of Eden to work the ground from which he was taken. He drove out the man, and at the east of the garden of Eden he placed the cherubim and a flaming sword that turned every way to guard the way to the tree of life.
Genesis 3:22-24

• Death is a consequence of sin.

And God said to Noah, "I have determined to make an end of all flesh, for the earth is filled with violence through them. Behold, I will destroy them with the earth."
Genesis 6:13

You sweep them away as with a flood; they are like a dream, like grass that is renewed in the morning: in the morning it flourishes and is renewed; in the evening it fades and withers. For we are brought to an end by your anger; by your wrath we are dismayed. You have set our iniquities before you, our secret sins in the light of your presence. For all our days pass away under your wrath; we bring our years to an end like a sigh.
Psalm 90:5-9

Therefore, just as sin came into the world through one man, and death through sin, and so death spread to all men because all sinned …
Romans 5:12

• Death is a tool of Satan.

Since therefore the children share in flesh and blood, he himself likewise partook of the same things, that through death he might destroy the one who has the power of death, that is, the devil, and deliver all those who through fear of death were subject to lifelong slavery.
Hebrews 2:14-15

- Death is multi-faceted.

> *"And do not fear those who kill the body but cannot kill the soul.*
> *Rather fear him who can destroy both soul and body in hell."*
> Matthew 10:28

> *… and the dust returns to the earth as it was, and the spirit returns to God who gave it.*
> Ecclesiastes 12:7

> *For as the body apart from the spirit is dead, so also faith apart from works is dead.*
> James 2:26

  ○ _____ death: The separation of a person from God.

> *Then the LORD God said, "Behold, the man has become like one of us in*
> *knowing good and evil. Now, lest he reach out his hand and take also of the tree*
> *of life and eat, and live forever—" therefore the LORD God sent him out from*
> *the garden of Eden to work the ground from which he was taken. He drove out*
> *the man, and at the east of the garden of Eden he placed the cherubim and a*
> *flaming sword that turned every way to guard the way to the tree of life.*
> Genesis 3:22-24

> *Behold, all souls are mine; the soul of the father as well as the*
> *soul of the son is mine: the soul who sins shall die.*
> Ezekiel 18:4

> *"But if a wicked person turns away from all his sins that he has committed and keeps*
> *all my statutes and does what is just and right, he shall surely live; he shall not die."*
> Ezekiel 18:21

  ○ _____ death: The cessation of life in our physical body.

> *This is the book of the generations of Adam. When God created man, he made him*
> *in the likeness of God. Male and female he created them, and he blessed them and*
> *named them Man when they were created. When Adam had lived 130 years, he*
> *fathered a son in his own likeness, after his image, and named him Seth. The days of*
> *Adam after he fathered Seth were 800 years; and he had other sons and daughters.*
> *Thus all the days that Adam lived were 930 years, and he died. When Seth had lived*
> *105 years, he fathered Enosh. Seth lived after he fathered Enosh 807 years and had*
> *other sons and daughters. Thus all the days of Seth were 912 years, and he died.*
> Genesis 5:1-8

  ○ _____ death: The finalization of separation from God.

"But as for the cowardly, the faithless, the detestable, as for murderers, the sexually immoral, sorcerers, idolaters, and all liars, their portion will be in the lake that burns with fire and sulfur, which is the second death."
Revelation 21:8

Blessed and holy is the one who shares in the first resurrection! Over such the second death has no power, but they will be priests of God and of Christ, and they will reign with him for a thousand years.
Revelation 20:6

Four Gospel Exhortations ...

The bad news: Death is our universal _____.

The last enemy to be destroyed is death.
1 Corinthians 15:26

○ We are all spiritually dead.

And you were dead in the trespasses and sins in which you once walked, following the course of this world, following the prince of the power of the air, the spirit that is now at work in the sons of disobedience—among whom we all once lived in the passions of our flesh, carrying out the desires of the body and the mind, and were by nature children of wrath, like the rest of mankind.
Ephesians 2:1-3

○ We will all experience physical death.

For as in Adam all die, so also in Christ shall all be made alive.
1 Corinthians 15:22

○ We all deserve eternal death.

For the wages of sin is death, but the free gift of God is eternal life in Christ Jesus our Lord.
Romans 6:23

The good news: Death has been ultimately _____.

When the perishable puts on the imperishable, and the mortal puts on immortality, then shall come to pass the saying that is written: "Death is swallowed up in victory. O death, where is your victory? O death, where is your sting?" The sting of death is sin, and the power of sin is the law. But thanks be to God, who gives us the victory through our Lord Jesus Christ.
1 Corinthians 15:54-57

○ Jesus has lived the life we could not live.

*Pilate said to him, "What is truth?" After he had said this, he went
back outside to the Jews and told them, "I find no guilt in him."*
John 18:38

*For we do not have a high priest who is unable to sympathize with our weaknesses,
but one who in every respect has been tempted as we are, yet without sin.*
Hebrews 4:15

You know that he appeared in order to take away sins, and in him there is no sin.
1 John 3:5

○ Jesus has _____ the death we deserve to die.

*Therefore he had to be made like his brothers in every respect, so that he might become a mercif
and faithful high priest in the service of God, to make propitiation for the sins of the people.*
Hebrews 2:17

*For while we were still weak, at the right time Christ died for the ungodly. For one will
scarcely die for a righteous person—though perhaps for a good person one would dare eve
to die—but God shows his love for us in that while we were still sinners, Christ died for u*
Romans 5:6-8

*Christ redeemed us from the curse of the law by becoming a curse for us—
for it is written, "Cursed is everyone who is hanged on a tree" ...*
Galatians 3:13

*He himself bore our sins in his body on the tree, that we might die to sin
and live to righteousness. By his wounds you have been healed.*
1 Peter 2:24

*For our sake he made him to be sin who knew no sin, so that
in him we might become the righteousness of God.*
2 Corinthians 5:21

○ Jesus has conquered the enemy we cannot conquer.

*For I delivered to you as of first importance what I also received: that Christ died for
our sins in accordance with the Scriptures, that he was buried, that he was raised on
the third day in accordance with the Scriptures, and that he appeared to Cephas, then
to the twelve. Then he appeared to more than five hundred brothers at one time, most
of whom are still alive, though some have fallen asleep. Then he appeared to James,
then to all the apostles. Last of all, as to one untimely born, he appeared also to me.*
1 Corinthians 15:3-8

ince therefore the children share in flesh and blood, he himself likewise partook of the same things, that through death he might destroy the one who has the power of death, that is, the devil, and deliver all those who through fear of death were subject to lifelong slavery.
Hebrews 2:14-15

And you, who were dead in your trespasses and the uncircumcision of your flesh, God made live together with him, having forgiven us all our trespasses, by canceling the record of debt that stood against us with its legal demands. This he set aside, nailing it to the cross. He disarmed the rulers and authorities and put them to open shame, by triumphing over them in him.
Colossians 2:13-15

The decisive question:

> *If you confess with your mouth that Jesus is Lord and believe in your heart that God raised him from the dead, you will be saved. For with the heart one believes and is justified, and with the mouth one confesses and is saved.*
> *Romans 10:9-10*

o Will you __turn__ from Jesus?

> *… when the Lord Jesus is revealed from heaven with his mighty angels in flaming fire, inflicting vengeance on those who do not know God and on those who do not obey the gospel of our Lord Jesus.*
> *2 Thessalonians 1:7b-8*

- Live without Christ now.

> *Do you not know that if you present yourselves to anyone as obedient slaves, you are slaves of the one whom you obey, either of sin, which leads to death, or of obedience, which leads to righteousness?*
> *Romans 6:16*

- Die without Christ forever.

They will suffer the punishment of eternal destruction, away from the presence of the Lord and from the glory of his might, when he comes on that day to be glorified in his saints, and to be marveled at among all who have believed, because our testimony to you was believed.
2 Thessalonians 1:9-10

- For the non-Christian, death remains an eternally dreaded __enemy__.

And I saw the dead, great and small, standing before the throne, and books were opened. Then another book was opened, which is the book of life. And the dead were judged by what was written in the books, according to what they had done. And the sea gave up

the dead who were in it, Death and Hades gave up the dead who were in them, and they were judged, each one of them, according to what they had done. Then Death and Hades were thrown into the lake of fire. This is the second death, the lake of fire. And if anyone's name was not found written in the book of life, he was thrown into the lake of fire.
Revelation 20:12-15

○ Or will you __trust__ in Jesus?

> *I have been crucified with Christ. It is no longer I who live, but Christ who lives in me. And the life I now live in the flesh I live by faith in the Son of God, who loved me and gave himself for me.*
> *Galatians 2:20*

■ Die with Christ now.

For if we have been united with him in a death like his, we shall certainly be united with him in a resurrection like his. We know that our old self was crucified with him in order that the body of sin might be brought to nothing, so that we would no longer be enslaved to sin. For one who has died has been set free from sin. Now if we have died with Christ, we believe that we will also live with him. We know that Christ, being raised from the dead, will never die again; death no longer has dominion over him. For the death he died he died to sin, once for all, but the life he lives he lives to God. So you also must consider yourselves dead to sin and alive to God in Christ Jesus.
Romans 6:5-11

■ Live with Christ forever.

> *Jesus said to her, "I am the resurrection and the life. Whoever believes in me, though he die, yet shall he live …"*
> *John 11:25*

■ For the Christian, death becomes a surprisingly helpful __Friend__.

One of the criminals who were hanged railed at him, saying, "Are you not the Christ? Save yourself and us!" But the other rebuked him, saying, "Do you not fear God, since you are under the same sentence of condemnation? And we indeed justly, for we are receiving the due reward of our deeds; but this man has done nothing wrong." And he said, "Jesus, remember me when you come into your kingdom." And he said to him, "Truly, I say to you, today you will be with me in Paradise."
Luke 23:39-43

And he said, "Behold, I see the heavens opened, and the Son
of Man standing at the right hand of God."
Acts 7:56

... as it is my eager expectation and hope that I will not be at all ashamed, but that
with full courage now as always Christ will be honored in my body, whether by life or
by death. For to me to live is Christ, and to die is gain. If I am to live in the flesh, that
means fruitful labor for me. Yet which I shall choose I cannot tell. I am hard pressed
between the two. My desire is to depart and be with Christ, for that is far better.
Philippians 1:20-23

The definitive conclusion:
  o Death is not the end.

And just as it is appointed for man to die once, and after that comes judgment ...
Hebrews 9:27

  o Death is only the beginning .

"Oh, God, this is the end; for me the beginning of life."
Dietrich Bonhoeffer

THE INTERMEDIATE STATE

For we know that if the tent that is our earthly home is destroyed, we have a building from God, a house not made with hands, eternal in the heavens. For in this tent we groan, longing to put on our heavenly dwelling, if indeed by putting it on we may not be found naked. For while we are still in this tent, we groan, being burdened—not that we would be unclothed, but that we would be further clothed, so that what is mortal may be swallowed up by life. He who has prepared us for this very thing is God, who has given us the Spirit as a guarantee. So we are always of good courage. We know that while we are at home in the body we are away from the Lord, for we walk by faith, not by sight. Yes, we are of good courage, and we would rather be away from the body and at home with the Lord. So whether we are at home or away, we make it our aim to please him. For we must all appear before the judgment seat of Christ, so that each one may receive what is due for what he has done in the body, whether good or evil.
2 Corinthians 5:1-10

A Definition ...

- The intermediate state refers to the condition of people between their bodily death and their bodily resurrection.

When he opened the fifth seal, I saw under the altar the souls of those who had been slain for the word of God and for the witness they had borne. They cried out with a loud voice, "O Sovereign Lord, holy and true, how long before you will judge and avenge our blood on those who dwell on the earth?" Then they were each given a white robe and told to rest a little longer, until the number of their fellow servants and their brothers should be complete, who were to be killed as they themselves had been.
Revelation 6:9-11

- All people possess both a body and a ___Soul___.

... then the LORD God formed the man of dust from the ground and breathed into his nostrils the breath of life, and the man became a living creature.
Genesis 2:7

  ○ When we die, our bodies are buried.

... and the dust returns to the earth as it was, and the spirit returns to God who gave it.
Ecclesiastes 12:7

  ○ When we die, our souls persist.

And as they were stoning Stephen, he called out, "Lord Jesus, receive my spirit." And falling to his knees he cried out with a loud voice, "Lord, do not hold this sin against them." And when he had said this, he fell asleep.
Acts 7:59-60

One day, our bodies will be resurrected and reunited _____ with our souls.

Do not marvel at this, for an hour is coming when all who are in the tombs will hear his voice and come out, those who have done good to the resurrection of life, and those who have done evil to the resurrection of judgment.
John 5:28-29

"When the Son of Man comes in his glory, and all the angels with him, then he will sit on his glorious throne. Before him will be gathered all the nations, and he will separate people one from another as a shepherd separates the sheep from the goats."
Matthew 25:31-32

"But this I confess to you, that according to the Way, which they call a sect, I worship the God of our fathers, believing everything laid down by the Law and written in the Prophets, having a hope in God, which these men themselves accept, that there will be a resurrection of both the just and the unjust."
Acts 24:14-15

And I saw the dead, great and small, standing before the throne, and books were opened. Then another book was opened, which is the book of life. And the dead were judged by what was written in the books, according to what they had done.
Revelation 20:12

But someone will ask, "How are the dead raised? With what kind of body do they come?" You foolish person! What you sow does not come to life unless it dies. And what you sow is not the body that is to be, but a bare kernel, perhaps of wheat or of some other grain. But God gives it a body as he has chosen, and to each kind of seed its own body. For not all flesh is the same, but there is one kind for humans, another for animals, another for birds, and another for fish. There are heavenly bodies and earthly bodies, but the glory of the heavenly is of one kind, and the glory of the earthly is of another.
1 Corinthians 15:35-40

Behold! I tell you a mystery. We shall not all sleep, but we shall all be changed, in a moment, in the twinkling of an eye, at the last trumpet. For the trumpet will sound, and the dead will be raised imperishable, and we shall be changed. For this perishable body must put on the imperishable, and this mortal body must put on immortality.
1 Corinthians 15:51-53

Some Questions ...

- So what happens at the moment of death?

One of the criminals who were hanged railed at him, saying, "Are you not the Christ? Save yourself and us!" But the other rebuked him, saying, "Do you not fear God, since you are under the same sentence of condemnation? And we indeed justly, for we are receiving the due reward of our deeds; but this man has done nothing wrong." And he said, "Jesus, remember me when you come into your kingdom." And he said to him, "Truly, I say to you, today you will be with me in Paradise."
Luke 23:39-43

○ The souls of believers immediately enter the _____ of God.

So we are always of good courage. We know that while we are at home in the body we are away from the Lord, for we walk by faith, not by sight. Yes, we are of good courage, and we would rather be away from the body and at home with the Lord.
2 Corinthians 5:6-8

I am hard pressed between the two. My desire is to depart and be with Christ, for that is far better.
Philippians 1:23

But you have come to Mount Zion and to the city of the living God, the heavenly Jerusalem, and to innumerable angels in festal gathering, and to the assembly of the firstborn who are enrolled in heaven, and to God, the judge of all, and to the spirits of the righteous made perfect, and to Jesus, the mediator of a new covenant, and to the sprinkled blood that speaks a better word than the blood of Abel.
Hebrews 12:22-24

○ The souls of unbelievers immediately experience the _____ of God.

"There was a rich man who was clothed in purple and fine linen and who feasted sumptuously every day. And at his gate was laid a poor man named Lazarus, covered with sores, who desired to be fed with what fell from the rich man's table. Moreover, even the dogs came and licked his sores. The poor man died and was carried by the angels to Abraham's side. The rich man also died and was buried, and in Hades, being in torment, he lifted up his eyes and saw Abraham far off and Lazarus at his side. And he called out, 'Father Abraham, have mercy on me, and send Lazarus to dip the end of his finger in water and cool my tongue, for I am in anguish in this flame.' But Abraham said, 'Child, remember that you in your lifetime received your good things, and Lazarus in like manner bad things; but now he is comforted here, and you are in anguish. And besides all this, between us and you a great chasm has been fixed, in order that those who would pass from here to you may not be able, and

none may cross from there to us.' And he said, 'Then I beg you, father, to send him to my father's house—for I have five brothers—so that he may warn them, lest they also come into this place of torment.' But Abraham said, 'They have Moses and the Prophets; let them hear them.' And he said, 'No, father Abraham, but if someone goes to them from the dead, they will repent.' He said to him, 'If they do not hear Moses and the Prophets, neither will they be convinced if someone should rise from the dead.'"

Luke 16:19-31

What about purgatory?
- o According to Catholicism …
  - ▪ Purgatory is the place where believers' souls go to be further purified from sin prior to admission into heaven.

"[Judas Maccabeus, the leader of the Jewish forces] also took a collection, man by man, to the amount of 2,000 drachmas of silver, and sent it to Jerusalem to provide for a sin offering. In doing this he acted very well and honorably, taking into account the resurrection. For if he were not expecting that those who had fallen would rise again, it would have been superfluous and foolish to pray for the dead. But if he was looking to the splendid reward that is laid up for those who fall asleep in godliness, it was a holy and pious thought. Therefore he made atonement for the dead, that they might be delivered from their sin."

2 Maccabees 12:42-45

  - ▪ The penalty of venial sins can be removed by:
    - Unconditional forgiveness from God
    - Contrition
    - Works of penance
  - ▪ Souls in purgatory can be helped in the process of purification by saints on earth through their participation in:
    - Mass
    - Prayers
    - Giving
    - Good Works

"Souls are cleansed by purgatorial pains after death, and in order that they may be rescued from these pains, they are benefitted by the suffrages of the living faith, viz: the sacrifice of the Mass, prayers, alms, and other works of piety."

Decree of Union, Council of Florence

- o According to Scripture …

- We are saved from our sins by _grace_ alone …

For by grace you have been saved through faith. And this is not your own doing; it is the gift of God, not a result of works, so that no one may boast.
Ephesians 2:8-9

- Through _Faith_ alone …

O foolish Galatians! Who has bewitched you? It was before your eyes that Jesus Christ was publicly portrayed as crucified. Let me ask you only this: Did you receive the Spirit by works of the law or by hearing with faith? Are you so foolish? Having begun by the Spirit, are you now being perfected by the flesh? Did you suffer so many things in vain—if indeed it was in vain? Does he who supplies the Spirit to you and works miracles among you do so by works of the law, or by hearing with faith— just as Abraham "believed God, and it was counted to him as righteousness"?

Know then that it is those of faith who are the sons of Abraham. And the Scripture, foreseeing that God would justify the Gentiles by faith, preached the gospel beforehand to Abraham, saying, "In you shall all the nations be blessed." So then, those who are of faith are blessed along with Abraham, the man of faith.

For all who rely on works of the law are under a curse; for it is written, "Cursed be everyone who does not abide by all things written in the Book of the Law, and do them." Now it is evident that no one is justified before God by the law, for "The righteous shall live by faith." But the law is not of faith, rather "The one who does them shall live by them." Christ redeemed us from the curse of the law by becoming a curse for us—for it is written, "Cursed is everyone who is hanged on a tree"—so that in Christ Jesus the blessing of Abraham might come to the Gentiles, so that we might receive the promised Spirit through faith.
Galatians 3:1-14

- In _Christ_ alone.

For there is one God, and there is one mediator between God and men, the man Christ Jesus, who gave himself as a ransom for all, which is the testimony given at the proper time.
1 Timothy 2:5-6

- What about soul sleep?
  - According to some …
    - Believers who die enter into a state of unconscious existence, and they stay unconscious until Christ returns and raises them to eternal life.

"The condition of man in death is one of unconsciousness [and] all men, good and evil alike, remain in the grave from death to the resurrection."
"Fundamental Beliefs," Seventh-Day Adventists

- After all, even Jesus describes death as sleep.

… he said, "Go away, for the girl is not dead but sleeping." And they laughed at him.
Matthew 9:24

And falling to his knees he cried out with a loud voice, "Lord, do not hold
this sin against them." And when he had said this, he fell asleep.
Acts 7:60

"For David, after he had served the purpose of God in his own generation,
fell asleep and was laid with his fathers and saw corruption …"
Acts 13:36

For God has not destined us for wrath, but to obtain salvation through our Lord Jesus
Christ, who died for us so that whether we are awake or asleep we might live with him.
1 Thessalonians 5:9-10

o According to Scripture …
- Sleep is clearly a _____ intended to depict the temporary
  nature of death for Christians.

After saying these things, he said to them, "Our friend Lazarus has
fallen asleep, but I go to awaken him." The disciples said to him, "Lord,
if he has fallen asleep, he will recover." Now Jesus had spoken of his
death, but they thought that he meant taking rest in sleep.
John 11:11-13

The dead do not praise the LORD, nor do any who go down into silence. But we
will bless the LORD from this time forth and forevermore. Praise the LORD!
Psalm 115:17-18

- Believers in heaven are clearly not sleeping.

And after six days Jesus took with him Peter and James, and John his brother,
and led them up a high mountain by themselves. And he was transfigured before
them, and his face shone like the sun, and his clothes became white as light.
And behold, there appeared to them Moses and Elijah, talking with him.
Matthew 17:1-3

And he said to him, "Truly, I say to you, today you will be with me in Paradise."
Luke 23:43

When he opened the fifth seal, I saw under the altar the souls of those who had been
slain for the word of God and for the witness they had borne. They cried out with
a loud voice, "O Sovereign Lord, holy and true, how long before you will judge and

avenge our blood on those who dwell on the earth?" Then they were each given a white robe and told to rest a little longer, until the number of their fellow servants and their brothers should be complete, who were to be killed as they themselves had been.
Revelation 6:9-11

- What are believers doing in the intermediate heaven?
  - They are Worshiping.

But you have come to Mount Zion and to the city of the living God, the heavenly Jerusalem, and to innumerable angels in festal gathering, and to the assembly of the firstborn who are enrolled in heaven, and to God, the judge of all, and to the spirits of the righteous made perfect, and to Jesus, the mediator of a new covenant, and to the sprinkled blood that speaks a better word than the blood of Abel.
Hebrews 12:22-24

After this I heard what seemed to be the loud voice of a great multitude in heaven, crying out, "Hallelujah! Salvation and glory and power belong to our God, for his judgments are true and just; for he has judged the great prostitute who corrupted the earth with her immorality, and has avenged on her the blood of his servants." Once more they cried out, "Hallelujah! The smoke from her goes up forever and ever." And the twenty-four elders and the four living creatures fell down and worshiped God who was seated on the throne, saying, "Amen. Hallelujah!" And from the throne came a voice saying, "Praise our God, all you his servants, you who fear him, small and great."
Revelation 19:1-5

  - They are watching.

Therefore, since we are surrounded by so great a cloud of witnesses, let us also lay aside every weight, and sin which clings so closely, and let us run with endurance the race that is set before us …
Hebrews 12:1

"Just so, I tell you, there will be more joy in heaven over one sinner who repents than over ninety-nine righteous persons who need no repentance."
Luke 15:7

"Rejoice over her, O heaven, and you saints and apostles and prophets, for God has given judgment for you against her!"
Revelation 18:20

  - They are ~~watching~~ waiting

When he opened the fifth seal, I saw under the altar the souls of those who had been slain for the word of God and for the witness they had borne. They cried out with a loud voice, "O Sovereign Lord, holy and true, how long before you will judge and

venge our blood on those who dwell on the earth?" Then they were each given a white robe and told to rest a little longer, until the number of their fellow servants and their brothers should be complete, who were to be killed as they themselves had been.
Revelation 6:9-11

- They are clearly <u>Concious</u>.
- They are audibly loud.
- They are emotionally passionate.
- They are distinctly individual.
- They are completely unified.
- They are continually <u>enterceding</u>.
- They thirst for final justice.
- They long for full redemption.
- They know God's character more deeply.
- They love God's church more fully.
- They are trusting God's promises in the present.
- They are <u>inticipatiun</u> God's plan for the future.

After this I looked, and behold, a great multitude that no one could number, from every nation, from all tribes and peoples and languages, standing before the throne and before the Lamb, clothed in white robes, with palm branches in their hands, and crying out with a loud voice, "Salvation belongs to our God who sits on the throne, and to the Lamb!"
Revelation 7:9-10

How then should we view our own death?
- All who follow Christ should <u>Confidence</u> death with confidence.

Even though I walk through the valley of the shadow of death, I will fear no evil, for you are with me; your rod and your staff, they comfort me.
Psalm 23:4

No, in all these things we are more than conquerors through him who loved us. For I am sure that neither death nor life, nor angels nor rulers, nor things present nor things to come, nor powers, nor height nor depth, nor anything else in all creation, will be able to separate us from the love of God in Christ Jesus our Lord.
Romans 8:37-39

... for I know that through your prayers and the help of the Spirit of Jesus Christ this will turn out for my deliverance, as it is my eager expectation and hope that I will not be at all ashamed, but that with full courage now as always Christ will be honored in my body, whether by life or by death. For to me to live is Christ, and to die is gain. If I am to live in the flesh, that means fruitful labor for me. Yet which I shall choose I cannot tell. I am hard pressed between the two. My desire is to depart and be with Christ, for that is far better.
Philippians 1:19-23

Since therefore the children share in flesh and blood, he himself likewise partook of the s[e]
things, that through death he might destroy the one who has the power of death, that i[s]
the devil, and deliver all those who through fear of death were subject to lifelong slaver[y]
Hebrews 2:14-15

- ○ All who do not follow Christ should ___Fear___ death with trepidation.

"The poor man died and was carried by the angels to Abraham's side. The rich man
also died and was buried, and in Hades, being in torment, he lifted up his eyes and
saw Abraham far off and Lazarus at his side. And he called out, 'Father Abraham,
have mercy on me, and send Lazarus to dip the end of his finger in water and cool
my tongue, for I am in anguish in this flame.' But Abraham said, 'Child, remember
that you in your lifetime received your good things, and Lazarus in like manner bad
things; but now he is comforted here, and you are in anguish. And besides all this,
between us and you a great chasm has been fixed, in order that those who would
pass from here to you may not be able, and none may cross from there to us.' And
he said, 'Then I beg you, father, to send him to my father's house—for I have five
brothers—so that he may warn them, lest they also come into this place of torment.'"
Luke 16:22-28

- And how should we view the deaths of others? _with Sorrow_

"At a funeral the church is perhaps at its most theological."
Russell Moore

- ○ How should we view the death of non-Christians? _weep and worship?_
  - ■ With biblical ___honesty___.

This is evidence of the righteous judgment of God, that you may be considered worthy
of the kingdom of God, for which you are also suffering—since indeed God considers
it just to repay with affliction those who afflict you, and to grant relief to you who are
afflicted as well as to us, when the Lord Jesus is revealed from heaven with his mighty
angels in flaming fire, inflicting vengeance on those who do not know God and on thos[e]
who do not obey the gospel of our Lord Jesus. They will suffer the punishment of eterna[l]
destruction, away from the presence of the Lord and from the glory of his might …
2 Thessalonians 1:5-9

  - ■ With personal humility.

And he said to him, "Truly, I say to you, today you will be with me in Paradise."
Luke 23:43

  - ■ With appropriate honor.

ur glory, O Israel, is slain on your high places! How the mighty have fallen! Tell it not ~ath, publish it not in the streets of Ashkelon, lest the daughters of the Philistines rejoice, the daughters of the uncircumcised exult. You mountains of Gilboa, let there be no dew rain upon you, nor fields of offerings! For there the shield of the mighty was defiled, the ~ld of Saul, not anointed with oil. From the blood of the slain, from the fat of the mighty, bow of Jonathan turned not back, and the sword of Saul returned not empty. Saul and ~athan, beloved and lovely! In life and in death they were not divided; they were swifter ~an eagles; they were stronger than lions. You daughters of Israel, weep over Saul, who ~othed you luxuriously in scarlet, who put ornaments of gold on your apparel. How the mighty have fallen in the midst of the battle! Jonathan lies slain on your high places."

2 Samuel 1:19-25

- With heart-breaking _____.

I am speaking the truth in Christ—I am not lying; my conscience bears me witness in the Holy Spirit—that I have great sorrow and unceasing anguish in my heart. For I could wish that I myself were accursed and cut off from Christ for the sake of my brothers, my kinsmen according to the flesh.

Romans 9:1-3

- With life-giving resolve.

"Surely those who know the great passionate heart of Jehovah must deny their own loves to share in the expression of His. Consider the call from the Throne above, 'Go ye,' and from round about, 'Come over and help us,' and even the call from the damned souls below, 'Send Lazarus to my brothers, that they come not to this place.' Impelled, then, by these voices, I dare not stay home while Quichuas perish. So what if the well-fed church in the homeland needs stirring? They have the Scriptures, Moses, and the Prophets, and a whole lot more. Their condemnation is written on their bank books and in the dust on their Bible covers. American believers have sold their lives to the service of Mammon, and God has His rightful way of dealing with those who succumb to the spirit of Laodicea."

Jim Elliot

- How should we view the death of Christians?
  - With profound _____.

Jesus wept.
John 11:35

And he said, "Behold, I see the heavens opened, and the Son of Man standing at the right hand of God." But they cried out with a loud voice and stopped their ears and rushed together at him. Then they cast him out of the city and stoned him. And the witnesses laid down their garments at the feet of a young man named Saul. And as they were stoning Stephen, he called out, "Lord Jesus, receive my spirit." And falling to his knees he cried out with a loud voice, "Lord, do not hold this sin against them."

And when he had said this, he fell asleep. And Saul approved of his execution. And there arose on that day a great persecution against the church in Jerusalem, and they were all scattered throughout the regions of Judea and Samaria, except the apostles. Devout men buried Stephen and made great lamentation over him.
Acts 7:56-8:2

And when he had said these things, he knelt down and prayed with them all. And there was much weeping on the part of all; they embraced Paul and kissed him, being sorrowful most of all because of the word he had spoken, that they would not see his face again. And they accompanied him to the ship.
Acts 20:36-38

I have thought it necessary to send to you Epaphroditus my brother and fellow worker and fellow soldier, and your messenger and minister to my need, for he has been longing for you all and has been distressed because you heard that he was ill. Indeed he was ill, near to death. But God had mercy on him, and not only on him but on me also, lest I should have sorrow upon sorrow.
Philippians 2:25-27

- With abiding _____.

"Truly, truly, I say to you, you will weep and lament, but the world will rejoice. You will be sorrowful, but your sorrow will turn into joy. When a woman is giving birth, she has sorrow because her hour has come, but when she has delivered the baby, she no longer remembers the anguish, for joy that a human being has been born into the world. So also you have sorrow now, but I will see you again, and your hearts will rejoice, and no one will take your joy from you. In that day you will ask nothing of me. Truly, truly, I say to you, whatever you ask of the Father in my name, he will give it to you. Until now you have asked nothing in my name. Ask, and you will receive, that your joy may be full."
John 16:20-24

"I have said these things to you, that in me you may have peace. In the world you will have tribulation. But take heart; I have overcome the world."
John 16:33

Precious in the sight of the LORD is the death of his saints.
Psalm 116:15

And I heard a voice from heaven saying, "Write this: Blessed are the dead who die in the Lord from now on." "Blessed indeed," says the Spirit, "that they may rest from their labors, for their deeds follow them!"
Revelation 14:13

"If any righteous man among the Christians passes from this world, they rejoice and offer thanks to God, and they escort his body with songs and thanksgiving as if he were setting out from one place to another nearby."
Aristides, 125 AD

- With sincere _____.

But when David saw that his servants were whispering together, David understood that the child was dead. And David said to his servants, "Is the child dead?" They said, "He is dead." Then David arose from the earth and washed and anointed himself and changed his clothes. And he went into the house of the LORD and worshiped. He then went to his own house. And when he asked, they set food before him, and he ate.
2 Samuel 12:19-20

While he was yet speaking, there came another and said, "Your sons and daughters were eating and drinking wine in their oldest brother's house, and behold, a great wind came across the wilderness and struck the four corners of the house, and it fell upon the young people, and they are dead, and I alone have escaped to tell you." Then Job arose and tore his robe and shaved his head and fell on the ground and worshiped. And he said, "Naked I came from my mother's womb, and naked shall I return. The LORD gave, and the LORD has taken away; blessed be the name of the LORD." In all this Job did not sin or charge God with wrong.
Job 1:18-22

- With unshakeable _____.

But we do not want you to be uninformed, brothers, about those who are asleep, that you may not grieve as others do who have no hope. For since we believe that Jesus died and rose again, even so, through Jesus, God will bring with him those who have fallen asleep. For this we declare to you by a word from the Lord, that we who are alive, who are left until the coming of the Lord, will not precede those who have fallen asleep. For the Lord himself will descend from heaven with a cry of command, with the voice of an archangel, and with the sound of the trumpet of God. And the dead in Christ will rise first. Then we who are alive, who are left, will be caught up together with them in the clouds to meet the Lord in the air, and so we will always be with the Lord. Therefore encourage one another with these words.
1 Thessalonians 4:13-18

THE RETURN OF CHRIST

And just as it is appointed for man to die once, and after that comes judgment,
so Christ, having been offered once to bear the sins of many, will appear a second
time, not to deal with sin but to save those who are eagerly waiting for him.
Hebrews 9:27-28

What We Know ...

• Jesus is coming _____.

"Then will appear in heaven the sign of the Son of Man, and then all the tribes of the
earth will mourn, and they will see the Son of Man coming on the clouds of heaven with
power and great glory. And he will send out his angels with a loud trumpet call, and
they will gather his elect from the four winds, from one end of heaven to the other."
Matthew 24:30-31

And when he had said these things, as they were looking on, he was lifted up, and
a cloud took him out of their sight. And while they were gazing into heaven as he
went, behold, two men stood by them in white robes, and said, "Men of Galilee,
why do you stand looking into heaven? This Jesus, who was taken up from you
into heaven, will come in the same way as you saw him go into heaven."
Acts 1:9-11

I give thanks to my God always for you because of the grace of God that was given
you in Christ Jesus, that in every way you were enriched in him in all speech and all
knowledge—even as the testimony about Christ was confirmed among you—so that
you are not lacking in any gift, as you wait for the revealing of our Lord Jesus Christ,
who will sustain you to the end, guiltless in the day of our Lord Jesus Christ.
1 Corinthians 1:4-8

For what is our hope or joy or crown of boasting before our Lord Jesus
at his coming? Is it not you? For you are our glory and joy.
1 Thessalonians 2:19-20

Now may our God and Father himself, and our Lord Jesus, direct our way to you,
and may the Lord make you increase and abound in love for one another and for
all, as we do for you, so that he may establish your hearts blameless in holiness
before our God and Father, at the coming of our Lord Jesus with all his saints.
1 Thessalonians 3:11-13

Now may the God of peace himself sanctify you completely, and may your whole
spirit and soul and body be kept blameless at the coming of our Lord Jesus Christ.
1 Thessalonians 5:23

Now concerning the coming of our Lord Jesus Christ and our
being gathered together to him, we ask you, brothers …
2 Thessalonians 2:1

charge you in the presence of God, who gives life to all things, and of Christ Jesus, who in
his testimony before Pontius Pilate made the good confession, to keep the commandment
unstained and free from reproach until the appearing of our Lord Jesus Christ …
1 Timothy 6:13-14

I charge you in the presence of God and of Christ Jesus, who is to judge the living and
the dead, and by his appearing and his kingdom: preach the word; be ready in season
and out of season; reprove, rebuke, and exhort, with complete patience and teaching.
2 Timothy 4:1-2

Henceforth there is laid up for me the crown of righteousness, which
the Lord, the righteous judge, will award to me on that Day, and
not only to me but also to all who have loved his appearing.
2 Timothy 4:8

Therefore, preparing your minds for action, and being sober-minded, set your hope
fully on the grace that will be brought to you at the revelation of Jesus Christ.
1 Peter 1:13

And now, little children, abide in him, so that when he appears we may
have confidence and not shrink from him in shame at his coming.
1 John 2:28

"And behold, I am coming soon. Blessed is the one who
keeps the words of the prophecy of this book."
Revelation 22:7

"Behold, I am coming soon, bringing my recompense with
me, to repay each one for what he has done."
Revelation 22:12

who testifies to these things says, "Surely I am coming soon." Amen. Come, Lord Jesus!
Revelation 22:20

His return will be _____.

"Therefore, stay awake, for you do not know on what day your Lord is
coming. But know this, that if the master of the house had known in what
part of the night the thief was coming, he would have stayed awake and

would not have let his house be broken into. Therefore you also must be
ready, for the Son of Man is coming at an hour you do not expect."
Matthew 24:42-44

"You also must be ready, for the Son of Man is coming at an hour you do not expect."
Luke 12:40

For you yourselves are fully aware that the day of the
Lord will come like a thief in the night.
1 Thessalonians 5:2

But the day of the Lord will come like a thief, and then the heavens will pass
away with a roar, and the heavenly bodies will be burned up and dissolved,
and the earth and the works that are done on it will be exposed.
2 Peter 3:10

- His return will be visible.

And when he had said these things, as they were looking on, he was lifted up, and
a cloud took him out of their sight. And while they were gazing into heaven as he
went, behold, two men stood by them in white robes, and said, "Men of Galilee,
why do you stand looking into heaven? This Jesus, who was taken up from you
into heaven, will come in the same way as you saw him go into heaven."
Acts 1:9-11

Behold, he is coming with the clouds, and every eye will see him, even those who
pierced him, and all tribes of the earth will wail on account of him. Even so. Amen.
Revelation 1:7

- His return will be personal.

"Let not your hearts be troubled. Believe in God; believe also in me. In my
Father's house are many rooms. If it were not so, would I have told you that I
go to prepare a place for you? And if I go and prepare a place for you, I will
come again and will take you to myself, that where I am you may be also."
John 14:1-3

For the Lord himself will descend from heaven with a cry of command, with the voice
of an archangel, and with the sound of the trumpet of God. And the dead in Christ
will rise first. Then we who are alive, who are left, will be caught up together with them
in the clouds to meet the Lord in the air, and so we will always be with the Lord.
1 Thessalonians 4:16-17

Beloved, we are God's children now, and what we will be has not yet appeared; but we know that when he appears we shall be like him, because we shall see him as he is.
1 John 3:2

His return will be _____.

"When the Son of Man comes in his glory, and all the angels with him, then he will sit on his glorious throne."
Matthew 25:31

○ He came the first time lying in a manger; He will come the second time riding on the clouds.

He lays the beams of his chambers on the waters; he makes the clouds his chariot; he rides on the wings of the wind …
Psalm 104:3

Behold, the LORD is riding on a swift cloud and comes to Egypt; and the idols of Egypt will tremble at his presence, and the heart of the Egyptians will melt within them.
Isaiah 19:1

"Then will appear in heaven the sign of the Son of Man, and then all the tribes of the earth will mourn, and they will see the Son of Man coming on the clouds of heaven with power and great glory."
Matthew 24:30

○ He came the first time in humility to provide salvation; He will come the second time in glory to execute judgment.

"Before him will be gathered all the nations, and he will separate people one from another as a shepherd separates the sheep from the goats. And he will place the sheep on his right, but the goats on the left."
Matthew 25:32-33

What We Don't Know …

_When_____ is Jesus coming back?

"But concerning that day or that hour, no one knows, not even the angels in heaven, nor the Son, but only the Father. Be on guard, keep awake. For you do not know when the time will come."
Mark 13:32-33

"Watch therefore, for you know neither the day nor the hour."
Matthew 25:13

> *So when they had come together, they asked him, "Lord, will you at this time restore the kingdom Israel?" He said to them, "It is not for you to know times or seasons that the Father has fixed by his own authority."*
> Acts 1:6-7

- What _____ have been fulfilled?
  - The preaching of the gospel to all nations.

> *"But be on your guard. For they will deliver you over to councils, and you will be beaten in synagogues, and you will stand before governors and kings for my sake, to bear witness before them. And the gospel must first be proclaimed to all nations."*
> Mark 13:9-10

> *"And this gospel of the kingdom will be proclaimed throughout the whole world as a testimony to all nations, and then the end will come."*
> Matthew 24:14

  - The great tribulation.

> *"And when you hear of wars and rumors of wars, do not be alarmed. This must take place, but the end is not yet. For nation will rise against nation, and kingdom against kingdom. There will be earthquakes in various places; there will be famines. These are but the beginning of the birth pains."*
> Mark 13:7-8

> *"For in those days there will be such tribulation as has not been from the beginning of the creation that God created until now, and never will be. And if the Lord had not cut short the days, no human being would be saved. But for the sake of the elect, whom he chose, he shortened the days."*
> Mark 13:19-20

> *"So when you see the abomination of desolation spoken of by the prophet Daniel, standing in the holy place (let the reader understand), then let those who are in Judea flee to the mountains. Let the one who is on the housetop not go down to take what is in his house, and let the one who is in the field not turn back to take his cloak. And alas for women who are pregnant and for those who are nursing infants in those days! Pray that your flight may not be in winter or on a Sabbath. For then there will be great tribulation, such as has not been from the beginning of the world until now, no, and never will be. And if those days had not been cut short, no human being would be saved. But for the sake of the elect those days will be cut short."*
> Matthew 24:15-22

  - False prophets and miracle workers.

"For false christs and false prophets will arise and perform signs and wonders, to lead astray, if possible, the elect. But be on guard; I have told you all things beforehand."
Mark 13:22-23

"Then if anyone says to you, 'Look, here is the Christ!' or 'There he is!' do not believe it. For false christs and false prophets will arise and perform great signs and wonders, so as to lead astray, if possible, even the elect."
Matthew 24:23-24

○ Signs in the heavens.

"But in those days, after that tribulation, the sun will be darkened, and the moon will not give its light, and the stars will be falling from heaven, and the powers in the heavens will be shaken. And then they will see the Son of Man coming in clouds with great power and glory."
Mark 13:24-26

"Immediately after the tribulation of those days the sun will be darkened, and the moon will not give its light, and the stars will fall from heaven, and the powers of the heavens will be shaken. Then will appear in heaven the sign of the Son of Man, and then all the tribes of the earth will mourn, and they will see the Son of Man coming on the clouds of heaven with power and great glory."
Matthew 24:29-30

"And there will be signs in sun and moon and stars, and on the earth distress of nations in perplexity because of the roaring of the sea and the waves, people fainting with fear and with foreboding of what is coming on the world. For the powers of the heavens will be shaken. And then they will see the Son of Man coming in a cloud with power and great glory."
Luke 21:25-27

○ The coming of the _____.

Now concerning the coming of our Lord Jesus Christ and our being gathered together to him, we ask you, brothers, not to be quickly shaken in mind or alarmed, either by a spirit or a spoken word, or a letter seeming to be from us, to the effect that the day of the Lord has come. Let no one deceive you in any way. For that day will not come, unless the rebellion comes first, and the man of lawlessness is revealed, the son of destruction, who opposes and exalts himself against every so-called god or object of worship, so that he takes his seat in the temple of God, proclaiming himself to be God. Do you not remember that when I was still with you I told you these things? And you know what is restraining him now so that he may be revealed in his time. For the mystery of lawlessness is already

at work. Only he who now restrains it will do so until he is out of the way. And then the lawless one will be revealed, whom the Lord Jesus will kill with the breath of his mouth and bring to nothing by the appearance of his coming. The coming of the lawless one is by the activity of Satan with all power and false signs and wonders, and with all wicked deception for those who are perishing, because they refused to love the truth and so be saved
2 Thessalonians 2:1-10

- The Spirit of Christ is on Christians as a guarantee of His future coming

And not only the creation, but we ourselves, who have the firstfruits of the Spirit, groan inwardly as we wait eagerly for adoption as sons, the redemption of our bodies.
Romans 8:23

In him you also, when you heard the word of truth, the gospel of your salvation, and believed in him, were sealed with the promised Holy Spirit, who is the guarantee of our inheritance until we acquire possession of it, to the praise of his glory.
Ephesians 1:13-14

- The spirit of the antichrist is in the world as a guarantee of his future coming.

By this you know the Spirit of God: every spirit that confesses that Jesus Christ has come the flesh is from God, and every spirit that does not confess Jesus is not from God. This i. the spirit of the antichrist, which you heard was coming and now is in the world already.
1 John 4:2-3

- The Christ was preceded and accompanied by a true prophet.

In those days John the Baptist came preaching in the wilderness of Judea, "Repent, for the kingdom of heaven is at hand." For this is he who was spoken of by the prophet Isaiah when he said, "The voice of one crying in the wilderness: 'Prepare the way of the Lord; make his paths straight.'"
Matthew 3:1-3

- The antichrist will be preceded and accompanied by a false prophet.

Children, it is the last hour, and as you have heard that antichrist is coming, so now many antichrists have come. Therefore we know that it is the last hour.
1 John 2:18

Then I saw another beast rising out of the earth. It had two horns like a lamb and it spoke like a dragon. It exercises all the authority of the first beast in its presence, and makes the earth and its inhabitants worship the first beast, whose mortal wound was healed. It performs great signs, even making fire come down from heaven to earth in front of people, and by the signs that it is allowed to work in the presence of the beast it

deceives those who dwell on earth, telling them to make an image for the beast that was wounded by the sword and yet lived. And it was allowed to give breath to the image of the beast, so that the image of the beast might even speak and might cause those who would not worship the image of the beast to be slain. Also it causes all, both small and great, both rich and poor, both free and slave, to be marked on the right hand or the forehead, so that no one can buy or sell unless he has the mark, that is, the name of the beast or the number of its name. This calls for wisdom: let the one who has understanding calculate the number of the beast, for it is the number of a man, and his number is 666.
Revelation 13:11-18

- The Christ speaks truth.

So Jesus said to the Jews who had believed him, "If you abide in my word, you are truly my disciples, and you will know the truth, and the truth will set you free."
John 8:31-32

- The antichrist spreads deception.

For many deceivers have gone out into the world, those who do not confess the coming of Jesus Christ in the flesh. Such a one is the deceiver and the antichrist.
2 John 7

It performs great signs, even making fire come down from heaven to earth in front of people, and by the signs that it is allowed to work in the presence of the beast it deceives those who dwell on earth, telling them to make an image for the beast that was wounded by the sword and yet lived.
Revelation 13:13-14

- The Christ builds the temple, the church, of which he is the cornerstone.

So then you are no longer strangers and aliens, but you are fellow citizens with the saints and members of the household of God, built on the foundation of the apostles and prophets, Christ Jesus himself being the cornerstone, in whom the whole structure, being joined together, grows into a holy temple in the Lord. In him you also are being built together into a dwelling place for God by the Spirit.
Ephesians 2:19-22

- The antichrist stands in the temple, claiming to be its center.

Let no one deceive you in any way. For that day will not come, unless the rebellion comes first, and the man of lawlessness is revealed, the son of destruction, who opposes and exalts himself against every so-called god or object of worship, so that he takes his seat in the temple of God, proclaiming himself to be God.
2 Thessalonians 2:3-4

○ The salvation of _____.

So I ask, did they stumble in order that they might fall? By no means! Rather through their trespass salvation has come to the Gentiles, so as to make Israel jealous. Now if their trespass means riches for the world, and if their failure means riches for the Gentiles, how much more will their full inclusion mean!
Romans 11:11-12

Lest you be wise in your own sight, I do not want you to be unaware of this mystery, brothers: a partial hardening has come upon Israel, until the fullness of the Gentiles has come in. And in this way all Israel will be saved, as it is written, "The Deliverer will come from Zion, he will banish ungodliness from Jacob"; "and this will be my covenant with them when I take away their sins."
Romans 11:25-27

- All Christians believe in a future for Israel.
- Many Christians disagree on the _____ of Israel.
  - An ethnic people?
  - A national state?
  - The church?
  - The Christ?
- We are heirs of a Jewish _____.

That is why it depends on faith, in order that the promise may rest on grace and be guarantee to all his offspring—not only to the adherent of the law but also to the one who shares the fait of Abraham, who is the father of us all, as it is written, "I have made you the father of many nations"—in the presence of the God in whom he believed, who gives life to the dead and call into existence the things that do not exist. In hope he believed against hope, that he should become the father of many nations, as he had been told, "So shall your offspring be." He did n weaken in faith when he considered his own body, which was as good as dead (since he was about a hundred years old), or when he considered the barrenness of Sarah's womb. No unbel made him waver concerning the promise of God, but he grew strong in his faith as he gave glo to God, fully convinced that God was able to do what he had promised. That is why his fait was "counted to him as righteousness." But the words "it was counted to him" were not writte for his sake alone, but for ours also. It will be counted to us who believe in him who raised fro the dead Jesus our Lord, who was delivered up for our trespasses and raised for our justificatic
Romans 4:16-25

Now the promises were made to Abraham and to his offspring. It does not say, "And to offsprings," referring to many, but referring to one, "And to your offspring," who is Chris
Galatians 3:16

But now that faith has come, we are no longer under a guardian, for in Christ Jesus you are all sons of God, through faith. For as many of you as were baptized into Christ have put on Christ. There is neither Jew nor Greek, there is neither slave

nor free, there is no male and female, for you are all one in Christ Jesus. And if
you are Christ's, then you are Abraham's offspring, heirs according to promise.
Galatians 3:25-29

In him also you were circumcised with a circumcision made without hands,
by putting off the body of the flesh, by the circumcision of Christ, having been
buried with him in baptism, in which you were also raised with him through
faith in the powerful working of God, who raised him from the dead.
Colossians 2:11-12

Here there is not Greek and Jew, circumcised and uncircumcised,
barbarian, Scythian, slave, free; but Christ is all, and in all.
Colossians 3:11

■ We are saved by a Jewish _____.

"I am the true vine, and my Father is the vinedresser. Every branch in me that does not
ear fruit he takes away, and every branch that does bear fruit he prunes, that it may bear
more fruit. Already you are clean because of the word that I have spoken to you. Abide
in me, and I in you. As the branch cannot bear fruit by itself, unless it abides in the vine,
neither can you, unless you abide in me. I am the vine; you are the branches. Whoever
abides in me and I in him, he it is that bears much fruit, for apart from me you can do
othing. If anyone does not abide in me he is thrown away like a branch and withers; and
the branches are gathered, thrown into the fire, and burned. If you abide in me, and my
ords abide in you, ask whatever you wish, and it will be done for you. By this my Father is
orified, that you bear much fruit and so prove to be my disciples. As the Father has loved
ne, so have I loved you. Abide in my love. If you keep my commandments, you will abide
in my love, just as I have kept my Father's commandments and abide in his love. These
things I have spoken to you, that my joy may be in you, and that your joy may be full."
John 15:1-11

For all the promises of God find their Yes in him. That is why it is through
him that we utter our Amen to God for his glory. And it is God who
establishes us with you in Christ, and has anointed us, and who has also
put his seal on us and given us his Spirit in our hearts as a guarantee.
2 Corinthians 1:20-22

■ We are passionate about Jewish _____.

m speaking the truth in Christ—I am not lying; my conscience bears me witness in the Holy
pirit—that I have great sorrow and unceasing anguish in my heart. For I could wish that I
self were accursed and cut off from Christ for the sake of my brothers, my kinsmen according
* the flesh. They are Israelites, and to them belong the adoption, the glory, the covenants, the*

giving of the law, the worship, and the promises. To them belong the patriarchs, and from their race, according to the flesh, is the Christ, who is God over all, blessed forever. Amen.
Romans 9:1-5

- Is the second coming one event or _____?
  - ○ Two events …
    - ■ First, a secret coming for His church before the tribulation.
    - ■ Second, a public coming with His church after the tribulation.
  - ○ One event …
    - ■ A single moment when Jesus returns for His church.
- Could Jesus come back at _____ moment?

Rejoice in the Lord always; again I will say, rejoice. Let your reasonableness be known to everyone. The Lord is at hand; do not be anxious about anything, but in everything by prayer and supplication with thanksgiving let your requests be made known to God. And the peace of God, which surpasses all understanding, will guard your hearts and your minds in Christ Jesus.
Philippians 4:4-7

For the grace of God has appeared, bringing salvation for all people, training us to renounce ungodliness and worldly passions, and to live self-controlled, upright, and godly lives in the present age, waiting for our blessed hope, the appearing of the glory of our great God and Savior Jesus Christ, who gave himself for us to redeem us from all lawlessness and to purify for himself a people for his own possession who are zealous for good works.
Titus 2:11-14

Be patient, therefore, brothers, until the coming of the Lord. See how the farmer waits for the precious fruit of the earth, being patient about it, until it receives the early and the late rains. You also, be patient. Establish your hearts, for the coming of the Lord is at hand. Do not grumble against one another, brothers, so that you may not be judged; behold, the Judge is standing at the door.
James 5:7-9

But you, beloved, building yourselves up in your most holy faith and praying in the Holy Spirit, keep yourselves in the love of God, waiting for the mercy of our Lord Jesus Christ that leads to eternal life.
Jude 20-21

"The prophets were little interested in chronology, and the future was always viewed as imminent …. The Old Testament prophets blended the near and the distant perspective so as to form a single canvas. Biblical prophecy is not primarily three-dimensional but two; it has height and breadth but is little concerned about depth, i.e., the chronology of future events …. The distant is viewed through the transparency of the immediate. It is true that the early church lived in expectancy of the return of the Lord, and it is the nature of biblical prophecy to make it possible for every generation to live in expectancy of the end.
George Ladd

What We Do Now ...

- We _____ in the authority of Christ.

  "Immediately after the tribulation of those days the sun will be darkened, and the moon will not give its light, and the stars will fall from heaven, and the powers of the heavens will be shaken. Then will appear in heaven the sign of the Son of Man, and then all the tribes of the earth will mourn, and they will see the Son of Man coming on the clouds of heaven with power and great glory."
  Matthew 24:29-30

  ○ The things of this world are passing.
  ○ The truth of His Word is permanent.

  "Heaven and earth will pass away, but my words will not pass away."
  Matthew 24:35

- We _____ in the power of Christ.
  ○ Followers of Jesus will face deception.

  And Jesus answered them, "See that no one leads you astray."
  Matthew 24:4

  "And if those days had not been cut short, no human being would be saved. But for the sake of the elect those days will be cut short. Then if anyone says to you, 'Look, here is the Christ!' or 'There he is!' do not believe it. For false christs and false prophets will arise and perform great signs and wonders, so as to lead astray, if possible, even the elect. See, I have told you beforehand."
  Matthew 24:22-25

  ○ Followers of Jesus will face _____.

  "And you will hear of wars and rumors of wars. See that you are not alarmed, for this must take place, but the end is not yet. For nation will rise against nation, and kingdom against kingdom, and there will be famines and earthquakes in various places. All these are but the beginning of the birth pains."
  Matthew 24:6-8

  - ■ Christians are not saved from trials.
  - ■ Christians are saved through trials.
  ○ Followers of Jesus will face temptation.

  "And then many will fall away and betray one another and hate one another. And many false prophets will arise and lead many astray. And because lawlessness will be increased, the love of many will grow cold. But the one who endures to the end will be saved."
  Matthew 24:10-13

○ Followers of Jesus will face _persecution_.

> *"Then they will deliver you up to tribulation and put you to death,*
> *and you will be hated by all nations for my name's sake."*
> Matthew 24:9

- Persecution inevitably follows kingdom proclamation.
- Proclamation inevitably results in kingdom consummation.

> *"And this gospel of the kingdom will be proclaimed throughout the whole*
> *world as a testimony to all nations, and then the end will come."*
> Matthew 24:14

• We _anticipation_ the coming of Christ.

> *"But concerning that day and hour no one knows, not even the angels of heaven, nor*
> *the Son, but the Father only. For as were the days of Noah, so will be the coming of*
> *the Son of Man. For as in those days before the flood they were eating and drinking,*
> *marrying and giving in marriage, until the day when Noah entered the ark, and*
> *they were unaware until the flood came and swept them all away, so will be the*
> *coming of the Son of Man. Then two men will be in the field; one will be taken and*
> *one left. Two women will be grinding at the mill; one will be taken and one left.*
> *Therefore, stay awake, for you do not know on what day your Lord is coming."*
> Matthew 24:36-42

○ His delay will be long.
○ His return will be sudden.
○ His judgment will be irreversible.
○ Our hearts will be _____.
○ Our sentence may be surprising.

> *"Not everyone who says to me, 'Lord, Lord,' will enter the kingdom of heaven, but*
> *the one who does the will of my Father who is in heaven. On that day many will*
> *say to me, 'Lord, Lord, did we not prophesy in your name, and cast out demons*
> *in your name, and do many mighty works in your name?' And then will I declare*
> *to them, 'I never knew you; depart from me, you workers of lawlessness.'"*
> Matthew 7:21-23

○ Our lives will stand _____.
○ We must be prepared …
- Are you keeping _____ for Christ?

> *"'For I was hungry and you gave me no food, I was thirsty and you gave*
> *me no drink, I was a stranger and you did not welcome me, naked and you*
> *did not clothe me, sick and in prison and you did not visit me.' Then they*

also will answer, saying, 'Lord, when did we see you hungry or thirsty or a
stranger or naked or sick or in prison, and did not minister to you?'"
Matthew 25:42-44

For you yourselves are fully aware that the day of the
Lord will come like a thief in the night.
1 Thessalonians 5:2

But the day of the Lord will come like a thief, and then the heavens will pass
away with a roar, and the heavenly bodies will be burned up and dissolved,
and the earth and the works that are done on it will be exposed.
2 Peter 3:10

"'Remember, then, what you received and heard. Keep it, and
repent. If you will not wake up, I will come like a thief, and you
will not know at what hour I will come against you.'"
Revelation 3:3

"Behold, I am coming like a thief! Blessed is the one who stays awake, keeping
his garments on, that he may not go about naked and be seen exposed!"
Revelation 16:15

- Are you faithfully ___Following___ Christ?

"Who then is the faithful and wise servant, whom his master has set over his
household, to give them their food at the proper time? Blessed is that servant
whom his master will find so doing when he comes. Truly, I say to you, he will
set him over all his possessions. But if that wicked servant says to himself, 'My
master is delayed,' and begins to beat his fellow servants and eats and drinks with
drunkards, the master of that servant will come on a day when he does not expect
him and at an hour he does not know and will cut him in pieces and put him
with the hypocrites. In that place there will be weeping and gnashing of teeth."
Matthew 24:45-51

"Then the kingdom of heaven will be like ten virgins who took their lamps and went
to meet the bridegroom. Five of them were foolish, and five were wise. For when the
foolish took their lamps, they took no oil with them, but the wise took flasks of oil with
their lamps. As the bridegroom was delayed, they all became drowsy and slept. But at
midnight there was a cry, 'Here is the bridegroom! Come out to meet him.' Then all
those virgins rose and trimmed their lamps. And the foolish said to the wise, 'Give us
some of your oil, for our lamps are going out.' But the wise answered, saying, 'Since there
will not be enough for us and for you, go rather to the dealers and buy for yourselves.'
And while they were going to buy, the bridegroom came, and those who were ready

went in with him to the marriage feast, and the door was shut. Afterward the other virgins came also, saying, 'Lord, lord, open to us.' But he answered, 'Truly, I say to you, I do not know you.' Watch therefore, for you know neither the day nor the hour."
Matthew 25:1-13

- The kingdom of heaven is not for those who …
  - Respond to an invitation, make a confession, or express some affection.
- The kingdom of heaven is for those who …
  - Endure in salvation.
- Are you serving _____ with what He has given you?

"For it will be like a man going on a journey, who called his servants and entrusted to them his property. To one he gave five talents, to another two, to another one, to each according to his ability. Then he went away. He who had received the five talents went at once and traded with them, and he made five talents more. So also he who had the two talents made two talents more. But he who had received the one talent went and dug in the ground and hid his master's money. Now after a long time the master of those servants came and settled accounts with them. And he who had received the five talents came forward, bringing five talents more, saying, 'Master, you delivered to me five talents; here I have made five talents more.' His master said to him, 'Well done, good and faithful servant. You have been faithful over a little; I will set you over much. Enter into the joy of your master.' And he also who had the two talents came forward, saying, 'Master, you delivered to me two talents; here I have made two talents more.' His master said to him, 'Well done, good and faithful servant. You have been faithful over a little; I will set you over much. Enter into the joy of your master.'

"He also who had received the one talent came forward, saying, 'Master, I knew you to be a hard man, reaping where you did not sow, and gathering where you scattered no seed, so I was afraid, and I went and hid your talent in the ground. Here you have what is yours.' But his master answered him, 'You wicked and slothful servant! You knew that I reap where I have not sown and gather where I scattered no seed? Then you ought to have invested my money with the bankers, and at my coming I should have received what was my own with interest. So take the talent from him and give it to him who has the ten talents. For to everyone who has will more be given, and he will have an abundance. But from the one who has not, even what he has will be taken away. And cast the worthless servant into the outer darkness. In that place there will be weeping and gnashing of teeth.'"
Matthew 25:14-30

- Jesus is our Master, and we are His stewards.
- Will you be commended in your _____ for Christ?
- Will you be condemned in your laziness before Christ?
- Are you serving _____ that God has put around you?

"When the Son of Man comes in his glory, and all the angels with him, then he will sit on his glorious throne. Before him will be gathered all the nations, and he will separate people one from another as a shepherd separates the sheep from the goats. And he will place the sheep on his right, but the goats on the left. Then the King will say to those on his right, 'Come, you who are blessed by my Father, inherit the kingdom prepared for you from the foundation of the world. For I was hungry and you gave me food, I was thirsty and you gave me drink, I was a stranger and you welcomed me, I was naked and you clothed me, I was sick and you visited me, I was in prison and you came to me.' Then the righteous will answer him, saying, 'Lord, when did we see you hungry and feed you, or thirsty and give you drink? And when did we see you a stranger and welcome you, or naked and clothe you? And when did we see you sick or in prison and visit you?' And the King will answer them, 'Truly, I say to you, as you did it to one of the least of these my brothers, you did it to me.'

"Then he will say to those on his left, 'Depart from me, you cursed, into the eternal fire prepared for the devil and his angels. For I was hungry and you gave me no food, I was thirsty and you gave me no drink, I was a stranger and you did not welcome me, naked and you did not clothe me, sick and in prison and you did not visit me.' Then they also will answer, saying, 'Lord, when did we see you hungry or thirsty or a stranger or naked or sick or in prison, and did not minister to you?' Then he will answer them, saying, 'Truly, I say to you, as you did not do it to one of the least of these, you did not do it to me.' And these will go away into eternal punishment, but the righteous into eternal life."
Matthew 25:31-46

- Not because you want to get to heaven.
- But because Jesus has changed your heart.
    - Sacrificial service is not a means of earning salvation.
    - Sacrificial service is necessary *evidence* of salvation.
- In the end …
    - His timing will confound our _____.

This is now the second letter that I am writing to you, beloved. In both of them I am stirring up your sincere mind by way of reminder, that you should remember the predictions of the holy prophets and the commandment of the Lord and Savior through your apostles, knowing this first of all, that scoffers will come in the last days with scoffing, following their own sinful desires. They will say, "Where is the promise of his coming? For ever since the fathers fell asleep, all things are continuing as they were from the beginning of creation." For they deliberately overlook this fact, that the heavens existed long ago, and the earth was formed out of water and through water by the word of God, and that by means of these the world that then existed was deluged with water and perished. But by the same word the heavens and earth that now exist are stored up for fire, being kept until the day of judgment and destruction of the ungodly.

But do not overlook this one fact, beloved, that with the Lord one day is as a thousand years, and a thousand years as one day. The Lord is not slow to fulfill his promise as some count slowness, but is patient toward you, not wishing that any should perish, but that all should reach repentance. But the day of the Lord will come like a thief, and then the heavens will pass away with a roar, and the heavenly bodies will be burned up and dissolved, and the earth and the works that are done on it will be exposed.
2 Peter 3:1-10

- His church (our lives!) will accomplish His _____.

"And this gospel of the kingdom will be proclaimed throughout the whole world as a testimony to all nations, and then the end will come."
Matthew 24:14

"God alone knows the definition of terms [here]. I cannot precisely define who all the nations are, but I do not need to know. I know only one thing: Christ has not yet returned therefore, the task is not yet done. When it is done, Christ will come. Our responsibility is not to insist on defining the terms; our responsibility is to complete the task. So long as Christ does not return, our work is undone. Let us get busy and complete our mission."
George Ladd

Since all these things are thus to be dissolved, what sort of people ought you to be in lives of holiness and godliness, waiting for and hastening the coming of the day of God, because of which the heavens will be set on fire and dissolved, and the heavenly bodies will melt as they burn!
2 Peter 3:11-12

- His return will exceed our *expectations*

Our Lord, come!
1 Corinthians 16:22b

He who testifies to these things says, "Surely I am coming soon." Amen. Come, Lord Jesus!
Revelation 22:20

"Lo! He comes, with clouds descending, once for favored sinners slain;
Thousand thousand saints attending swell the triumph of his train:
Alleluia! Alleluia! God appears on earth to reign.

"Ev'ry eye shall now behold him, robed in dreadful majesty;
Those who set at naught and sold him, pierced, and nailed him to the tree,
Deeply wailing, deeply wailing, shall the true Messiah see.

"Ev'ry island, sea, and mountain, heav'n and earth, shall flee away;
All who hate him must, confounded, hear the trump proclaim the Day;
Come to judgment! Come to judgment! Come to judgment, come away!

"Now redemption, long expected, see in solemn pomp appear!
All his saints, by man rejected, now shall meet him in the air:
Alleluia! Alleluia! See the Day of God appear!

"Yea, amen! Let all adore thee, high on thine eternal throne;
Savior, take the pow'r and glory, claim the kingdom for thine own:
O come quickly; O come quickly; alleluia! Come, Lord, come."

Charles Wesley and John Cennick

THE RESURRECTION OF THE DEAD

"For I know that my Redeemer lives, and at the last he will stand upon the earth. And after my skin has been thus destroyed, yet in my flesh I shall see God, whom I shall see for myself, and my eyes shall behold, and not another. My heart faints within me!"
Job 19:25-27

"Your dead shall live; their bodies shall rise. You who dwell in the dust, awake and sing for joy! For your dew is a dew of light, and the earth will give birth to the dead."
Isaiah 26:19

Jesus said to her, "I am the resurrection and the life. Whoever believes in me, though he die, yet shall he live, and everyone who lives and believes in me shall never die. Do you believe this?"
John 11:25-26

And not only the creation, but we ourselves, who have the firstfruits of the Spirit, groan inwardly as we wait eagerly for adoption as sons, the redemption of our bodies. For in this hope we were saved. Now hope that is seen is not hope. For who hopes for what he sees? But if we hope for what we do not see, we wait for it with patience.
Romans 8:23-25

"Christianity is not a platonic religion that regards material things as mere shadows of reality, which will be sloughed off as soon as possible. Not the mere immortality of the soul, but rather the resurrection of the body and renewal of all creation is the hope of the Christian faith."
John Piper

"[The resurrection of the body] is the Christian's brightest hope. Many believers make a mistake when they long to die and long for Heaven. Those things may be desirable, but they are not the ultimate for the saints. The saints in Heaven are perfectly free from sin and, so far as they are capable of it, are perfectly happy. But a disembodied spirit never can be perfect until it is reunited to its body. God made man not pure spirit but body and spirit, and the spirit alone will never be content until it sees its physical frame raised to its own condition of holiness and glory. Think not that our longings here below are not shared in by the saints in Heaven. They do not groan so far as any pain can be, but they long with greater intensity than you and I for the 'adoption ... the redemption of our bodies.' People have said there is no faith in Heaven, and no hope. They know not what they say— in Heaven faith and hope have their fullest swing and their brightest sphere, for glorified saints believe in God's promise and hope for the resurrection of the body."
Charles Spurgeon

Jesus rose from the dead.

For I delivered to you as of first importance what I also received: that Christ died for our sins in accordance with the Scriptures, that he was buried, that he was raised on the third day in accordance with the Scriptures, and that he appeared to Cephas, then to the twelve. Then he appeared to more than five hundred brothers at one time, most of whom are still alive, though some have fallen asleep. Then he appeared to James, then to all the apostles. Last of all, as to one untimely born, he appeared also to me.
1 Corinthians 15:3-8

Now when Paul perceived that one part were Sadducees and the other Pharisees, he cried out in the council, "Brothers, I am a Pharisee, a son of Pharisees. It is with respect to the hope and the resurrection of the dead that I am on trial."
Acts 23:6

Possible Explanations for Jesus' Resurrection ...
- ○ Jesus didn't _____ on the cross.
- ○ Jesus' tomb was not empty.
- ○ The disciples _____ the body of Jesus.
- ○ The disciples were delusional when they claimed to see Jesus.
- ○ Jesus died on the cross and _____ rose from the grave.
  - ■ Not resuscitation.
  - ■ Not reincarnation.
  - ■ Resurrection.

Startling Implications of Jesus' Resurrection ...
- ○ He is Lord over life and _death_.

"No one takes it from me, but I lay it down of my own accord. I have authority to lay it down, and I have authority to take it up again. This charge I have received from my Father."
John 10:18

- ○ He is Lord over sin and Satan.

"O death, where is your victory? O death, where is your sting?" The sting of death is sin, and the power of sin is the law. But thanks be to God, who gives us the victory through our Lord Jesus Christ.
1 Corinthians 15:55-57

- ○ He is Lord over _you_ and me.

... because, if you confess with your mouth that Jesus is Lord and believe in your heart that God raised him from the dead, you will be saved. For with the heart one believes and is justified, and with the mouth one confesses and is saved.
Romans 10:9-10

- Believe in the resurrection of Christ.
- _____ to the Lordship of Christ.

For as the Father raises the dead and gives them life, so also the Son gives life to whom he will. The Father judges no one, but has given all judgment to the Son, that all may honor the Son, just as they honor the Father. Whoever does not honor the Son does not honor the Father who sent him. Truly, truly, I say to you, whoever hears my word and believes him who sent me has eternal life. He does not come into judgment, but has passed from death to life. "Truly, truly, I say to you, an hour is coming, and is now here, when the dead will hear the voice of the Son of God, and those who hear will live. For as the Father has life in himself, so he has granted the Son also to have life in himself. And he has given him authority to execute judgment, because he is the Son of Man. Do not marvel at this, for an hour is coming when all who are in the tombs will hear his voice and come out, those who have done good to the resurrection of life, and those who have done evil to the resurrection of judgment."
John 5:21-29

When the resurrected Christ returns, Christians will experience physical resurrection with Him.

For as in Adam all die, so also in Christ shall all be made alive. But each in his own order: Christ the firstfruits, then at his coming those who belong to Christ.
1 Corinthians 15:22-23

"Thou wilt come to raise my body from the dust, and re-unite it to my soul, by a wonderful work of infinite power and love, greater than that which bounds the ocean's waters, ebbs and flows the tides, keeps the stars in their courses, and gives life to all creatures."
"Valley of Vision: A Collection of Puritan Prayers and Devotions"

- __Most__ believers will die.

Behold! I tell you a mystery. We shall not all sleep, but we shall all be changed, in a moment, in the twinkling of an eye, at the last trumpet. For the trumpet will sound, and the dead will be raised imperishable, and we shall be changed.
1 Corinthians 15:51-52

- __All__ believers will be resurrected.

For since we believe that Jesus died and rose again, even so, through Jesus, God will bring with him those who have fallen asleep. For this we declare to you by a word from the Lord, that we who are alive, who are left until the coming of the Lord, will not precede those who have fallen asleep. For the Lord himself will descend from heaven with a cry of command, with the voice of an archangel, and with the sound of the trumpet of God. And the dead in

Christ will rise first. Then we who are alive, who are left, will be caught up together with them in the clouds to meet the Lord in the air, and so we will always be with the Lord.
1 Thessalonians 4:14-17

- ○ Those who are alive when Christ returns will be physically transformed in their bodies.
- ○ Those who are dead when Christ returns will be physically reunited with their bodies.

Our resurrection bodies will be <u>Christ-like</u>.

But our citizenship is in heaven, and from it we await a Savior, the Lord Jesus Christ, who will transform our lowly body to be like his glorious body, by the power that enables him even to subject all things to himself.
Philippians 3:20-21

Beloved, we are God's children now, and what we will be has not yet appeared; but we know that when he appears we shall be like him, because we shall see him as he is.
1 John 3:2

Our resurrection bodies will be _____.

And he said to them, "Why are you troubled, and why do doubts arise in your hearts? See my hands and my feet, that it is I myself. Touch me, and see. For a spirit does not have flesh and bones as you see that I have."
Luke 24:38-39

Then he said to Thomas, "Put your finger here, and see my hands; and put out your hand, and place it in my side. Do not disbelieve, but believe."
John 20:27

"All things are lawful for me," but not all things are helpful. "All things are lawful for me," but I will not be dominated by anything. "Food is meant for the stomach and the stomach for food"—and God will destroy both one and the other. The body is not meant for sexual immorality, but for the Lord, and the Lord for the body. And God raised the Lord and will also raise us up by his power. Do you not know that your bodies are members of Christ? Shall I then take the members of Christ and make them members of a prostitute? Never! Or do you not know that he who is joined to a prostitute becomes one body with her? For, as it is written, "The two will become one flesh." But he who is joined to the Lord becomes one spirit with him. Flee from sexual immorality. Every other sin a person commits is outside the body, but the sexually immoral person sins against his own body. Or do you not know that your body is a temple of the Holy Spirit within you, whom you have from God? You are not your own, for you were bought with a price. So glorify God in your body.
1 Corinthians 6:12-20

- The Bible views the physical body (apart from sin) as holy, good, and valuable
  - Implications for our lives …
    - We dare not _____ the care of our bodies.

"Because we believe in the resurrection of the body, we know our bodies are not expendable vehicles for our souls, and they are certainly not playthings for our amusement."
Russell Moore

    - We must not _____ the care of bodies.

If you put these things before the brothers, you will be a good servant of Christ Jesus, being trained in the words of the faith and of the good doctrine that you have followed. Have nothing to do with irreverent, silly myths. Rather train yourself for godliness; for while bodily training is of some value, godliness is of value in every way, as it holds promise for the present life and also for the life to come. The saying is trustworthy and deserving of full acceptance. For to this end we toil and strive, because we have our hope set on the living God, who is the Savior of all people, especially of those who believe.
1 Timothy 4:6-10

  - Implications for our death …
    - _____ is biblical.

For I delivered to you as of first importance what I also received: that Christ died for our sins in accordance with the Scriptures, that he was buried, that he was raised on the third day in accordance with the Scriptures …
1 Corinthians 15:3-4

We were buried therefore with him by baptism into death, in order that, just as Christ was raised from the dead by the glory of the Father, we too might walk in newness of life
Romans 6:4

By faith Joseph, at the end of his life, made mention of the exodus of the Israelites and gave directions concerning his bones.
Hebrews 11:22

    - _____ undercuts resurrection.

"Since we believe in the resurrection of the body, we do not see a corpse as garbage. From the time of our earliest ancestors in the faith, we have buried our dead, committing them to the earth from which they came with the conviction that they will one day be summoned from it once more. The image of sleep is useful—not because the dead are unconscious but because they will one day be awakened. God deems as faith Joseph committing his bones to his brothers for future transport into the land of promise. In the same way the act of burial is a testimony of the entire community to the resurrection of the body. Cremation is a horrifying testimony of the burning up of the flesh and bones, a testimony

that is decidedly pagan in both origin and in practice. Of course, God can resurrect a cremated Christian (or a Christian torn to pieces by lions, etc.), but how we deal with the body of a Christian teaches us—and the watching world—what we really believe about the gospel. Cremation ought then to be shunned by those who hope in Christ."
Russell Moore

○ Christians look forward to the restoration of the body, not relief from the body.

So is it with the resurrection of the dead. What is sown is perishable; what is raised is imperishable. It is sown in dishonor; it is raised in glory. It is sown in weakness; it is raised in power. It is sown a natural body; it is raised a spiritual body. If there is a natural body, there is also a spiritual body. Thus it is written, "The first man Adam became a living being"; the last Adam became a life-giving spirit. But it is not the spiritual that is first but the natural, and then the spiritual. The first man was from the earth, a man of dust; the second man is from heaven. As was the man of dust, so also are those who are of the dust, and as is the man of heaven, so also are those who are of heaven. Just as we have borne the image of the man of dust, we shall also bear the image of the man of heaven.

I tell you this, brothers: flesh and blood cannot inherit the kingdom of God, nor does the perishable inherit the imperishable. Behold! I tell you a mystery. We shall not all sleep, but we shall all be changed, in a moment, in the twinkling of an eye, at the last trumpet. For the trumpet will sound, and the dead will be raised imperishable, and we shall be changed. For this perishable body must put on the imperishable, and this mortal body must put on immortality. When the perishable puts on the imperishable, and the mortal puts on immortality, then shall come to pass the saying that is written: "Death is swallowed up in victory. O death, where is your victory? O death, where is your sting?" The sting of death is sin, and the power of sin is the law. But thanks be to God, who gives us the victory through our Lord Jesus Christ.
1 Corinthians 15:42-57

• Our resurrection bodies will be _____ (entirely Spirit-filled).
• Our resurrection bodies will be eternal.

So we do not lose heart. Though our outer self is wasting away, our inner self is being renewed day by day. For this light momentary affliction is preparing for us an eternal weight of glory beyond all comparison, as we look not to the things that are seen but to the things that are unseen. For the things that are seen are transient, but the things that are unseen are eternal.
2 Corinthians 4:16-18

"I hope in some way I can take my wheelchair to heaven. With my new glorified body I will stand up on resurrected legs, and I will be next to the Lord Jesus. And I will feel those nail prints in his hands, and I will say, 'Thank you, Jesus!' He will know I mean it, because he will recognize me from the inner sanctum of sharing in the fellowship of

his sufferings. He will see that I was one who identified with him in the sharing of his sufferings, so my gratitude will not be hollow. And then I will say, 'Lord Jesus, do you see that wheelchair over there? Well, you were right. When you put me in it, it was a lot of trouble. But the weaker I was in that thing, the harder I leaned on you. And the harder I leaned on you, the stronger I discovered you to be. I do not think I would ever have known the glory of your grace were it not for the weakness of that wheelchair. So thank you, Lord Jesus, for that. Now, if you like, you can send that thing off to hell.'"
Joni Eareckson Tada

- Our resurrection bodies will be _____.

> *Whenever Moses went in before the LORD to speak with him, he would remove the veil, until he came out. And when he came out and told the people of Israel what he was commanded, the people of Israel would see the face of Moses, that the skin of Moses' face was shining. And Moses would put the veil over his face again, until he went in to speak with him.*
> Exodus 34:34-35

> *"And those who are wise shall shine like the brightness of the sky above; and those who turn many to righteousness, like the stars forever and ever."*
> Daniel 12:3

> *"Then the righteous will shine like the sun in the kingdom of their Father. He who has ears, let him hear."*
> Matthew 13:43

- Our resurrection bodies will be powerful.

> *"Watch and pray that you may not enter into temptation. The spirit indeed is willing, but the flesh is weak."*
> Matthew 26:41

> *"All things which the Savior did, He did in the first place in order that what was spoken concerning Him in the prophets might be fulfilled, that the blind should receive sight, and the deaf hear (Isaiah 35:5), and so on; but also to induce the belief that in the resurrection the flesh shall arise entire. For if on earth He healed the sicknesses of the flesh, and made the body whole, much more will He do this in the resurrection, so that the flesh shall rise perfect and entire."*
> Justin Martyr

> *"I said of this poor body, 'You have not yet been newly created. The venom of the old serpent still taints you. But you shall yet be delivered. You shall rise again if you die and are buried, or you shall be changed if the Lord should suddenly come today. You, poor body, which drags me down to the dust in pain and sorrow, even you shall rise and be remade in the redemption of the body. For*

the new creation has begun in me, with God's down payment of his Spirit.' Oh
beloved, can't you rejoice in this? I encourage you to do so. Rejoice in what God
is doing in this new creation! Let your whole spirit be glad! Leap down, you
waterfalls of joy! Overflow with gladness! Let loose the torrents of praise!"
Charles Spurgeon

"I still can hardly believe it. I, with shriveled, bent fingers, atrophied muscles, gnarled
knees, and no feeling from the shoulders down, will one day have a new body, light,
bright, and clothed in righteousness—powerful and dazzling. Can you imagine the
hope this gives someone spinal-cord injured like me? Or someone who is cerebral palsied,
brain-injured, or who has multiple sclerosis? Imagine the hope this gives someone who
is manic-depressive. No other religion, no other philosophy promises new bodies, hearts,
and minds. Only in the Gospel of Christ do hurting people find such incredible hope."
Joni EarecksonTada

Our resurrection bodies will be _recognizeable_

Jesus answered them, "Destroy this temple, and in three days I will raise it up."
John 2:19

If the Spirit of him who raised Jesus from the dead dwells in you,
he who raised Christ Jesus from the dead will also give life to your
mortal bodies through his Spirit who dwells in you.
Romans 8:11

And what you sow is not the body that is to be, but a bare kernel,
perhaps of wheat or of some other grain. But God gives it a body
as he has chosen, and to each kind of seed its own body.
1 Corinthians 15:37-38

"I tell you, many will come from east and west and recline at table with
Abraham, Isaac, and Jacob in the kingdom of heaven …"
Matthew 8:11

And behold, two men were talking with him, Moses and Elijah, who appeared in glory
and spoke of his departure, which he was about to accomplish at Jerusalem. Now Peter
and those who were with him were heavy with sleep, but when they became fully awake
they saw his glory and the two men who stood with him. And as the men were parting
from him, Peter said to Jesus, "Master, it is good that we are here. Let us make three
tents, one for you and one for Moses and one for Elijah"—not knowing what he said.
Luke 9:30-33

"The glorified body is not a different body, but a different form of the same body."
Thomas Oden

- We will reflect our uniqueness.

So God created man in his own image, in the image of God he created him; male and female he created them. And God blessed them. And God said to them, "Be fruitful and multiply and fill the earth and subdue it, and have dominion over the fish of the sea and over the birds of the heavens and over every living thing that moves on the earth."
Genesis 1:27-28

- We will retain various distinctions.

After this I looked, and behold, a great multitude that no one could number, from every nation, from all tribes and peoples and languages, standing before the throne and before the Lamb, clothed in white robes, with palm branches in their hands, and crying out with a loud voice, "Salvation belongs to our God who sits on the throne, and to the Lamb!"
Revelation 7:9-10

"Ten thousand times ten thousand in sparkling raiment bright,
The armies of the ransomed saints throng up the steeps of light:
'Tis finished, all is finished, their fight with death and sin:
Fling open wide the golden gates, and let the victors in.

"What rush of alleluias fills all the earth and sky!
What ringing of a thousand harps bespeaks the triumph nigh!
O day, for which creation and all its tribes were made;
O joy, for all its former woes a thousand-fold repaid!

"O then what raptured greetings on Canaan's happy shore;
What knitting severed friendships up where partings are no more!
Then eyes with joy shall sparkle, that brimmed with tears of late;
Orphans no longer fatherless, nor widows desolate.

"Bring near thy great salvation, thou Lamb for sinners slain;
Fill up the roll of thine elect, then take thy pow'r, and reign:
Appear, desire of nations, thine exiles long for home;
Show in the heav'n thy promised sign; thou Prince and Saviour, come."

Henry Alford

- The return of Christ and the resurrection of Christians will usher in the _____ of creation.

For the creation waits with eager longing for the revealing of the sons of God. For the creation was subjected to futility, not willingly, but because of him who subjected it, in hope that the creation itself will be set free from its bondage to corruption and obtain the freedom of the glory of the children of God. For we know that the whole

creation has been groaning together in the pains of childbirth until now. And not only the creation, but we ourselves, who have the firstfruits of the Spirit, groan inwardly as we wait eagerly for adoption as sons, the redemption of our bodies. For in this hope we were saved. Now hope that is seen is not hope. For who hopes for what he sees? But if we hope for what we do not see, we wait for it with patience.
Romans 8:19-25

"Our Lord has written the promise of the resurrection not in books alone, but in every leaf in springtime."
Martin Luther

"Do you ever sense creation's restlessness? Do you hear groaning in the cold night wind? Do you feel the forests' loneliness, the oceans' agitation? Do you hear longing in the cries of the whales? Do you see blood and pain in the eyes of wild animals, or the mixture of pleasure and pain in the eyes of your pets? Despite vestiges of beauty and joy, something on this earth is terribly wrong .... The creation hopes for, even anticipates, resurrection."
Randy Alcorn

When the resurrected Christ returns, all people (Christians and non-Christians alike) will be resurrected for the day of final _____.

"And many of those who sleep in the dust of the earth shall awake, some to everlasting life, and some to shame and everlasting contempt."
Daniel 12:2

"Do not marvel at this, for an hour is coming when all who are in the tombs will hear his voice and come out, those who have done good to the resurrection of life, and those who have done evil to the resurrection of judgment."
John 5:28-29

"When the Son of Man comes in his glory, and all the angels with him, then he will sit on his glorious throne. Before him will be gathered all the nations, and he will separate people one from another as a shepherd separates the sheep from the goats. And he will place the sheep on his right, but the goats on the left."
Matthew 25:31-33

"But this I confess to you, that according to the Way, which they call a sect, I worship the God of our fathers, believing everything laid down by the Law and written in the Prophets, having a hope in God, which these men themselves accept, that there will be a resurrection of both the just and the unjust."
Acts 24:14-15

THE FINAL JUDGMENT

And just as it is appointed for man to die once, and after that comes judgment,
so Christ, having been offered once to bear the sins of many, will appear a second
time, not to deal with sin but to save those who are eagerly waiting for him.
Hebrews 9:27-28

"There are few things stressed more strongly in the Bible
than the reality of God's work as Judge."
J.I. Packer

Biblical Truths ...

• A day of final judgment is coming.

"The times of ignorance God overlooked, but now he commands all people
everywhere to repent, because he has fixed a day on which he will judge
the world in righteousness by a man whom he has appointed; and of
this he has given assurance to all by raising him from the dead."
Acts 17:30-31

But because of your hard and impenitent heart you are storing up wrath for yourself
on the day of wrath when God's righteous judgment will be revealed. He will render
to each one according to his works: to those who by patience in well-doing seek for
glory and honor and immortality, he will give eternal life; but for those who are self-
seeking and do not obey the truth, but obey unrighteousness, there will be wrath
and fury. There will be tribulation and distress for every human being who does
evil, the Jew first and also the Greek, but glory and honor and peace for everyone
who does good, the Jew first and also the Greek. For God shows no partiality.
Romans 2:5-11

Then I saw a great white throne and him who was seated on it. From his presence
earth and sky fled away, and no place was found for them. And I saw the dead, great
and small, standing before the throne, and books were opened. Then another book was
opened, which is the book of life. And the dead were judged by what was written in
the books, according to what they had done. And the sea gave up the dead who were
in it, Death and Hades gave up the dead who were in them, and they were judged,
each one of them, according to what they had done. Then Death and Hades were
thrown into the lake of fire. This is the second death, the lake of fire. And if anyone's
name was not found written in the book of life, he was thrown into the lake of fire.
Revelation 20:11-15

○ The _____ for judgment is instinctual.

*O LORD, how long shall I cry for help, and you will not hear? Or cry to you
"Violence!" and you will not save? Why do you make me see iniquity, and
why do you idly look at wrong? Destruction and violence are before me; strife
and contention arise. So the law is paralyzed, and justice never goes forth.
For the wicked surround the righteous; so justice goes forth perverted.*
Habakkuk 1:2-4

"I always say to my skeptical, secular friends that, even if they can't believe in the
resurrection, they should want it to be true. Most of them care deeply about justice for the
poor, alleviating hunger and disease, and caring for the environment. Yet many of them
believe that the material world was caused by accident and that the world and everything
in it will eventually simply burn up. They find it discouraging that so few people care
about justice without realizing that their own worldview undermines any motivation to
make the world a better place. Why sacrifice for the needs of others if in the end nothing
we do will make any difference? However, if the resurrection of Jesus happened, that
means there's infinite hope and reason to pour ourselves out for the needs of the world."
Tim Keller

○ The fact of judgment is inevitable.

*And I saw the dead, great and small, standing before the throne, and books were
opened. Then another book was opened, which is the book of life. And the dead
were judged by what was written in the books, according to what they had done.*
Revelation 20:12

"The only natural argument of any weight, for the immortality of the
soul, takes its rise from this observation, that justice is not extended to
the good, nor executed upon the bad, man in this life; and that, as the
Governor of the world is just, man must live hereafter to be judged."
Jonathan Edwards

○ The _____ of judgment are undeniable.

*For if God did not spare angels when they sinned, but cast them into hell and committed
them to chains of gloomy darkness to be kept until the judgment; if he did not spare
the ancient world, but preserved Noah, a herald of righteousness, with seven others,
when he brought a flood upon the world of the ungodly; if by turning the cities of
Sodom and Gomorrah to ashes he condemned them to extinction, making them an
example of what is going to happen to the ungodly; and if he rescued righteous Lot,
greatly distressed by the sensual conduct of the wicked (for as that righteous man
lived among them day after day, he was tormenting his righteous soul over their
lawless deeds that he saw and heard); then the Lord knows how to rescue the godly
from trials, and to keep the unrighteous under punishment until the day of judgment,*

and especially those who indulge in the lust of defiling passion and despise authority.
Bold and willful, they do not tremble as they blaspheme the glorious ones …
2 Peter 2:4-10

○ The scope of judgment will be universal.

"For behold, the LORD will come in fire, and his chariots like the whirlwind,
to render his anger in fury, and his rebuke with flames of fire. For by fire will
the LORD enter into judgment, and by his sword, with all flesh; and those
slain by the LORD shall be many. Those who sanctify and purify themselves
to go into the gardens, following one in the midst, eating pig's flesh and the
abomination and mice, shall come to an end together, declares the LORD.

"For I know their works and their thoughts, and the time is coming to gather all nation.
and tongues. And they shall come and shall see my glory, and I will set a sign among the
And from them I will send survivors to the nations, to Tarshish, Pul, and Lud, who dra
the bow, to Tubal and Javan, to the coastlands far away, that have not heard my fame o
seen my glory. And they shall declare my glory among the nations. And they shall bring
all your brothers from all the nations as an offering to the LORD, on horses and in chario
and in litters and on mules and on dromedaries, to my holy mountain Jerusalem, says th
LORD, just as the Israelites bring their grain offering in a clean vessel to the house of the
LORD. And some of them also I will take for priests and for Levites, says the LORD.

"For as the new heavens and the new earth that I make shall remain before
me, says the LORD, so shall your offspring and your name remain. From new
moon to new moon, and from Sabbath to Sabbath, all flesh shall come to worship
before me, declares the LORD. And they shall go out and look on the dead bodies
of the men who have rebelled against me. For their worm shall not die, their
fire shall not be quenched, and they shall be an abhorrence to all flesh."
Isaiah 66:15-24

○ The nature of judgment will be personal.

"Not everyone who says to me, 'Lord, Lord,' will enter the kingdom of heaven, but
the one who does the will of my Father who is in heaven. On that day many will
say to me, 'Lord, Lord, did we not prophesy in your name, and cast out demons
in your name, and do many mighty works in your name?' And then will I declare
to them, 'I never knew you; depart from me, you workers of lawlessness.'"
Matthew 7:21-23

- The day of judgment will not ultimately determine our spiritual conditio
- The day of judgment will truly _____ our spiritual conditio

"In the day that we stand before our Master and Maker, it will not matter how many people on earth knew our name, how many called us great, and how many considered us fools. It will not matter whether schools and hospitals were named after us, whether our estate was large or small, whether our funeral drew ten thousand or no one. It will not matter what the newspapers or history books said or didn't say. What will matter is one thing and one thing only—what the Master thinks of us."
Randy Alcorn

○ The impartiality of judgment will be unquestionable.

There will be tribulation and distress for every human being who does evil, the Jew first and also the Greek, but glory and honor and peace for everyone who does good, the Jew first and also the Greek. For God shows no partiality.
Romans 2:9-11

For the wrongdoer will be paid back for the wrong he has done, and there is no partiality.
Colossians 3:25

○ The effects of judgment will be **eternal**.

"And these will go away into eternal punishment, but the righteous into eternal life."
Matthew 25:46

The final Judge will be **Christ**.

For to us a child is born, to us a son is given; and the government shall be upon his shoulder, and his name shall be called Wonderful Counselor, Mighty God, Everlasting Father, Prince of Peace. Of the increase of his government and of peace there will be no end, on the throne of David and over his kingdom, to establish it and to uphold it with justice and with righteousness from this time forth and forevermore. The zeal of the LORD of hosts will do this.
Isaiah 9:6-7

Behold my servant, whom I uphold, my chosen, in whom my soul delights; I have put my Spirit upon him; he will bring forth justice to the nations.
Isaiah 42:1

"The Father judges no one, but has given all judgment to the Son, that all may honor the Son, just as they honor the Father. Whoever does not honor the Son does not honor the Father who sent him. Truly, truly, I say to you, whoever hears my word and believes him who sent me has eternal life. He does not come into judgment, but has passed from death to life. Truly, truly, I say to you, an hour is coming, and is now here, when the dead will hear the voice of the Son of God, and those who hear will live. For as the

Father has life in himself, so he has granted the Son also to have life in himself. And he has given him authority to execute judgment, because he is the Son of Man."
John 5:22-27

"When the Son of Man comes in his glory, and all the angels with him, then he will sit on his glorious throne. Before him will be gathered all the nations, and he will separate people one from another as a shepherd separates the sheep from the goats. And he will place the sheep on his right, but the goats on the left."
Matthew 25:31-33

And he commanded us to preach to the people and to testify that he is the one appointed by God to be judge of the living and the dead.
Acts 10:42

… on that day when, according to my gospel, God judges the secrets of men by Christ Jesus.
Romans 2:16

I charge you in the presence of God and of Christ Jesus, who is to judge the living and the dead, and by his appearing and his kingdom …
2 Timothy 4:1

For we must all appear before the judgment seat of Christ, so that each one may receive what is due for what he has done in the body, whether good or evil.
2 Corinthians 5:10

- All __Angels__ will be involved in this judgment.
  - Holy angels will gather the judged.

"The Son of Man will send his angels, and they will gather out of his kingdom all causes of sin and all law-breakers, and throw them into the fiery furnace. In that place there will be weeping and gnashing of teeth."
Matthew 13:41-42

"And he will send out his angels with a loud trumpet call, and they will gather his elect from the four winds, from one end of heaven to the other."
Matthew 24:31

  - Fallen angels will all be judged.

For if God did not spare angels when they sinned, but cast them into hell and committed them to chains of gloomy darkness to be kept until the judgment …
2 Peter 2:4

ow I want to remind you, although you once fully knew it, that Jesus, who saved a people out of the land of Egypt, afterward destroyed those who did not believe. And the angels who did not stay within their own position of authority, but left their proper dwelling, he *as kept in eternal chains under gloomy darkness until the judgment of the great day …*
Jude 5-6

All people (and ___all___ they have done) will be involved in this judgment.

Why do you pass judgment on your brother? Or you, why do you despise your brother? For we will all stand before the judgment seat of God; for it is written, "As I live, says the Lord, every knee shall bow to me, and every tongue shall confess to God." So then each of us will give an account of himself to God.
Romans 14:10-12

Rejoice, O young man, in your youth, and let your heart cheer you in the days of your youth. Walk in the ways of your heart and the sight of your eyes. But know that for all these things God will bring you into judgment.
Ecclesiastes 11:9

God will bring every deed into judgment, with every secret thing, whether good or evil.
Ecclesiastes 12:14

I tell you, on the day of judgment people will give account for every careless word they *eak, for by your words you will be justified, and by your words you will be condemned."*
Matthew 12:36-37

"Nothing is covered up that will not be revealed, or hidden that will not be known."
Luke 12:2

o Two Realities:

"The nations raged, but your wrath came, and the time for the dead to be judged, and for rewarding your servants, the prophets and saints, and those who fear your name, both small and great, and for destroying the destroyers of the earth."
Revelation 11:18

▪ God will justify every saint who has ___trusted___ in Him.

Then what becomes of our boasting? It is excluded. By what kind of law? By a law of works? No, but by the law of faith. For we hold that one is justified by faith apart from works of the law. Or is God the God of Jews only? Is he not the God of Gentiles also? Yes, of Gentiles also, since God is one—who will justify the

circumcised by faith and the uncircumcised through faith. Do we then overthrow the law by this faith? By no means! On the contrary, we uphold the law.
Romans 3:27-31

There is therefore now no condemnation for those who are in Christ Jesus. For the law of the Spirit of life has set you free in Christ Jesus from the law of sin and death.
Romans 8:1-2

"God's Word treats the judgment of believers with great sobriety. It does not portray it as a meaningless formality, going through the motions before we get on to the real business of heavenly bliss. Rather, Scripture presents it as a monumental event in which things of eternal significance are brought to light and things of eternal consequence are put into effect.
Randy Alcorn

- Every sin will have been ̲f̲o̲r̲g̲i̲v̲e̲n̲.

He will not always chide, nor will he keep his anger forever. He does not deal with us according to our sins, nor repay us according to our iniquities. For as high as the heavens are above the earth, so great is his steadfast love toward those who fear him; as far as the east is from the west, so far does he remove our transgressions from us. As a father shows compassion to his children, so the LORD shows compassion to those who fear him.
Psalm 103:9-13

"I, I am he who blots out your transgressions for my own sake, and I will not remember your sins."
Isaiah 43:25

He will again have compassion on us; he will tread our iniquities underfoot. You will cast all our sins into the depths of the sea.
Micah 7:19

"For I will be merciful toward their iniquities, and I will remember their sins no more."
Hebrews 8:12

And the Holy Spirit also bears witness to us; for after saying, "This is the covenant that I will make with them after those days, declares the Lord: I will put my laws on their hearts, and write them on their minds," then he adds, "I will remember their sins and their lawless deeds no more." Where there is forgiveness of these, there is no longer any offering for sin.
Hebrews 10:15-18

- Varying rewards for faithfulness will be distributed.

"And he said to him, 'Well done, good servant! Because you have been faithful in a very little, you shall have authority over ten cities.' And the second came, saying, 'Lord, your mina has made five minas.' And he said to him, 'And you are to be over five cities.'"
Luke 19:17-19

Now if anyone builds on the foundation with gold, silver, precious stones, wood, hay, straw—each one's work will become manifest, for the Day will disclose it, because it will be revealed by fire, and the fire will test what sort of work each one has done. If the work that anyone has built on the foundation survives, he will receive a reward. If anyone's work is burned up, he will suffer loss, though he himself will be saved, but only as through fire.
1 Corinthians 3:12-15

Whatever you do, work heartily, as for the Lord and not for men, knowing that from the Lord you will receive the inheritance as your reward. You are serving the Lord Christ.
Colossians 3:23-24

    ○ We're not competing with one another for rewards.

If one member suffers, all suffer together; if one member is honored, all rejoice together. Now you are the body of Christ and individually members of it.
1 Corinthians 12:26-27

    ○ We're _____ one another toward reward.

And let us consider how to stir up one another to love and good works, not neglecting to meet together, as is the habit of some, but encouraging one another, and all the more as you see the Day drawing near.
Hebrews 10:24-25

For what is our hope or joy or crown of boasting before our Lord Jesus at his coming? Is it not you? For you are our glory and joy.
1 Thessalonians 2:19-20

Therefore, my brothers, whom I love and long for, my joy and crown, stand firm thus in the Lord, my beloved.
Philippians 4:1

    ■ God will condemn every sinner who has _____ from Him.

"For God so loved the world, that he gave his only Son, that whoever believes in him should not perish but have eternal life. For God did not send his Son into the world to condemn the world, but in order that the world might be saved through him. Whoever believes in him is not condemned, but whoever does not believe is condemned already, because he has not believed in the name of the only Son of God."
John 3:16-18

And I saw the dead, great and small, standing before the throne, and books were opened. Then another book was opened, which is the book of life. And the dead were judged by what was written in the books, according to what they had done. And the sea gave up the dead who were in it, Death and Hades gave up the dead who were in them, and they were judged, each one of them, according to what they had done. Then Death and Hades were thrown into the lake of fire. This is the second death, the lake of fire. And if anyone's name was not found written in the book of life, he was thrown into the lake of fire.
Revelation 20:12-15

- Every sin will come to __light__.

Therefore do not pronounce judgment before the time, before the Lord comes, who will bring to light the things now hidden in darkness and will disclose the purposes of the heart
1 Corinthians 4:5a

- Varying degrees of punishment will be enforced.

"But I tell you, it will be more bearable on the day of judgment for Tyre and Sidon than for you. And you, Capernaum, will you be exalted to heaven? You will be brought down to Hades. For if the mighty works done in you had been done in Sodom, it would have remained until this day. But I tell you that it will be more tolerable on the day of judgment for the land of Sodom than for you."
Matthew 11:22-24

"And that servant who knew his master's will but did not get ready or act according to his will, will receive a severe beating. But the one who did not know, and did what deserved a beating, will receive a light beating. Everyone to whom much was given, of him much will be required, and from him to whom they entrusted much, they will demand the more."
Luke 12:47-48

And in the hearing of all the people he said to his disciples, "Beware of the scribes, who like to walk around in long robes, and love greetings in the marketplaces and the best seats in the synagogues and the places of honor at feasts, who devour widows' houses and for a pretense make long prayers. They will receive the greater condemnation."
Luke 20:45-47

- Two Questions:
  - Did we put our faith in __Christ's__ work?

We ourselves are Jews by birth and not Gentile sinners; yet we know that a person is not justified by works of the law but through faith in Jesus Christ, so we also have believed in Christ Jesus, in order to be justified by faith in Christ and not by works of the law, because by works of the law no one will be justified. But if, in our endeavor to be justified in Christ, we too were found to be sinners, is Christ then a servant of sin?

Certainly not! For if I rebuild what I tore down, I prove myself to be a transgressor. For through the law I died to the law, so that I might live to God. I have been crucified with Christ. It is no longer I who live, but Christ who lives in me. And the life I now live in the flesh I live by faith in the Son of God, who loved me and gave himself for me.
Galatians 2:15-20

… and all who dwell on earth will worship it, everyone whose name has not been written before the foundation of the world in the book of life of the Lamb who was slain.
Revelation 13:8

- Was there evidence of faith in _____ *Our* _____ work?

"Not everyone who says to me, 'Lord, Lord,' will enter the kingdom of heaven, but the one who does the will of my Father who is in heaven. On that day many will say to me, 'Lord, Lord, did we not prophesy in your name, and cast out demons in your name, and do many mighty works in your name?' And then will I declare to them, 'I never knew you; depart from me, you workers of lawlessness.' Everyone then who hears these words of mine and does them will be like a wise man who built his house on the rock. And the rain fell, and the floods came, and the winds blew and beat on that house, but it did not fall, because it had been founded on the rock. And everyone who hears these words of mine and does not do them will be like a foolish man who built his house on the sand. And the rain fell, and the floods came, and the winds blew and beat against that house, and it fell, and great was the fall of it."
Matthew 7:21-27

"For the Son of Man is going to come with his angels in the glory of his Father, and then he will repay each person according to what he has done."
Matthew 16:27

'When the Son of Man comes in his glory, and all the angels with him, then he will sit on his glorious throne. Before him will be gathered all the nations, and he will separate people one from another as a shepherd separates the sheep from the goats. And he will place the sheep on his right, but the goats on the left. Then the King will say to those on his right, 'Come, you who are blessed by my Father, inherit the kingdom prepared for you from the foundation of the world. For I was hungry and you gave me food, I was thirsty and you gave me drink, I was a stranger and you welcomed me, I was naked and you clothed me, I was sick and you visited me, I was in prison and you came to me.' Then the righteous will answer him, saying, 'Lord, when did we see you hungry and feed you, or thirsty and give you drink? And when did we see you a stranger and welcome you, or naked and clothe you? And when did we see you sick or in prison and visit you?' And the King will answer them, 'Truly, I say to you, as you did it to one of the least of these my brothers, you did it to me.'

"Then he will say to those on his left, 'Depart from me, you cursed, into the eternal fire prepared for the devil and his angels. For I was hungry and you gave me no food, I was thirsty and you gave me no drink, I was a stranger and you did not welcome me, naked and you did not clothe me, sick and in prison and you did not visit me.' Then they also

will answer, saying, 'Lord, when did we see you hungry or thirsty or a stranger or naked or sick or in prison, and did not minister to you?' Then he will answer them, saying, 'Truly, I say to you, as you did not do it to one of the least of these, you did not do it to me.' And these will go away into eternal punishment, but the righteous into eternal life."
Matthew 25:31-46

For we must all appear before the judgment seat of Christ, so that each one may receive what is due for what he has done in the body, whether good or evil.
2 Corinthians 5:10

What good is it, my brothers, if someone says he has faith but does not have works? Can that faith save him? If a brother or sister is poorly clothed and lacking in daily food, and one of you says to them, "Go in peace, be warmed and filled," without giving them the things needed for the body, what good is that? So also faith by itself, if it does not have works, is dead. But someone will say, "You have faith and I have works." Show me your faith apart from your works, and I will show you my faith by my works. You believe that God is one; you do well. Even the demons believe—and shudder! Do you want to be shown, you foolish person, that faith apart from works is useless? Was not Abraham our father justified by works when he offered up his son Isaac on the altar? You see that faith was active along with his works, and faith was completed by his works; and the Scripture was fulfilled that says, "Abraham believed God, and it was counted to him as righteousness"—and he was called a friend of God. You see that a person is justified by works and not by faith alone. And in the same way was not also Rahab the prostitute justified by works when she received the messengers and sent them out by another way? For as the body apart from the spirit is dead, so also faith apart from works is dead.
James 2:14-26

But you, beloved, building yourselves up in your most holy faith and praying in the Holy Spirit, keep yourselves in the love of God, waiting for the mercy of our Lord Jesus Christ that leads to eternal life. And have mercy on those who doubt; save others by snatching them out of the fire; to others show mercy with fear, hating even the garment stained by the flesh. Now to him who is able to keep you from stumbling and to present you blameless before the presence of his glory with great joy, to the only God, our Savior, through Jesus Christ our Lord, be glory, majesty, dominion, and authority, before all time and now and forever. Amen.
Jude 20-25

Here is a call for the endurance of the saints, those who keep the commandments of God and their faith in Jesus. And I heard a voice from heaven saying, "Write this: Blessed are the dead who die in the Lord from now on." "Blessed indeed," says the Spirit, "that they may rest from their labors, for their deeds follow them!"
Revelation 14:12-13

○ Two Destinations:

And he said to me, "It is done! I am the Alpha and the Omega, the beginning and the end. To the thirsty I will give from the spring of the water of life without payment. The one who conquers will have this heritage, and I will be his God and he will be my son. But as for the cowardly, the faithless, the detestable, as for murderers, the sexually immoral, sorcerers, idolaters, and all liars, their portion will be in the lake that burns with fire and sulfur, which is the second death."
Revelation 21:6-8

- Everlasting _____.

Then I heard what seemed to be the voice of a great multitude, like the roar of many waters and like the sound of mighty peals of thunder, crying out, "Hallelujah! For the Lord our God the Almighty reigns. Let us rejoice and exult and give him the glory, for the marriage of the Lamb has come, and his Bride has made herself ready; it was granted her to clothe herself with fine linen, bright and pure"—for the fine linen is the righteous deeds of the saints. And the angel said to me, "Write this: Blessed are those who are invited to the marriage supper of the Lamb." And he said to me, "These are the true words of God."
Revelation 19:6-9

- Eternal torment.

And another angel, a third, followed them, saying with a loud voice, "If anyone worships the beast and its image and receives a mark on his forehead or on his hand, he also will drink the wine of God's wrath, poured full strength into the cup of his anger, and he will be tormented with fire and sulfur in the presence of the holy angels and in the presence of the Lamb. And the smoke of their torment goes up forever and ever, and they have no rest, day or night, these worshipers of the beast and its image, and whoever receives the mark of its name."
Revelation 14:9-11

God will be _____ for His justice.

And I saw what appeared to be a sea of glass mingled with fire—and also those who had conquered the beast and its image and the number of its name, standing beside the sea of glass with harps of God in their hands. And they sing the song of Moses, the servant of God, and the song of the Lamb, saying, "Great and amazing are your deeds, O Lord God the Almighty! Just and true are your ways, O King of the nations! Who will not fear, O Lord, and glorify your name? For you alone are holy. All nations will come and worship you, for your righteous acts have been revealed."
Revelation 15:2-4

Then I heard a loud voice from the temple telling the seven angels, "Go and pour out on the earth the seven bowls of the wrath of God." So the first angel went and poured out his bowl on the earth, and harmful and painful sores came upon the people who bore the mark of the beast and worshiped its image. The second angel poured out his bowl into the sea, and

it became like the blood of a corpse, and every living thing died that was in the sea. The third angel poured out his bowl into the rivers and the springs of water, and they became blood. And I heard the angel in charge of the waters say, "Just are you, O Holy One, who is and who was, for you brought these judgments. For they have shed the blood of saints and prophets, and you have given them blood to drink. It is what they deserve!" And I heard the altar saying, "Yes, Lord God the Almighty, true and just are your judgments!"
Revelation 16:1-7

After this I heard what seemed to be the loud voice of a great multitude in heaven, crying out, "Hallelujah! Salvation and glory and power belong to our God, for his judgments are true and just; for he has judged the great prostitute who corrupted the earth with her immorality, and has avenged on her the blood of his servants."
Revelation 19:1-2

○ We will finally have a _____ view of God.

"Who is like you, O LORD, among the gods? Who is like you, majestic in holiness, awesome in glorious deeds, doing wonders?"
Exodus 15:11

■ He is sovereign over all.

The earth is the LORD's and the fullness thereof, the world and those who dwell therein, for he has founded it upon the seas and established it upon the rivers.
Psalm 24:1-2

"You are the LORD, you alone. You have made heaven, the heaven of heavens, with all their host, the earth and all that is on it, the seas and all that is in them; and you preserve all of them; and the host of heaven worships you."
Nehemiah 9:6

O LORD, how manifold are your works! In wisdom have you made them all; the earth is full of your creatures. Here is the sea, great and wide, which teems with creatures innumerable, living things both small and great. There go the ships, and Leviathan, which you formed to play in it. These all look to you, to give them their food in due season. When you give it to them, they gather it up; when you open your hand, they are filled with good things. When you hide your face, they are dismayed; when you take away their breath, they die and return to their dust. When you send forth your Spirit, they are created, and you renew the face of the ground.
Psalm 104:24-30

■ He is glorified above all.

*"Be still, and know that I am God. I will be exalted among
the nations, I will be exalted in the earth!"*
Psalm 46:10

*All the nations you have made shall come and worship before you, O Lord, and shall
glorify your name. For you are great and do wondrous things; you alone are God.*
Psalm 86:9-10

"Turn to me and be saved, all the ends of the earth! For I am God, and there is no other."
Isaiah 45:22

- He is _____ in all His attributes.

*"There is none holy like the LORD: for there is none
besides you; there is no rock like our God."*
1 Samuel 2:2

*And one called to another and said: "Holy, holy, holy is the
LORD of hosts; the whole earth is full of his glory!"*
Isaiah 6:3

*And the four living creatures, each of them with six wings, are full of eyes
all around and within, and day and night they never cease to say, "Holy,
holy, holy, is the Lord God Almighty, who was and is and is to come!"*
Revelation 4:8

- He is righteous in all His ways.

*"Far be it from you to do such a thing, to put the righteous to death
with the wicked, so that the righteous fare as the wicked! Far be that
from you! Shall not the Judge of all the earth do what is just?"*
Genesis 18:25

*"The Rock, his work is perfect, for all his ways are justice. A God of
faithfulness and without iniquity, just and upright is he."*
Deuteronomy 32:4

*"Therefore, hear me, you men of understanding: far be it from God that he should
do wickedness, and from the Almighty that he should do wrong. For according to the
work of a man he will repay him, and according to his ways he will make it befall him.
Of a truth, God will not do wickedly, and the Almighty will not pervert justice."*
Job 34:10-12

*"Out of the north comes golden splendor; God is clothed with awesome
majesty. The Almighty—we cannot find him; he is great in power; justice*

and abundant righteousness he will not violate. Therefore men fear
him; he does not regard any who are wise in their own conceit."
Job 37:22-24

But if our unrighteousness serves to show the righteousness of God, what
shall we say? That God is unrighteous to inflict wrath on us? (I speak in a
human way.) By no means! For then how could God judge the world?
Romans 3:5-6

This is evidence of the righteous judgment of God, that you may be considered worthy
of the kingdom of God, for which you are also suffering—since indeed God considers
it just to repay with affliction those who afflict you, and to grant relief to you who are
afflicted as well as to us, when the Lord Jesus is revealed from heaven with his mighty
angels in flaming fire, inflicting vengeance on those who do not know God and on
those who do not obey the gospel of our Lord Jesus. They will suffer the punishment
of eternal destruction, away from the presence of the Lord and from the glory of his
might, when he comes on that day to be glorified in his saints, and to be marveled
at among all who have believed, because our testimony to you was believed.
2 Thessalonians 1:5-10

- He is _____ toward all His creation.

The LORD passed before him and proclaimed, "The LORD, the LORD, a God
merciful and gracious, slow to anger, and abounding in steadfast love and faithfulness,
keeping steadfast love for thousands, forgiving iniquity and transgression and sin,
but who will by no means clear the guilty, visiting the iniquity of the fathers on the
children and the children's children, to the third and the fourth generation."
Exodus 34:6-7

The LORD is merciful and gracious, slow to anger and abounding in steadfast love.
Psalm 103:8

So we have come to know and to believe the love that God has for us. God is
love, and whoever abides in love abides in God, and God abides in him.
1 John 4:16

- The clear conclusion …
  • God is infinitely worthy of eternal _____.

"Worthy are you, our Lord and God, to receive glory and honor and power,
for you created all things, and by your will they existed and were created."
Revelation 4:11

And I heard every creature in heaven and on earth and under the earth and in
the sea, and all that is in them, saying, "To him who sits on the throne and to

the Lamb be blessing and honor and glory and might forever and ever!" And the
four living creatures said, "Amen!" and the elders fell down and worshiped.
Revelation 5:13-14

○ We will finally have a _____ view of man.

Humble yourselves before the Lord, and he will exalt you.
James 4:10

■ We have denounced the sovereignty of God.

So when the woman saw that the tree was good for food, and that it was a
delight to the eyes, and that the tree was to be desired to make one wise, she took
of its fruit and ate, and she also gave some to her husband who was with her,
and he ate. Then the eyes of both were opened, and they knew that they were
naked. And they sewed fig leaves together and made themselves loincloths.
Genesis 3:6-7

And Aaron shall lay both his hands on the head of the live goat, and confess
over it all the iniquities of the people of Israel, and all their transgressions,
all their sins. And he shall put them on the head of the goat and send it
away into the wilderness by the hand of a man who is in readiness.
Leviticus 16:21

■ We have defamed the glory of God.

For the wrath of God is revealed from heaven against all ungodliness and unrighteousness
of men, who by their unrighteousness suppress the truth. For what can be known about
God is plain to them, because God has shown it to them. For his invisible attributes,
namely, his eternal power and divine nature, have been clearly perceived, ever since the
creation of the world, in the things that have been made. So they are without excuse.
For although they knew God, they did not honor him as God or give thanks to him, but
they became futile in their thinking, and their foolish hearts were darkened. Claiming
to be wise, they became fools, and exchanged the glory of the immortal God for images
resembling mortal man and birds and animals and creeping things. Therefore God
gave them up in the lusts of their hearts to impurity, to the dishonoring of their bodies
among themselves, because they exchanged the truth about God for a lie and worshiped
and served the creature rather than the Creator, who is blessed forever! Amen.
Romans 1:18-25

For, as it is written, "The name of God is blasphemed among the Gentiles because of you."
Romans 2:24

■ We have _____ the holiness of God.

*"Therefore say to the house of Israel, Thus says the Lord GOD: It is not for your sake,
O house of Israel, that I am about to act, but for the sake of my holy name, which
you have profaned among the nations to which you came. And I will vindicate the
holiness of my great name, which has been profaned among the nations, and which
you have profaned among them. And the nations will know that I am the LORD,
declares the Lord GOD, when through you I vindicate my holiness before their eyes."*
Ezekiel 36:22-23

- We have despised the righteousness of God.

*... as it is written: "None is righteous, no, not one; no one understands;
no one seeks for God. All have turned aside; together they have
become worthless; no one does good, not even one."*
Romans 3:10-12

- We have _____ the love of God.

*Or do you presume on the riches of his kindness and forbearance and patience,
not knowing that God's kindness is meant to lead you to repentance?*
Romans 2:4

- The clear conclusion ...
  - We are infinitely worthy of God's eternal _____.

*And you were dead in the trespasses and sins in which you once walked,
following the course of this world, following the prince of the power of the air,
the spirit that is now at work in the sons of disobedience—among whom we all
once lived in the passions of our flesh, carrying out the desires of the body and
the mind, and were by nature children of wrath, like the rest of mankind.*
Ephesians 2:1-3

"Do you really want nothing but totally effective, instantaneous justice? Then go to hell."
D.A. Carson

- We will finally understand the depth of _____ in the gospel.

*But now the righteousness of God has been manifested apart from the law, although
the Law and the Prophets bear witness to it—the righteousness of God through faith
in Jesus Christ for all who believe. For there is no distinction: for all have sinned
and fall short of the glory of God, and are justified by his grace as a gift, through the
redemption that is in Christ Jesus, whom God put forward as a propitiation by his
blood, to be received by faith. This was to show God's righteousness, because in his divine
forbearance he had passed over former sins. It was to show his righteousness at the
present time, so that he might be just and the justifier of the one who has faith in Jesus.*
Romans 3:21-26

- At the cross, God expressed His wrath toward sin.
- At the cross, God endured His wrath against sin.
- At the cross, God enabled _____ for sinners.

For our sake he made him to be sin who knew no sin, so that
in him we might become the righteousness of God.
2 Corinthians 5:21

Practical Takeaways …

- Those who are not followers of Christ …
  o __Repent__ and receive the mercy of God before it is too late.

"Repent therefore, and turn back, that your sins may be blotted out, that times of
refreshing may come from the presence of the Lord, and that he may send the Christ
appointed for you, Jesus, whom heaven must receive until the time for restoring all
the things about which God spoke by the mouth of his holy prophets long ago."
Acts 3:19-21

"Behold, I am coming like a thief!"
Revelation 16:15a

- Those who are followers of Christ …
  o _____ God completely.

God also said to Moses, "Say this to the people of Israel, 'The LORD, the God of your
fathers, the God of Abraham, the God of Isaac, and the God of Jacob, has sent me to you.'
This is my name forever, and thus I am to be remembered throughout all generations.
Go and gather the elders of Israel together and say to them, 'The LORD, the God of your
fathers, the God of Abraham, of Isaac, and of Jacob, has appeared to me, saying, "I have
observed you and what has been done to you in Egypt, and I promise that I will bring you
up out of the affliction of Egypt to the land of the Canaanites, the Hittites, the Amorites,
the Perizzites, the Hivites, and the Jebusites, a land flowing with milk and honey."' And
they will listen to your voice, and you and the elders of Israel shall go to the king of Egypt
and say to him, 'The LORD, the God of the Hebrews, has met with us; and now, please let
us go a three days' journey into the wilderness, that we may sacrifice to the LORD our God.'
But I know that the king of Egypt will not let you go unless compelled by a mighty hand.
So I will stretch out my hand and strike Egypt with all the wonders that I will do in it;
after that he will let you go. And I will give this people favor in the sight of the Egyptians;
and when you go, you shall not go empty, but each woman shall ask of her neighbor, and
any woman who lives in her house, for silver and gold jewelry, and for clothing. You shall
put them on your sons and on your daughters. So you shall plunder the Egyptians."
Exodus 3:15-22

- Be careful not to evaluate God's justice in the short-term.
- God will assert His justice ultimately and completely in His perfect time.

When he opened the fifth seal, I saw under the altar the souls of those who had been slain for the word of God and for the witness they had borne. They cried out with a loud voice, "O Sovereign Lord, holy and true, how long before you will judge and avenge our blood on those who dwell on the earth?" Then they were each given a white robe and told to rest a little longer, until the number of their fellow servants and their brothers should be complete, who were to be killed as they themselves had been.
Revelation 6:9-11

Then a mighty angel took up a stone like a great millstone and threw it into the sea, saying, "So will Babylon the great city be thrown down with violence, and will be found no more; and the sound of harpists and musicians, of flute players and trumpeters, will be heard in you no more, and a craftsman of any craft will be found in you no more, and the sound of the mill will be heard in you no more, and the light of a lamp will shine in you no more, and the voice of bridegroom and bride will be heard in you no more, for your merchants were the great ones of the earth, and all nations were deceived by your sorcery. And in her was found the blood of prophets and of saints, and of all who have been slain on earth."
Revelation 18:21-24

○ **Forgive** others freely.

"For if you forgive others their trespasses, your heavenly Father will also forgive you, but if you do not forgive others their trespasses, neither will your Father forgive your trespasses."
Matthew 6:14-15

Beloved, never avenge yourselves, but leave it to the wrath of God, for it is written, "Vengeance is mine, I will repay, says the Lord." To the contrary, "if your enemy is hungry, feed him; if he is thirsty, give him something to drink; for by so doing you will heap burning coals on his head." Do not be overcome by evil, but overcome evil with good.
Romans 12:19-21

- Forgive Christians, whose sin has been paid for by the cross of Christ.
- Forgive non-Christians, whose sin will be paid for at the judgment seat of Christ.
○ **Discipline** consistently and compassionately.

And have you forgotten the exhortation that addresses you as sons? "My son, do not regard lightly the discipline of the Lord, nor be weary when reproved by him. For the Lord disciplines the one he loves, and chastises every son whom he receives." It is for discipline that you have to endure. God is treating you as sons. For what son is there whom his father does not discipline? If you are left without discipline, in which all have participated, then you are illegitimate children and not sons. Besides this, we have had earthly fathers who disciplined us and we respected them. Shall we not much

more be subject to the Father of spirits and live? For they disciplined us for a short time as it seemed best to them, but he disciplines us for our good, that we may share his holiness. For the moment all discipline seems painful rather than pleasant, but later it yields the peaceful fruit of righteousness to those who have been trained by it.
Hebrews 12:5-11

- In the church.

"If your brother sins against you, go and tell him his fault, between you and him alone. If he listens to you, you have gained your brother. But if he does not listen, take one or two others along with you, that every charge may be established by the evidence of two or three witnesses. If he refuses to listen to them, tell it to the church. And if he refuses to listen even to the church, let him be to you as a Gentile and a tax collector. Truly, I say to you, whatever you bind on earth shall be bound in heaven, and whatever you loose on earth shall be loosed in heaven. Again I say to you, if two of you agree on earth about anything they ask, it will be done for them by my Father in heaven. For where two or three are gathered in my name, there am I among them."
Matthew 18:15-20

- In the home.

Children, obey your parents in the Lord, for this is right. "Honor your father and mother" (this is the first commandment with a promise), "that it may go well with you and that you may live long in the land." Fathers, do not provoke your children to anger, but bring them up in the discipline and instruction of the Lord.
Ephesians 6:1-4

○ __Walk__ in purity.

Therefore, preparing your minds for action, and being sober-minded, set your hope fully on the grace that will be brought to you at the revelation of Jesus Christ. As obedient children, do not be conformed to the passions of your former ignorance, but as he who called you is holy, you also be holy in all your conduct, since it is written, "You shall be holy, for I am holy." And if you call on him as Father who judges impartially according to each one's deeds, conduct yourselves with fear throughout the time of your exile, knowing that you were ransomed from the futile ways inherited from your forefathers, not with perishable things such as silver or gold, but with the precious blood of Christ, like that of a lamb without blemish or spot. He was foreknown before the foundation of the world but was made manifest in the last times for the sake of you who through him are believers in God, who raised him from the dead and gave him glory, so that your faith and hope are in God.
1 Peter 1:13-21

- Not because we fear God's wrath toward sinners, but because we feel God's wrath toward sin.

- Not because we're worried about eternal condemnation, but because we want eternal reward.

Not that I have already obtained this or am already perfect, but I press on to make it my own, because Christ Jesus has made me his own. Brothers, I do not consider that I have made it my own. But one thing I do: forgetting what lies behind and straining forward to what lies ahead, I press on toward the goal for the prize of the upward call of God in Christ Jesus. Let those of us who are mature think this way, and if in anything you think otherwise, God will reveal that also to you. Only let us hold true to what we have attained. Brothers, join in imitating me, and keep your eyes on those who walk according to the example you have in us. For many, of whom I have often told you and now tell you even with tears, walk as enemies of the cross of Christ. Their end is destruction, their god is their belly, and they glory in their shame, with minds set on earthly things. But our citizenship is in heaven, and from it we await a Savior, the Lord Jesus Christ, who will transform our lowly body to be like his glorious body, by the power that enables him even to subject all things to himself.
Philippians 3:12-21

For I am already being poured out as a drink offering, and the time of my departure has come. I have fought the good fight, I have finished the race, I have kept the faith. Henceforth there is laid up for me the crown of righteousness, which the Lord, the righteous judge, will award to me on that Day, and not only to me but also to all who have loved his appearing.
2 Timothy 4:6-8

o **Witness** with urgency.

How then will they call on him in whom they have not believed? And how are they to believe in him of whom they have never heard? And how are they to hear without someone preaching? And how are they to preach unless they are sent? As it is written, "How beautiful are the feet of those who preach the good news!" But they have not all obeyed the gospel. For Isaiah says, "Lord, who has believed what he has heard from us?" So faith comes from hearing, and hearing through the word of Christ.
Romans 10:14-17

- To everyone you know.
- To the ends of the earth.

o **Worship** with sincerity.

After this I heard what seemed to be the loud voice of a great multitude in heaven, crying out, "Hallelujah! Salvation and glory and power belong to our God, for his judgments are true and just; for he has judged the great prostitute who corrupted the earth with her immorality, and has avenged on her the blood of his servants." Once more they cried out, "Hallelujah! The smoke from her goes up forever and ever." And the twenty-four elders and the four living creatures fell down and worshiped God

who was seated on the throne, saying, "Amen. Hallelujah!" And from the throne came a voice saying, "Praise our God, all you his servants, you who fear him, small and great."
Revelation 19:1-5

- God's love without wrath would be indifferent.
- God's justice without wrath would be ineffective.
- God's love, justice, and wrath *together* _____ are inscrutable.

"God's wrath is not a cranky explosion, but his settled opposition to the cancer of sin which is eating out the insides of the human race he loves with his whole being."
Becky Pippert

Oh, the depth of the riches and wisdom and knowledge of God! How unsearchable are his judgments and how inscrutable his ways! "For who has known the mind of the Lord, or who has been his counselor?" "Or who has given a gift to him that he might be repaid?" For from him and through him and to him are all things. To him be glory forever. Amen.
Romans 11:33-36

THE HORROR OF HELL

*And if anyone's name was not found written in the book
of life, he was thrown into the lake of fire.*
Revelation 20:15

Introductory Cautions ...

- We must approach this doctrine __Biblically__.

> *"Let's be eager to leave what is familiar for what is true. Nothing outside of God and His truth should be sacred to us. And so it is with hell. If hell is some primitive myth left over from conservative tradition, then let's set it on that dusty shelf next to other traditional beliefs that have no basis in Scripture. But if it is true, if the Bible does teach that there is a literal hell awaiting those who don't believe in Jesus, then this reality must change us. It should certainly purge our souls of all complacency."*
> Francis Chan

   - The Bible speaks clearly about hell.

> *"If Jesus, the Lord of Love and Author of Grace spoke about hell more often, and in a more vivid, blood-curdling manner than anyone else, it must be a crucial truth."*
> Tim Keller

> *"All the language that strikes terror into our hearts—weeping and gnashing of teeth, outer darkness, the worm, the fire, gehenna, the great gulf fixed—is all directly taken from our Lord's teaching. It is from Jesus Christ that we learn the doctrine of eternal punishment."*
> J.I. Packer

   - The Bible speaks comprehensively about hell.

> *"If there is any truth in Scripture at all, this is true—that those who stubbornly refuse to submit to the Gospel, and to love and obey Jesus Christ incur at the Last Advent an infinite and irreparable loss. They pass into a night on which no morning dawns."*
> James Denney

   - The aim of Scripture is not primarily to inform people about the details of hell.
   - The aim of Scripture is primarily to warn people about the __danger__ of hell.
      - That we might repent of sin.
      - That we might live in righteousness.

> *"Hell is not in the Bible for us to debate it or to reject it.
> It is there so that we might escape from it!"*
> Richard Brooks

We must approach this doctrine _humbly_.

What shall we say then? Is there injustice on God's part? By no means! For he says to Moses, "I will have mercy on whom I have mercy, and I will have compassion on whom I have compassion." So then it depends not on human will or exertion, but on God, who has mercy. For the Scripture says to Pharaoh, "For this very purpose I have raised you up, that I might show my power in you, and that my name might be proclaimed in all the earth." So then he has mercy on whomever he wills, and he hardens whomever he wills. You will say to me then, "Why does he still find fault? For who can resist his will?" But who are you, O man, to answer back to God? Will what is molded say to its molder, "Why have you made me like this?" Has the potter no right over the clay, to make out of the same lump one vessel for honorable use and another for dishonorable use? What if God, desiring to show his wrath and to make known his power, has endured with much patience vessels of wrath prepared for destruction, in order to make known the riches of his glory for vessels of mercy, which he has prepared beforehand for glory—even us whom he has called, not from the Jews only but also from the Gentiles?
Romans 9:14-24

o We do not deserve God's mercy.

And when Moses saw that the people had broken loose (for Aaron had let them break loose, to the derision of their enemies), then Moses stood in the gate of the camp and said, "Who is on the LORD's side? Come to me." And all the sons of Levi gathered around him. And he said to them, "Thus says the LORD God of Israel, 'Put your sword on your side each of you, and go to and fro from gate to gate throughout the camp, and each of you kill his brother and his companion and his neighbor.'" And the sons of Levi did according to the word of Moses. And that day about three thousand men of the people fell.
Exodus 32:25-28

Moses said, "Please show me your glory." And he said, "I will make all my goodness pass before you and will proclaim before you my name 'The LORD.' And I will be gracious to whom I will be gracious, and will show mercy on whom I will show mercy."
Exodus 33:18-19

- He would be just to condemn all people.
- He is gracious to save some people.

o We dare not _question_ God's authority.

- He is Creator; we are creature.
- He is Owner; we are owned.
- He is God; we are not.

*Then the LORD answered Job out of the whirlwind and said: "Dress for action
like a man; I will question you, and you make it known to me. Will you even
put me in the wrong? Will you condemn me that you may be in the right?"*
Job 40:6-8

*Then Job answered the LORD and said: "I know that you can do all things, and
that no purpose of yours can be thwarted. 'Who is this that hides counsel without
knowledge?' Therefore I have uttered what I did not understand, things too wonderful
for me, which I did not know. 'Hear, and I will speak; I will question you, and
you make it known to me.' I had heard of you by the hearing of the ear, but now
my eye sees you; therefore I despise myself, and repent in dust and ashes."*
Job 42:1-6

- We do not have the right to judge His ways.

*"Who are we to pass judgment on the justice of the decision of the All-Wise? Who are w
to say what is consistent or inconsistent with God's righteousness? Sin has so enfeebled ou
power of righteous judgment, so darkened our understanding, so dulled our conscience, s
perverted our wills, so corrupted our hearts, that we are quite incompetent to decide. W
are ourselves so infected and affected by sin that we are altogether incapable of estimating
due merits. Imagine a company of criminals passing judgment on the equity and goodne
of the law which had condemned them!"*
A.W. Pink

- God has the right to do what He <u>Wants</u>.

*Not to us, O LORD, not to us, but to your name give glory, for the sake of
your steadfast love and your faithfulness! Why should the nations say, "Where
is their God?" Our God is in the heavens; he does all that he pleases.*
Psalm 115:1-3

- We must approach this doctrine <u>personally</u>.
  - We are not considering a stale theological doctrine.
  - We are contemplating a real eternal destiny.
- We must approach this doctrine <u>passionately</u>.

*"I'm scared [to write a book on hell] because so much is at stake. Think about it. If I sa
there is no hell, and it turns out that there is a hell, I may lead people into the very plac
I convinced them did not exist! If I say there is a hell, and I'm wrong, I may persuade
people to spend their lives frantically warning loved ones about a terrifying place that
isn't real! When it comes to hell, we can't afford to be wrong. This is not one of those
doctrines where you can toss in your two cents, shrug your shoulders, and move on. Too
much is at stake. Too many people are at stake. And the Bible has too much to say."*
Francis Chan

Ten Biblical Realities ...

Hell is a place of ultimate _justice_ .

When he opened the fifth seal, I saw under the altar the souls of those who had been slain for the word of God and for the witness they had borne. They cried out with a loud voice, "O Sovereign Lord, holy and true, how long before you will judge and avenge our blood on those who dwell on the earth?" Then they were each given a white robe and told to rest a little longer, until the number of their fellow servants and their brothers should be complete, who were to be killed as they themselves had been.
Revelation 6:9-11

hen I heard a loud voice from the temple telling the seven angels, "Go and pour out on the arth the seven bowls of the wrath of God." So the first angel went and poured out his bowl on the earth, and harmful and painful sores came upon the people who bore the mark of the beast and worshiped its image. The second angel poured out his bowl into the sea, and it became like the blood of a corpse, and every living thing died that was in the sea. The third angel poured out his bowl into the rivers and the springs of water, and they became blood. And I heard the angel in charge of the waters say, "Just are you, O Holy One, who is and who was, for you brought these judgments. For they have shed the blood of saints and prophets, and you have given them blood to drink. It is what they deserve!" And I heard the altar saying, "Yes, Lord God the Almighty, true and just are your judgments!"
Revelation 16:1-7

After this I heard what seemed to be the loud voice of a great multitude in heaven, crying out, "Hallelujah! Salvation and glory and power belong to our God, for his judgments are true and just; for he has judged the great prostitute who corrupted the earth with her immorality, and has avenged on her the blood of his servants." Once more they cried out, "Hallelujah! The smoke from her goes up forever and ever." And the twenty-four elders and the four living creatures fell down and worshiped God who was seated on the throne, saying, "Amen. Hallelujah!"
Revelation 19:1-4

Then I saw a great white throne and him who was seated on it. From his presence earth and sky fled away, and no place was found for them. And I saw the dead, great and small, standing before the throne, and books were opened. Then another book was opened, which is the book of life. And the dead were judged by what was written in the books, according to what they had done.
Revelation 20:11-12

"If God is supremely just, and just in a sense which is recognizable as just by his human creatures, and if hell exists because it is ordained by God, then hell must be just."
Paul Helm

- Hell is a place of ~~firey~~ Fiery agony.

> "And if your hand causes you to sin, cut it off. It is better for you to enter life crippled than with two hands to go to hell, to the unquenchable fire. And if your foot causes you to sin, cut it off. It is better for you to enter life lame than with two feet to be thrown into hell. And if your eye causes you to sin, tear it out. It is better for you to enter the kingdom of God with one eye than with two eyes to be thrown into hell, 'where their worm does not die and the fire is not quenched.'"
> Mark 9:43-48

> "Just as the weeds are gathered and burned with fire, so will it be at the end of the age. The Son of Man will send his angels, and they will gather out of his kingdom all causes of sin and all law-breakers, and throw them into the fiery furnace."
> Matthew 13:40-42

> "So it will be at the end of the age. The angels will come out and separate the evil from the righteous and throw them into the fiery furnace."
> Matthew 13:49-50a

> "And if your hand or your foot causes you to sin, cut it off and throw it away. It is better for you to enter life crippled or lame than with two hands or two feet to be thrown into the eternal fire. And if your eye causes you to sin, tear it out and throw it away. It is better for you to enter life with one eye than with two eyes to be thrown into the hell of fire."
> Matthew 18:8-9

> "Then he will say to those on his left, 'Depart from me, you cursed, into the eternal fire prepared for the devil and his angels.'"
> Matthew 25:41

> And the angels who did not stay within their own position of authority, but left their proper dwelling, he has kept in eternal chains under gloomy darkness until the judgment of the great day—just as Sodom and Gomorrah and the surrounding cities, which likewise indulged in sexual immorality and pursued unnatural desire, serve as an example by undergoing a punishment of eternal fire.
> Jude 6-7

> And have mercy on those who doubt; save others by snatching them out of the fire; to others show mercy with fear, hating even the garment stained by the flesh.
> Jude 22-23

> And if anyone's name was not found written in the book of life, he was thrown into the lake of fire.
> Revelation 20:15

Hell is a place of conscious ___*torment*___.

> "The poor man died and was carried by the angels to Abraham's side. The rich man also died and was buried, and in Hades, being in torment, he lifted up his eyes and saw Abraham far off and Lazarus at his side. And he called out, 'Father Abraham, have mercy on me, and send Lazarus to dip the end of his finger in water and cool my tongue, for I am in anguish in this flame.' But Abraham said, 'Child, remember that you in your lifetime received your good things, and Lazarus in like manner bad things; but now he is comforted here, and you are in anguish. And besides all this, between us and you a great chasm has been fixed, in order that those who would pass from here to you may not be able, and none may cross from there to us.' And he said, 'Then I beg you, father, to send him to my father's house—for I have five brothers—so that he may warn them, lest they also come into this place of torment.'"
> Luke 16:22-28

> And another angel, a third, followed them, saying with a loud voice, "If anyone worships the beast and its image and receives a mark on his forehead or on his hand, he also will drink the wine of God's wrath, poured full strength into the cup of his anger, and he will be tormented with fire and sulfur in the presence of the holy angels and in the presence of the Lamb."
> Revelation 14:9-10

> And they marched up over the broad plain of the earth and surrounded the camp of the saints and the beloved city, but fire came down from heaven and consumed them, and the devil who had deceived them was thrown into the lake of fire and sulfur where the beast and the false prophet were, and they will be tormented day and night forever and ever.
> Revelation 20:9-10

Hell is a place of outer ___*darkness*___.

> "I tell you, many will come from east and west and recline at table with Abraham, Isaac, and Jacob in the kingdom of heaven, while the sons of the kingdom will be thrown into the outer darkness."
> Matthew 8:11-12a

> "Then the king said to the attendants, 'Bind him hand and foot and cast him into the outer darkness.'"
> Matthew 22:13

> "'And cast the worthless servant into the outer darkness.'"
> Matthew 25:30a

> These are waterless springs and mists driven by a storm. For them the gloom of utter darkness has been reserved.
> 2 Peter 2:17

These are hidden reefs at your love feasts, as they feast with you without fear, shepherds feeding themselves; waterless clouds, swept along by winds; fruitless trees in late autumn, twice dead, uprooted; wild waves of the sea, casting up the foam of their own shame; wandering stars, for whom the gloom of utter darkness has been reserved forever.
Jude 12-13

• Hell is a place of weeping and gnashing of teeth.

> *"In that place there will be weeping and gnashing of teeth."*
> *Matthew 8:12b*

> *"In that place there will be weeping and gnashing of teeth."*
> *Matthew 13:42b*

> *"In that place there will be weeping and gnashing of teeth."*
> *Matthew 13:50b*

> *"'In that place there will be weeping and gnashing of teeth.'"*
> *Matthew 22:13b*

> *"'In that place there will be weeping and gnashing of teeth.'"*
> *Matthew 25:30b*

• Hell is a place of continual *Weeping and gnashing of teeth rebellion*

> *Therefore God has highly exalted him and bestowed on him the name that is above every name, so that at the name of Jesus every knee should bow, in heaven and on earth and under the earth, and every tongue confess that Jesus Christ is Lord, to the glory of God the Father.*
> *Philippians 2:9-11*

> *"The sinner in hell does not become morally neutral upon his sentence to hell. We must n* *imagine the damned sinner displaying gospel repentance and longing for the presence of Christ. The damned indeed are longing for an escape from punishment, but they are no 'new creations.' They do not, in hell, love the Lord their God with heart, mind, soul, and strength. Instead, they are now handed over to the full display of their natures apart from grace, natures that are satanic (John 8:44). Thus, the condemnation continues forever and ever and ever, with no end in view either for the sin or the punishment thereof."*
> *Russell Moore*

• Hell is a place of vile association.

> *"Then he will say to those on his left, 'Depart from me, you cursed, into the eternal fire prepared for the devil and his angels.'"*
> *Matthew 25:41*

"But as for the cowardly, the faithless, the detestable, as for murderers, the sexually immoral, sorcerers, idolaters, and all liars, their portion will be in the lake that burns with fire and sulfur, which is the second death."
Revelation 21:8

Hell is a place of divine destruction.

But by the same word the heavens and earth that now exist are stored up for fire, being kept until the day of judgment and destruction of the ungodly.
2 Peter 3:7

"They will suffer the punishment of eternal destruction, away from the presence of the Lord and from the glory of his might …"
2 Thessalonians 1:9

Hell is a place of complete _Seperation_.

"… so that you may be sons of your Father who is in heaven. For he makes his sun rise on the evil and on the good, and sends rain on the just and on the unjust."
Matthew 5:45

The true light, which gives light to everyone, was coming into the world.
John 1:9

"Yet he did not leave himself without witness, for he did good by giving you rains from heaven and fruitful seasons, satisfying your hearts with food and gladness."
Acts 14:17

"… that they should seek God, and perhaps feel their way toward him and find him. Yet he is actually not far from each one of us, for 'In him we live and move and have our being'; as even some of your own poets have said, 'For we are indeed his offspring.'"
Acts 17:27-28

"Not everyone who says to me, 'Lord, Lord,' will enter the kingdom of heaven, but the one who does the will of my Father who is in heaven. On that day many will say to me, 'Lord, Lord, did we not prophesy in your name, and cast out demons in your name, and do many mighty works in your name?' And then will I declare to them, 'I never knew you; depart from me, you workers of lawlessness.'"
Matthew 7:21-23

They will suffer the punishment of eternal destruction, away from the presence of the Lord and from the glory of his might …
2 Thessalonians 1:9

"So what is a 'totaled' human soul? It does not cease to exist, but rather becomes completely incapable of all the things a human soul is for—reasoning, feeling, choosing, giving or receiving love or joy. Why? Because the human soul was built for worshipping and enjoying the true God, and all truly human life flows from that. In this world, all of humanity, even those who have turned away from God, still are supported by 'kindly providences' or 'common grace' (Acts 14:16-17; Psalm 104:10-30; James 1:17) keeping us still capable of wisdom, love, joy, and goodness. But when we lose God's supportive presence all together, the result is hell."
Tim Keller

"None but one who really knows God can begin to estimate what it will mean to be eternally banished from the Lord. Forever separated from the Fount of all goodness! Never to enjoy the light of God's countenance! Never to bask in the sunshine of His presence. This, this is the most awful of all."
A.W. Pink

• Hell is a place of __eternal__ duration.

"And many of those who sleep in the dust of the earth shall awake, some to everlasting life, and some to shame and everlasting contempt."
Daniel 12:2

The sinners in Zion are afraid; trembling has seized the godless: "Who among us can dwell with the consuming fire? Who among us can dwell with everlasting burnings?"
Isaiah 33:14

"And they shall go out and look on the dead bodies of the men who have rebelled against me. For their worm shall not die, their fire shall not be quenched, and they shall be an abhorrence to all flesh."
Isaiah 66:24

"And if your hand causes you to sin, cut it off. It is better for you to enter life crippled than with two hands to go to hell, to the unquenchable fire. And if your foot causes you to sin, cut it off. It is better for you to enter life lame than with two feet to be thrown into hell. And if your eye causes you to sin, tear it out. It is better for you to enter the kingdom of God with one eye than with two eyes to be thrown into hell, 'where their worm does not die and the fire is not quenched.'"
Mark 9:43-48

"And if your hand or your foot causes you to sin, cut it off and throw it away. It is better for you to enter life crippled or lame than with two hands or two feet to be thrown into the eternal fire."
Matthew 18:8

"Then he will say to those on his left, 'Depart from me, you cursed, into the eternal fire prepared for the devil and his angels.'"
Matthew 25:41

"And these will go away into eternal punishment, but the righteous into eternal life."
Matthew 25:46

And the angels who did not stay within their own position of authority, but left their proper dwelling, he has kept in eternal chains under gloomy darkness until the judgment of the great day—just as Sodom and Gomorrah and the surrounding cities, which likewise indulged in sexual immorality and pursued unnatural desire, serve as an example by undergoing a punishment of eternal fire.
Jude 6-7

nd another angel, a third, followed them, saying with a loud voice, "If anyone worships the ast and its image and receives a mark on his forehead or on his hand, he also will drink the ine of God's wrath, poured full strength into the cup of his anger, and he will be tormented ith fire and sulfur in the presence of the holy angels and in the presence of the Lamb. And the smoke of their torment goes up forever and ever, and they have no rest, day or night, these worshipers of the beast and its image, and whoever receives the mark of its name."
Revelation 14:9-11

Once more they cried out, "Hallelujah! The smoke from her goes up forever and ever."
Revelation 19:3

And they marched up over the broad plain of the earth and surrounded the camp of the ints and the beloved city, but fire came down from heaven and consumed them, and the evil who had deceived them was thrown into the lake of fire and sulfur where the beast and the false prophet were, and they will be tormented day and night forever and ever.
Revelation 20:9-10

"Thus it is in Hell; they would die, but they cannot. The wicked shall be always dying but never dead; the smoke of the furnace ascends for ever and ever. Oh! Who can endure thus to be ever upon the rack? This word 'ever' breaks the heart."
Thomas Watson

"To help your conception, imagine yourself to be cast into a fiery oven, all of a glowing heat, or into the midst of a blowing brick-kiln, or of a great furnace, where your pain uld be as much greater than that occasioned by accidentally touching a coal of fire, as the eat is greater. Imagine also that your body were to lie there for a quarter of an hour, full f fire, as full within and without as a bright coal of fire, all the while full of quick sense; what horror would you feel at the entrance of such a furnace! And how long would that quarter of an hour seem to you! If it were to be measured by a glass, how long would the lass seem to be running! And after you had endured it for one minute, how overbearing ould it be to you to think that you had yet to endure the other fourteen. But what would

be the effect on your soul, if you knew you must lie there enduring that torment to the fu
for twenty-four hours! And how much greater would be the effect, if you knew you mus
endure it for a whole year, and how vastly greater still, if you knew you must endure it f
a thousand years! O then, how would your heart sink, if you thought, if you knew, that y
must bear it forever and ever! That there would be no end! That after millions of million
of ages, your torment would be no nearer to an end, than ever it was; and that you neve
never should be delivered! But your torment in Hell will be immeasurably greater than
this illustration represents. How then will the heart of a poor creature sink under it! Ho
utterly inexpressible and inconceivable must the sinking of the soul be in such a case."
Jonathan Edwards

"When you look forward, you shall see a long forever, a boundless duration before
you, which will swallow up your thoughts, and amaze your soul; and you will
absolutely despair of ever having any deliverance, any end, any mitigation, any
rest at all; you will know certainly that you must wear out long ages, millions and
millions of ages, in wrestling and conflicting with this almighty merciless vengeance;
and then you will have so done, when so many ages have actually been spent by
you in this manner, you will know that all is but a point to what remains."
Jonathan Edwards

Five Controversial Questions ...

• Is the Bible's description of hell _____ or metaphorical?
   ○ The Bible's descriptions of hell are possibly literal.

"Many say this is merely a figurative expression. We ask, How do they know that? Whe
has God told them so in His Word? Personally, we believe that when God says 'fire' He
means 'fire.' We refuse to blunt the sharp edge of His Word. Was the Deluge figurative?
Was it figurative 'fire and brimstone' which descended from heaven and destroyed
Sodom and Gomorrah? Were the plagues upon Egypt figurative ones? Is it figurative fir
which shall yet burn this earth, and cause the very elements to 'melt with fervent heat?'
No; in each of these cases we are obliged to take the words of Scripture in their literal
signification. Let those who dare affirm that Hell-fire is non-literal answer to God."
A.W. Pink

   ○ The Bible's descriptions of hell are _____ metaphorical.
      ■ This is not very comforting.

"When metaphors are used in Scripture about spiritual
things ... they fall short of the literal truth."
Jonathan Edwards

"To say that the Scriptural image of hell-fire is not wholly literal is of no
comfort whatsoever. The reality will be far worse than the image. What, then,
are the 'fire' and 'darkness' symbols for? They are vivid ways to describe what

happens when we lose the presence of God. Darkness refers to the isolation, and fire to the disintegration of being separated from God. Away from the favor and face of God, we literally, horrifically, and endlessly fall apart."
Tim Keller

- This is extremely frightening.

Isn't Gehenna just another word for a garbage dump?

"People tossed their garbage and waste into this valley. There was a fire there, burning constantly to consume the trash. Wild animals fought over the scraps of food along the edges of the heap. When they fought, their teeth would make a gnashing sound. Gehenna was the place with the gnashing of teeth, where the fire never went out. Gehenna was an actual place that Jesus's listeners would have been familiar with. So the next time someone asks if you believe in an actual hell, you can always say, 'Yes, I do believe that my garbage goes somewhere …'"
Rob Bell

o The idea of Gehenna as a simple garbage dump is deceptively *misleading*.

"But I say to you that everyone who is angry with his brother will be liable to judgment; whoever insults his brother will be liable to the council; and whoever says, 'You fool!' will be liable to the hell of fire."
Matthew 5:22

"If your right eye causes you to sin, tear it out and throw it away. For it is better that you lose one of your members than that your whole body be thrown into hell."
Matthew 5:29

"And do not fear those who kill the body but cannot kill the soul. Rather fear him who can destroy both soul and body in hell."
Matthew 10:28

"And if your eye causes you to sin, tear it out and throw it away. It is better for you to enter life with one eye than with two eyes to be thrown into the hell of fire."
Matthew 18:9

o The idea of Gehenna as a simple garbage dump is biblically _____.

Ahaz was twenty years old when he began to reign, and he reigned sixteen years in Jerusalem. And he did not do what was right in the eyes of the LORD, as his father David had done, but he walked in the ways of the kings of Israel. He even made metal images for the Baals, and he made offerings in the Valley of the Son of Hinnom and burned his sons as an offering, according to the abominations of the nations whom the LORD drove out before the people of Israel.
2 Chronicles 28:1-3

And he burned his sons as an offering in the Valley of the Son of Hinnom, and used fortune-telling and omens and sorcery, and dealt with mediums and with necromancers. He did much evil in the sight of the LORD, provoking him to anger.
2 Chronicles 33:6

"For the sons of Judah have done evil in my sight, declares the LORD. They have set their detestable things in the house that is called by my name, to defile it. And they have built the high places of Topheth, which is in the Valley of the Son of Hinnom, to burn their sons and their daughters in the fire, which I did not command, nor did it come into my mind. Therefore, behold, the days are coming, declares the LORD, when it will no more be called Topheth, or the Valley of the Son of Hinnom, but the Valley of Slaughter; for they will bury in Topheth, because there is no room elsewhere. And the dead bodies of this people will be food for the birds of the air, and for the beasts of the earth, and none will frighten them away. And I will silence in the cities of Judah and in the streets of Jerusalem the voice of mirth and the voice of gladness, the voice of the bridegroom and the voice of the bride, for the land shall become a waste."
Jeremiah 7:30-34

"... therefore, behold, days are coming, declares the LORD, when this place shall no more be called Topheth, or the Valley of the Son of Hinnom, but the Valley of Slaughter. And in this place I will make void the plans of Judah and Jerusalem, and will cause their people to fall by the sword before their enemies, and by the hand of those who seek their life. I will give their dead bodies for food to the birds of the air and to the beasts of the earth. And I will make this city a horror, a thing to be hissed at. Everyone who passes by it will be horrified and will hiss because of all its wounds. And I will make them eat the flesh of their sons and their daughters, and everyone shall eat the flesh of his neighbor in the siege and in the distress, with which their enemies and those who seek their life afflict them."
Jeremiah 19:6-9

"They built the high places of Baal in the Valley of the Son of Hinnom, to offer up their sons and daughters to Molech, though I did not command them, nor did it enter into my mind, that they should do this abomination, to cause Judah to sin."
Jeremiah 32:35

○ The idea of Gehenna as a simple garbage dump is historically _____

"Gehenna is a repugnant place, into which filth and cadavers are thrown, and in which fires perpetually burn in order to consume the filth and bones; on which account, by analogy, the judgment of the wicked is called 'Gehenna.'"
David Kimhi, Rabbi, AD 1200

○ The image of Gehenna as a violent picture of divine punishment is abundantly clear.

What about annihilationism?

- ○ The idea that after unbelievers have suffered the penalty of God's wrath for a time, God will annihilate them so that they no longer exist.

> *Their end is destruction, their god is their belly, and they glory*
> *in their shame, with minds set on earthly things.*
> Philippians 3:19

> *They will suffer the punishment of eternal destruction, away from*
> *the presence of the Lord and from the glory of his might.*
> 2 Thessalonians 1:9

> *But by the same word the heavens and earth that now exist are stored up for*
> *fire, being kept until the day of judgment and destruction of the ungodly.*
> 2 Peter 3:7

- ○ Biblically … One sin against an infinite God warrants infinite judgment.
  - ■ The gravity of sin is not determined by the gauge of the one who sins.
  - ■ The gravity of sin is determined by the *Greatness* of the One who is sinned against.

> *"Sin against the Creator is heinous to a degree utterly beyond our*
> *sin-warped imaginations' ability to conceive of …. Who would have*
> *the temerity to suggest to God what the punishment should be?"*
> David Kingdom

  - ■ Biblically, annihilation is unsupportable.

> *"And these will go away into eternal punishment, but the righteous into eternal life."*
> Matthew 25:46

> *"The Son of Man goes as it is written of him, but woe to that man by whom the Son*
> *of Man is betrayed! It would have been better for that man if he had not been born."*
> Matthew 26:24

- ○ Practically … Does temporary punishment pay the sinner's price?
  - ■ If so, then the price for sin has been paid, and the sinner goes to heaven.
  - ■ If not, then the price for sin is still unpaid, and the sinner remains in hell.
  - ■ Practically, annihilationism is _____.

- • What about universalism?
  - ○ The idea that all people will eventually be saved and experience eternity with God.

*"At the heart of this perspective is the belief that, given enough time, everybody
will turn to God and find themselves in the joy and peace of God's presence.
The love of God will melt every hard heart, and even the most 'depraved
sinners' will eventually give up their resistance and turn to God."*
Rob Bell

- ■ "Non-Christian" Universalists: Jesus is only _____ way to
  God/heaven.
- ■ "Christian" Universalists: Jesus is the only way to God/heaven,
  and _____ all people will be saved through Jesus.
- ○ Consider Philippians 2 …

*Therefore God has highly exalted him and bestowed on him the name that is above every
name, so that at the name of Jesus every knee should bow, in heaven and on earth and under
the earth, and every tongue confess that Jesus Christ is Lord, to the glory of God the Father.*
Philippians 2:9-11

- ■ This is not universal salvation.
- ■ This is universal Submission.

*"Turn to me and be saved, all the ends of the earth! For I am God, and there is
no other. By myself I have sworn; from my mouth has gone out in righteousness
a word that shall not return: 'To me every knee shall bow, every tongue shall
swear allegiance.' Only in the LORD, it shall be said of me, are righteousness and
strength; to him shall come and be ashamed all who were incensed against him.
In the LORD all the offspring of Israel shall be justified and shall glory."*
Isaiah 45:22-25

- ■ Paul does not nullify the distinction between the saved and the condemned
- ■ Instead, Paul highlights the destiny of both the saved and the condemned

*… and not frightened in anything by your opponents. This is a clear sign to
them of their destruction, but of your salvation, and that from God.*
Philippians 1:28

*Their end is destruction, their god is their belly, and they glory in their shame, with
minds set on earthly things. But our citizenship is in heaven, and from it we await
a Savior, the Lord Jesus Christ, who will transform our lowly body to be like his
glorious body, by the power that enables him even to subject all things to himself.*
Philippians 3:19-21

- ○ Consider 1 Corinthians 15 …

For as in Adam all die, so also in Christ shall all be made alive.
1 Corinthians 15:22

- Keep reading to the next verses.

But each in his own order: Christ the firstfruits, then at his coming those who belong to Christ. Then comes the end, when he delivers the kingdom to God the Father after destroying every rule and every authority and power. For he must reign until he has put all his enemies under his feet. The last enemy to be destroyed is death.
1 Corinthians 15:23-26

- Don't stop until you get to the last verses.

If anyone has no love for the Lord, let him be accursed. Our Lord, come! The grace of the Lord Jesus be with you. My love be with you all in Christ Jesus. Amen.
1 Corinthians 16:22-24

○ Consider 1 Timothy 2 …

This is good, and it is pleasing in the sight of God our Savior, who desires all people to be saved and to come to the knowledge of the truth.
1 Timothy 2:3-4

The logic of the situation is simple. Either God could not or would not save all. If he could not, he is not sovereign, then not all things are possible with God. If he would not, again the New Testament is wrong, for it openly claims that God would have all to be saved."
Nels Ferre

- This does NOT mean that all people will be saved.
  - We pray for all __types__ of people …

First of all, then, I urge that supplications, prayers, intercessions, and thanksgivings be made for all people, for kings and all who are in high positions, that we may lead a peaceful and quiet life, godly and dignified in every way.
1 Timothy 2:1-2

  - Because God saves all types of people.

For there is one God, and there is one mediator between God and men, the man Christ Jesus, who gave himself as a ransom for all, which is the testimony given at the proper time.
1 Timothy 2:5-6

- This does NOT mean that God's will has been thwarted.

  Then Job answered the LORD and said: "I know that you can do all things, and that no purpose of yours can be thwarted."
  Job 42:1-2

The LORD of hosts has sworn: "As I have planned, so shall it
be, and as I have purposed, so shall it stand …"
Isaiah 14:24

- Remember the revealed will of God: what He _____

"You shall not murder. You shall not commit adultery. You shall not
steal. You shall not bear false witness against your neighbor."
Exodus 20:13-16

For this is the will of God, your sanctification: that you abstain from sexual immorality …
1 Thessalonians 4:3

- Remember the secret will of God: what He _____.

"As for you, you meant evil against me, but God meant it for good, to bring
it about that many people should be kept alive, as they are today."
Genesis 50:20

Yet it was the will of the LORD to crush him; he has put him to grief;
when his soul makes an offering for guilt, he shall see his offspring; he shall
prolong his days; the will of the LORD shall prosper in his hand.
Isaiah 53:10

"… this Jesus, delivered up according to the definite plan and foreknowledge
of God, you crucified and killed by the hands of lawless men."
Acts 2:23

- This does NOT mean that God's love is in question.

"Say to them, As I live, declares the Lord GOD, I have no pleasure in the
death of the wicked, but that the wicked turn from his way and live; turn back,
turn back from your evil ways, for why will you die, O house of Israel?"
Ezekiel 33:11

Anyone who does not love does not know God, because God is love.
1 John 4:8

"For God so loved the world, that he gave his only Son, that whoever
believes in him should not perish but have eternal life."
John 3:16

He is the propitiation for our sins, and not for ours only
but also for the sins of the whole world.
1 John 2:2

The Lord is not slow to fulfill his promise as some count slowness, but is patient toward you, not wishing that any should perish, but that all should reach repentance.
2 Peter 3:9

- Remember the mystery …
  - God is sovereign.
  - We are <u>responsible</u>.

"Scripture sees hell as self-chosen … Hell appears as God's gesture of respect for human choice. All receive what they actually chose, either to be with God forever, worshipping him, or without God forever, worshipping themselves."
J.I. Packer

○ Consider the silence …

"That death seals the doom of the lost, we may prove negatively by the fact— and this is conclusive of itself—that we have not a single instance described in either the Old Testament or the New of a sinner being saved after death. Nor is there a single passage which holds out any promise of this in the future."
A.W. Pink

He went on his way through towns and villages, teaching and journeying toward Jerusalem. And someone said to him, "Lord, will those who are saved be few?" And he said to them, "Strive to enter through the narrow door. For many, I tell you, will seek to enter and will not be able. When once the master of the house has risen and shut the door, and you begin to stand outside and to knock at the door, saying, 'Lord, open to us,' then he will answer you, 'I do not know where you come from.' Then you will begin to say, 'We ate and drank in your presence, and you taught in our streets.' But he will say, 'I tell you, I do not know where you come from. Depart from me, all you workers of evil!' In that place there will be weeping and gnashing of teeth, when you see Abraham and Isaac and Jacob and all the prophets in the kingdom of God but you yourselves cast out. And people will come from east and west, and from north and south, and recline at table in the kingdom of God. And behold, some are last who will be first, and some are first who will be last."
Luke 13:22-30

Do people who never have a chance to hear the gospel go to hell?
  ○ All people have _____ of God the Father.

For the wrath of God is revealed from heaven against all ungodliness and unrighteousness of men, who by their unrighteousness suppress the truth. For what can be known about God is plain to them, because God has shown it to them. For his invisible attributes, namely, his eternal power and divine nature, have been clearly perceived, ever since the creation of the world, in the things that have been made. So they are without excuse.
Romans 1:18-20

○ All people _____ true knowledge of God.

For although they knew God, they did not honor him as God or give thanks to him, but they became futile in their thinking, and their foolish hearts were darkened. Claiming to be wise, they became fools, and exchanged the glory of the immortal God for images resembling mortal man and birds and animals and creeping things. Therefore God gave them up in the lusts of their hearts to impurity, to the dishonoring of their bodies among themselves, because they exchanged the truth about God for a lie and worshiped and served the creature rather than the Creator, who is blessed forever! Amen.
Romans 1:21-25

○ There are no ᴉnnocent people in the world.

What then? Are we Jews any better off? No, not at all. For we have already charged that all, both Jews and Greeks, are under sin, as it is written: "None is righteous, no, not one; no one understands; no one seeks for God. All have turned aside; together they have become worthless; no one does good, not even one. Their throat is an open grave; they use their tongues to deceive. The venom of asps is under their lips. Their mouth is full of curses and bitterness. Their feet are swift to shed blood; in their paths are ruin and misery, and the way of peace they have not known. There is no fear of God before their eyes."
Romans 3:9-18

○ All people are condemned for rejecting God.

Now we know that whatever the law says it speaks to those who are under the law, so that every mouth may be stopped, and the whole world may be held accountable to God. For by works of the law no human being will be justified in his sight, since through the law comes knowledge of sin.
Romans 3:19-20

○ God has made a way of Salvation for the lost.

But now the righteousness of God has been manifested apart from the law, although the Law and the Prophets bear witness to it—the righteousness of God through faith in Jesus Christ for all who believe. For there is no distinction: for all have sinned and fall short of the glory of God, and are justified by his grace as a gift, through the redemption that is in Christ Jesus, whom God put forward as a propitiation by his blood, to be received by faith. This was to show God's righteousness, because in his divine forbearance he had passed over former sins. It was to show his righteousness at the present time, so that he might be just and the justifier of the one who has faith in Jesus.
Romans 3:21-26

○ People cannot come to God apart from _____ in Christ.

Then what becomes of our boasting? It is excluded. By what kind of law? By a law of works? No, but by the law of faith. For we hold that one is justified by faith apart from works of the law. Or is God the God of Jews only? Is he not the God of Gentiles also? Yes, of Gentiles also, since God is one—who will justify the circumcised by faith and the uncircumcised through faith. Do we then overthrow the law by this faith? By no means! On the contrary, we uphold the law.
Romans 3:27-31

Therefore, since we have been justified by faith, we have peace with God through our Lord Jesus Christ. Through him we have also obtained access by faith into this grace in which we stand, and we rejoice in hope of the glory of God. Not only that, but we rejoice in our sufferings, knowing that suffering produces endurance, and endurance produces character, and character produces hope, and hope does not put us to shame, because God's love has been poured into our hearts through the Holy Spirit who has been given to us. For while we were still weak, at the right time Christ died for the ungodly. For one will scarcely die for a righteous person—though perhaps for a good person one would dare even to die—but God shows his love for us in that while we were still sinners, Christ died for us. Since, therefore, we have now been justified by his blood, much more shall we be saved by him from the wrath of God. For if while we were enemies we were reconciled to God by the death of his Son, much more, now that we are reconciled, shall we be saved by his life. More than that, we also rejoice in God through our Lord Jesus Christ, through whom we have now received reconciliation.
Romans 5:1-11

o Christ commands the church to _____ the gospel to all peoples.

… because, if you confess with your mouth that Jesus is Lord and believe in your heart that God raised him from the dead, you will be saved. For with the heart one believes and is justified, and with the mouth one confesses and is saved. For the Scripture says, "Everyone who believes in him will not be put to shame." For there is no distinction between Jew and Greek; for the same Lord is Lord of all, bestowing his riches on all who call on him. For "everyone who calls on the name of the Lord will be saved." How then will they call on him in whom they have not believed? And how are they to believe in him of whom they have never heard? And how are they to hear without someone preaching? And how are they to preach unless they are sent? As it is written, "How beautiful are the feet of those who preach the good news!"
Romans 10:9-15

Final Conclusions ...

- We must declare this doctrine _____.

"Evangelicals are often apologetic about the biblical view of retribution. They say that they wish that what the Bible says about the punishment of sinners is not true, that they find it hard to accept this doctrine emotionally, but that because the Bible teaches it they are forced to believe it. This type of thinking is understandable, given our human frailty and inability to fully understand God's ways. We do not see the seriousness of sin as strongly as God sees it. But many today seem to be proud that their hearts rebel against the judgment of God. The message they convey to an outsider is that they think God is wrong and unfair, but that's what he is going to do, so they reluctantly include it in their statement of faith."
Ajith Fernando

  ○ We need to stop apologizing for God.

  "Like the nervous kid who tries to keep his friends from seeing his drunken father, I have tried to hide God at times. Who do I think I am? The truth is, God is perfect and right in all that He does. I am a fool for thinking otherwise. He does not need nor want me to 'cover' for Him. There's nothing to be covered. Everything about Him and all He does is perfect."
  Francis Chan

  ○ We need to start apologizing to God.

  "Would you have thought to rescue sinful people from their sins by sending your Son to take on human flesh? Would you have thought to enter creation through the womb of a young Jewish woman and be born in a feeding trough? Would you have thought to allow your created beings to torture your Son, lacerate His flesh with whips, and then drive nails through His hands and feet? It's incredibly arrogant to pick and choose which incomprehensible truths we embrace. No one wants to ditch God's plan of redemption, even though it doesn't make sense to us. Neither should we erase God's revealed plan of punishment because it doesn't sit well with us. As soon as we do this, we are putting God's actions in submission to our own reasoning, which is a ridiculous thing for clay to do."
  Francis Chan

- We must declare this doctrine _____.
  ○ In view of God's sovereignty.

  Look, O LORD, and see! With whom have you dealt thus? Should women eat the fruit of their womb, the children of their tender care? Should priest and prophet be killed in the sanctuary of the Lord? In the dust of the streets lie the young and the old; my young women and my young men have fallen by the sword; you have killed them in the day of your anger, slaughtering without pity.
  Lamentations 2:20-21

○ In view of our salvation.

Remember my affliction and my wanderings, the wormwood and the gall! My soul
continually remembers it and is bowed down within me. But this I call to mind,
and therefore I have hope: The steadfast love of the LORD never ceases; his mercies
never come to an end; they are new every morning; great is your faithfulness.
"The LORD is my portion," says my soul, "therefore I will hope in him."
Lamentations 3:19-24

"Think lightly of hell, and you will think lightly of the cross. Think little of the sufferings
of lost souls, and you will soon think little of the Savior who delivers you from them."
Charles Spurgeon

We must declare this doctrine _____.

"The times of ignorance God overlooked, but now he commands all people
everywhere to repent, because he has fixed a day on which he will judge
the world in righteousness by a man whom he has appointed; and of
this he has given assurance to all by raising him from the dead."
Acts 17:30-31

"What is most needed today is a wide proclamation of those truths which are the least
acceptable to the flesh. What is needed today is a scriptural setting forth of the character
of God—His absolute sovereignty, His ineffable holiness, His inflexible justice, His
unchanging veracity. What is needed today is a scriptural setting forth of the condition
of the natural man—his total depravity, his spiritual insensibility, his inveterate hostility
to God, the fact that he is 'condemned already' and that the wrath of a sin-hating
God is even now abiding upon him. What is needed today is a scriptural setting forth
of the alarming danger in which sinners are—the indescribably awful doom which
awaits them, the fact that if they follow only a little further their present course they
shall most certainly suffer the due reward of their iniquities. What is needed today is
a scriptural setting forth of the nature of that punishment which awaits the lost—the
awfulness of it, the hopelessness of it, the unendurableness of it, the endlessness of it."
A.W. Pink

○ We need to be reminded that divine judgment is coming.

In those days John the Baptist came preaching in the wilderness of Judea, "Repent,
for the kingdom of heaven is at hand." For this is he who was spoken of by the
prophet Isaiah when he said, "The voice of one crying in the wilderness: 'Prepare
the way of the Lord; make his paths straight.'" Now John wore a garment of camel's
hair and a leather belt around his waist, and his food was locusts and wild honey.
Then Jerusalem and all Judea and all the region about the Jordan were going out to
him, and they were baptized by him in the river Jordan, confessing their sins.

But when he saw many of the Pharisees and Sadducees coming to his baptism, he said to them, "You brood of vipers! Who warned you to flee from the wrath to come? Bear fruit in keeping with repentance. And do not presume to say to yourselves, 'We have Abraham as our father,' for I tell you, God is able from these stones to raise up children for Abraham. Even now the axe is laid to the root of the trees. Every tree therefore that does not bear good fruit is cut down and thrown into the fire. "I baptize you with water for repentance, but he who is coming after me is mightier than I, whose sandals I am not worthy to carry. He will baptize you with the Holy Spirit and fire. His winnowing fork is in his hand, and he will clear his threshing floor and gather his wheat into the barn, but the chaff he will burn with unquenchable fire."
Matthew 3:1-12

"The vague and tenuous hope that God is too kind to punish the ungodly has become a deadly opiate for the consciences of millions. It hushes their fears and allows them to practice all pleasant forms of iniquity while death draws every day nearer and the command to repent goes unheeded."
A.W. Tozer

○ We need to be reminded that the pleasures of sin are fleeting.

By faith Moses, when he was grown up, refused to be called the son of Pharaoh's daughter, choosing rather to be mistreated with the people of God than to enjoy the fleeting pleasures of sin. He considered the reproach of Christ greater wealth than the treasures of Egypt, for he was looking to the reward.
Hebrews 11:24-26

"It doesn't matter how small the sins are provided that their cumulative effect is to edge the man way from the Light and out into the Nothing. Murder is no better than cards if cards can do the trick. Indeed the safest road to Hell is the gradual one—the gentle slope, soft underfoot, without sudden turnings, without milestones, without signposts."
Wormwood (The Demon), "The Screwtape Letters", C.S. Lewis

○ We need to be reminded that wealth in this world is passing.

But those who desire to be rich fall into temptation, into a snare, into many senseless and harmful desires that plunge people into ruin and destruction. For the love of money is a root of all kinds of evils. It is through this craving that some have wandered away from the faith and pierced themselves with many pangs.
1 Timothy 6:9-10

Come now, you rich, weep and howl for the miseries that are coming upon you. Your riches have rotted and your garments are moth-eaten. Your gold and silver have corroded and their corrosion will be evidence against you and will eat your flesh like fire. You have laid up treasure in the last days. Behold, the wages of the laborers who mowed

*your fields, which you kept back by fraud, are crying out against you, and the cries of
the harvesters have reached the ears of the Lord of hosts. You have lived on the earth in
luxury and in self-indulgence. You have fattened your hearts in a day of slaughter.*
James 5:1-5

○ We need to be reminded that unrighteousness is unrewarding.

*"But as for the cowardly, the faithless, the detestable, as for murderers, the
sexually immoral, sorcerers, idolaters, and all liars, their portion will be in
the lake that burns with fire and sulfur, which is the second death."*
Revelation 21:8

*"It is just because these truths have been withheld so much from public ministrations to
the saints that we now find so many backboneless, sentimental, lopsided Christians in our
assemblies. A clearer vision of the awe-inspiring attributes of God would banish much
of our levity and irreverence. A better understanding of our depravity by nature would
humble us, and make us see our deep need of using the appointed means of grace. A facing
of the alarming danger of the sinner would cause us to 'consider our ways' and make us
more diligent to make our 'calling and election sure.' A realization of the unspeakable
misery which awaits the lost (and which each, of us fully merited) would immeasurably
deepen our gratitude, and bring us to thank God more fervently that we have been
snatched as brands from the burning and delivered from the wrath to come; and too, it will
make us far more earnest in our prayers as we supplicate God on behalf of the unsaved."*
A.W. Pink

We must declare this doctrine with _____.

*"And if your hand causes you to sin, cut it off. It is better for you to enter life
crippled than with two hands to go to hell, to the unquenchable fire. And if your
foot causes you to sin, cut it off. It is better for you to enter life lame than with
two feet to be thrown into hell. And if your eye causes you to sin, tear it out. It is
better for you to enter the kingdom of God with one eye than with two eyes to be
thrown into hell, 'where their worm does not die and the fire is not quenched.'"*
Mark 9:43-48

• We must declare this doctrine with _____.

*For the wound of the daughter of my people is my heart wounded; I mourn,
and dismay has taken hold on me. Is there no balm in Gilead? Is there no
physician there? Why then has the health of the daughter of my people not been
restored? Oh that my head were waters, and my eyes a fountain of tears, that
I might weep day and night for the slain of the daughter of my people!*
Jeremiah 8:21-9:1

And when he drew near and saw the city, he wept over it, saying, "Would that you, even you, had known on this day the things that make for peace! But now they are hidden from your eyes. For the days will come upon you, when your enemies will set up a barricade around you and surround you and hem you in on every side and tear you down to the ground, you and your children within you. And they will not leave one stone upon another in you, because you did not know the time of your visitation."
Luke 19:41-44

"If you can witness, unmoved, men and women hurrying down the broad road which leadeth to destruction, then it is seriously to be doubted if you have within you the Spirit of that One who wept over Jerusalem."
A.W. Pink

I am speaking the truth in Christ—I am not lying; my conscience bears me witness in the Holy Spirit—that I have great sorrow and unceasing anguish in my heart. For I could wish that I myself were accursed and cut off from Christ for the sake of my brothers, my kinsmen according to the flesh. They are Israelites, and to them belong the adoption, the glory, the covenants, the giving of the law, the worship, and the promises. To them belong the patriarchs, and from their race, according to the flesh, is the Christ, who is God over all, blessed forever. Amen.
Romans 9:1-5

"I have never heard D.L. Moody refer to hell without tears in his voice."
R.W. Dale

- We must declare this doctrine with _____.
    - In the hardest, most trying, most stretching, most challenging, most difficult, most dangerous, most deadly places in the world …
    - For the salvation of the peoples of the world.

"And now, behold, I am going to Jerusalem, constrained by the Spirit, not knowing what will happen to me there, except that the Holy Spirit testifies to me in every city that imprisonment and afflictions await me. But I do not account my life of any value nor as precious to myself, if only I may finish my course and the ministry that I received from the Lord Jesus, to testify to the gospel of the grace of God."
Acts 20:22-24

THE HOPE OF HEAVEN

But our citizenship is in heaven, and from it we await a Savior, the Lord
Jesus Christ, who will transform our lowly body to be like his glorious body,
by the power that enables him even to subject all things to himself.
Philippians 3:20-21

If then you have been raised with Christ, seek the things that are
above, where Christ is, seated at the right hand of God.
Colossians 3:1

"The man who is about to sail for Australia or New Zealand as a settler, is naturally
anxious to know something about his future home, its climate, its employments,
its inhabitants, its ways, its customs. All these are subjects of deep interest to him.
You are leaving the land of your nativity, you are going to spend the rest of your life
in a new hemisphere. It would be strange indeed if you did not desire information
about your new abode. Now surely, if we hope to dwell forever in that 'better
country, even a heavenly one,' we ought to seek all the knowledge we can get about
it. Before we go to our eternal home we should try to become acquainted with it."
J.C. Ryle

"It becomes us to spend this life only as a journey toward heaven ... to which we
should subordinate all other concerns of life. Why should we labor for or set our
hearts on anything else, but that which is our proper end and true happiness?"
Jonathan Edwards

Heaven Contemplated ...

• We hold fast to biblical _____.

Then I saw a new heaven and a new earth, for the first heaven and the first
earth had passed away, and the sea was no more. And I saw the holy city,
new Jerusalem, coming down out of heaven from God, prepared as a bride
adorned for her husband. And I heard a loud voice from the throne saying,
"Behold, the dwelling place of God is with man. He will dwell with them, and
they will be his people, and God himself will be with them as their God."
Revelation 21:1-3

But, as it is written, "What no eye has seen, nor ear heard, nor the heart of man imagined,
what God has prepared for those who love him"—these things God has revealed to us
through the Spirit. For the Spirit searches everything, even the depths of God. For who
knows a person's thoughts except the spirit of that person, which is in him? So also no
one comprehends the thoughts of God except the Spirit of God. Now we have received

not the spirit of the world, but the Spirit who is from God, that we might understand the things freely given us by God. And we impart this in words not taught by human wisdom but taught by the Spirit, interpreting spiritual truths to those who are spiritual.
1 Corinthians 2:9-13

- We tread carefully into theological _____.

Love never ends. As for prophecies, they will pass away; as for tongues, they will cease; as for knowledge, it will pass away. For we know in part and we prophesy in part, but when the perfect comes, the partial will pass away. When I was a child, I spoke like a child, I thought like a child, I reasoned like a child. When I became a man, I gave up childish ways. For now we see in a mirror dimly, but then face to face. Now I know in part; then I shall know fully, even as I have been fully known.
1 Corinthians 13:8-12

Beloved, we are God's children now, and what we will be has not yet appeared; but we know that when he appears we shall be like him, because we shall see him as he is.
1 John 3:2

"Speculation is a legitimate theological activity, as long as we are aware that we are speculating.
Millard Erickson

- We leave room for personal _____.

Now to him who is able to do far more abundantly than all that we ask or think, according to the power at work within us, to him be glory in the church and in Christ Jesus throughout all generations, forever and ever. Amen.
Ephesians 3:20-21

  ○ Imagination must never fly away from truth.
  ○ Imagination must always fly upon the truth.

Heaven Defined ...

- The expanse of God's _____.

In the beginning, God created the heavens and the earth.
Genesis 1:1

"For truly, I say to you, until heaven and earth pass away, not an iota, not a dot, will pass from the Law until all is accomplished."
Matthew 5:18

"Heaven and earth will pass away, but my words will not pass away."
Matthew 24:35

A synonym for God's _____.

"But when he came to himself, he said, 'How many of my father's hired servants have more than enough bread, but I perish here with hunger! I will arise and go to my father, and I will say to him, "Father, I have sinned against heaven and before you. I am no longer worthy to be called your son. Treat me as one of your hired servants."' And he arose and came to his father. But while he was still a long way off, his father saw him and felt compassion, and ran and embraced him and kissed him. And the son said to him, 'Father, I have sinned against heaven and before you. I am no longer worthy to be called your son.'"
Luke 15:17-21

John answered, "A person cannot receive even one thing unless it is given him from heaven."
John 3:27

The baptism of John, from where did it come? From heaven or from man?" And they discussed it among themselves, saying, "If we say, 'From heaven,' he will say to us, 'Why then did you not believe him?'"
Matthew 21:25

From that time Jesus began to preach, saying, "Repent, for the kingdom of heaven is at hand."
Matthew 4:17

Now after John was arrested, Jesus came into Galilee, proclaiming the gospel of God, and saying, "The time is fulfilled, and the kingdom of God is at hand; repent and believe in the gospel."
Mark 1:14-15

The place where God _____.

Thus says the LORD: "Heaven is my throne, and the earth is my footstool; what is the house that you would build for me, and what is the place of my rest?"
Isaiah 66:1

Pray then like this: "Our Father in heaven, hallowed be your name."
Matthew 6:9

"Not everyone who says to me, 'Lord, Lord,' will enter the kingdom of heaven, but the one who does the will of my Father who is in heaven."
Matthew 7:21

"So everyone who acknowledges me before men, I also will acknowledge before my Father who is in heaven, but whoever denies me before men, I also will deny before my Father who is in heaven."
Matthew 10:32-33

And Jesus answered him, "Blessed are you, Simon Bar-Jonah! For flesh and blood has not revealed this to you, but my Father who is in heaven."
Matthew 16:17

"See that you do not despise one of these little ones. For I tell you that in heaven their angels always see the face of my Father who is in heaven."
Matthew 18:10

"Again I say to you, if two of you agree on earth about anything they ask, it will be done for them by my Father in heaven."
Matthew 18:19

○ Angels come from heaven.

And behold, there was a great earthquake, for an angel of the Lord descended from heaven and came and rolled back the stone and sat on it.
Matthew 28:2

And there appeared to him an angel from heaven, strengthening him.
Luke 22:43

When the angels went away from them into heaven, the shepherds said to one another, "Let us go over to Bethlehem and see this thing that has happened, which the Lord has made known to us."
Luke 2:15

○ The Son came from heaven.

"No one has ascended into heaven except he who descended from heaven, the Son of Man.
John 3:13

He who comes from above is above all. He who is of the earth belongs to the earth and speaks in an earthly way. He who comes from heaven is above all.
John 3:31

They said, "Is not this Jesus, the son of Joseph, whose father and mother we know? How does he now say, 'I have come down from heaven'?"
John 6:42

○ The Son returned to heaven.

And when he had said these things, as they were looking on, he was lifted up, and a cloud took him out of their sight. And while they were gazing into heaven as he went, behold, two men stood by them in white robes, and said, "Men of Galilee,

why do you stand looking into heaven? This Jesus, who was taken up from you into heaven, will come in the same way as you saw him go into heaven."
Acts 1:9-11

Baptism, which corresponds to this, now saves you, not as a removal of dirt from the body but as an appeal to God for a good conscience, through the resurrection of Jesus Christ, who has gone into heaven and is at the right hand of God, with angels, authorities, and powers having been subjected to him.
1 Peter 3:21-22

For Christ has entered, not into holy places made with hands, which are copies of the true things, but into heaven itself, now to appear in the presence of God on our behalf.
Hebrews 9:24

○ The Son resides in heaven.

But he, full of the Holy Spirit, gazed into heaven and saw the glory of God, and Jesus standing at the right hand of God. And he said, "Behold, I see the heavens opened, and the Son of Man standing at the right hand of God."
Acts 7:55-56

Who is to condemn? Christ Jesus is the one who died—more than that, who was raised—who is at the right hand of God, who indeed is interceding for us.
Romans 8:34

○ The Son will return from heaven.

"In my Father's house are many rooms. If it were not so, would I have told you that I go to prepare a place for you? And if I go and prepare a place for you, I will come again and will take you to myself, that where I am you may be also."
John 14:2-3

And when he had said these things, as they were looking on, he was lifted up, and a cloud took him out of their sight. And while they were gazing into heaven as he went, behold, two men stood by them in white robes, and said, "Men of Galilee, why do you stand looking into heaven? This Jesus, who was taken up from you into heaven, will come in the same way as you saw him go into heaven."
Acts 1:9-11

For the Lord himself will descend from heaven with a cry of command, with the voice of an archangel, and with the sound of the trumpet of God. And the dead in Christ will rise first. Then we who are alive, who are left, will be caught up together with them in the clouds to meet the Lord in the air, and so we will always be with the Lord. Therefore encourage one another with these words.
1 Thessalonians 4:16-18

○ We look forward to heaven.

- A _____ to come …

> *For he was looking forward to the city that has foundations,*
> *whose designer and builder is God.*
> *Hebrews 11:10*

> *For here we have no lasting city, but we seek the city that is to come.*
> *Hebrews 13:14*

- A country to come …

> *But as it is, they desire a better country, that is, a heavenly one. Therefore God*
> *is not ashamed to be called their God, for he has prepared for them a city.*
> *Hebrews 11:16*

- A _____ to come …

> *Pray then like this: "Our Father in heaven, hallowed be your name. Your*
> *kingdom come, your will be done, on earth as it is in heaven."*
> *Matthew 6:9-10*

> *"Then the King will say to those on his right, 'Come, you who are blessed by my*
> *Father, inherit the kingdom prepared for you from the foundation of the world.'"*
> *Matthew 25:34*

- The eternal Heaven is the _____ _____ where God and His angels will dwell with His people in unhindered communion and unimaginable joy.

> *"For behold, I create new heavens and a new earth, and the former things*
> *shall not be remembered or come into mind. But be glad and rejoice forever in*
> *that which I create; for behold, I create Jerusalem to be a joy, and her people*
> *to be a gladness. I will rejoice in Jerusalem and be glad in my people; no*
> *more shall be heard in it the sound of weeping and the cry of distress."*
> *Isaiah 65:17-19*

> *"For as the new heavens and the new earth that I make shall remain before me, says the*
> *LORD, so shall your offspring and your name remain. From new moon to new moon, and*
> *from Sabbath to Sabbath, all flesh shall come to worship before me, declares the LORD."*
> *Isaiah 66:22-23*

> *But according to his promise we are waiting for new heavens*
> *and a new earth in which righteousness dwells.*
> *2 Peter 3:13*

Then I saw a new heaven and a new earth, for the first heaven and the first earth had passed away, and the sea was no more. And I saw the holy city, new Jerusalem, coming down out of heaven from God, prepared as a bride adorned for her husband. And I heard a loud voice from the throne saying, "Behold, the dwelling place of God is with man. He will dwell with them, and they will be his people, and God himself will be with them as their God. He will wipe away every tear from their eyes, and death shall be no more, neither shall there be mourning, nor crying, nor pain anymore, for the former things have passed away."
Revelation 21:1-4

○ The ultimate end of the gospel is not that we will go to heaven, but that heaven will _____ to us.

"God will make the new earth his dwelling place …. Heaven and earth will then no longer be separated as they are now, but they will be one. But to leave the new earth out of consideration when we think of the final state of believers is greatly to impoverish biblical teaching about the life to come."
Anthony Hoekema

○ Careful questions …
  ■ Will the earth as we know it be obliterated?

Of old you laid the foundation of the earth, and the heavens are the work of your hands. They will perish, but you will remain; they will all wear out like a garment. You will change them like a robe, and they will pass away, but you are the same, and your years have no end.
Psalm 102:25-27

"Heaven and earth will pass away, but my words will not pass away."
Luke 21:33

And, "You, Lord, laid the foundation of the earth in the beginning, and the heavens are the work of your hands; they will perish, but you remain; they will all wear out like a garment, like a robe you will roll them up, like a garment they will be changed. But you are the same, and your years will have no end."
Hebrews 1:10-12

But the day of the Lord will come like a thief, and then the heavens will pass away with a roar, and the heavenly bodies will be burned up and dissolved, and the earth and the works that are done on it will be exposed.
2 Peter 3:10

Then I saw a great white throne and him who was seated on it. From his presence earth and sky fled away, and no place was found for them.
Revelation 20:11

Then I saw a new heaven and a new earth, for the first heaven and the first earth had passed away, and the sea was no more. And I saw the holy city, new Jerusalem, coming down out of heaven from God, prepared as a bride adorned for her husband.
Revelation 21:1-2

- Or will the earth as we know it be _____?

And God saw everything that he had made, and behold, it was very good. And there was evening and there was morning, the sixth day.
Genesis 1:31

A generation goes, and a generation comes, but the earth remains forever.
Ecclesiastes 1:4

He built his sanctuary like the high heavens, like the earth, which he has founded forever.
Psalm 78:69

"When Revelation 21:2 and 2 Peter 3:10 say that the present earth and heavens will 'pass away,' it does not have to mean that they go out of existence, but may mean that there will be such a change in them that their present condition passes away. We might say, 'The caterpillar passes away, and the butterfly emerges.' There is a real passing away, and there is a real continuity, a real connection."
John Piper

For in him all the fullness of God was pleased to dwell, and through him to reconcile to himself all things, whether on earth or in heaven, making peace by the blood of his cross.
Colossians 1:19-20

"In the beginning God created the heavens and the earth and declared it 'good.' God does not surrender this good creation to Satan but wins it back through the blood of Christ, which frees creation's rulers from the sentence of death for sin."
Russell Moore

"But truly, as I live, and as all the earth shall be filled with the glory of the LORD …"
Numbers 14:21

The heavens declare the glory of God, and the sky above proclaims his handiwork.
Psalm 19:1

And behold, the glory of the God of Israel was coming from the east. And the sound of his coming was like the sound of many waters, and the earth shone with his glory.
Ezekiel 43:2

They shall not hurt or destroy in all my holy mountain; for the earth shall be full of the knowledge of the LORD as the waters cover the sea. In that day the root of Jesse, who shall stand as a signal for the peoples—of him shall the nations inquire, and his resting place shall be glorious.
Isaiah 11:9-10

"For the earth will be filled with the knowledge of the glory of the LORD as the waters cover the sea."
Habakkuk 2:14

■ Will the earth as we know it be the same?

For the LORD comforts Zion; he comforts all her waste places and makes her wilderness like Eden, her desert like the garden of the LORD; joy and gladness will be found in her, thanksgiving and the voice of song.
Isaiah 51:3

"And they will say, 'This land that was desolate has become like the garden of Eden, and the waste and desolate and ruined cities are now fortified and inhabited.'"
Ezekiel 36:35

Then the LORD God said, "Behold, the man has become like one of us in knowing good and evil. Now, lest he reach out his hand and take also of the tree of life and eat, and live forever—" therefore the LORD God sent him out from the garden of Eden to work the ground from which he was taken. He drove out the man, and at the east of the garden of Eden he placed the cherubim and a flaming sword that turned every way to guard the way to the tree of life.
Genesis 3:22-24

Then the angel showed me the river of the water of life, bright as crystal, flowing from the throne of God and of the Lamb through the middle of the street of the city; also, on either side of the river, the tree of life with its twelve kinds of fruit, yielding its fruit each month. The leaves of the tree were for the healing of the nations. No longer will there be anything accursed, but the throne of God and of the Lamb will be in it, and his servants will worship him.
Revelation 22:1-3

A river flowed out of Eden to water the garden, and there it divided and became four rivers. The name of the first is the Pishon. It is the one that flowed around the whole land of Havilah, where there is gold. And the gold of that land is good; bdellium and onyx stone are there. The name of the second river is the Gihon. It is the one that flowed around the whole land of Cush. And the name of the third river is the Tigris, which flows east of Assyria. And the fourth river is the Euphrates.
Genesis 2:10-14

"You were in Eden, the garden of God; every precious stone was your covering, sardius, topaz, and diamond, beryl, onyx, and jasper, sapphire, emerald, and carbuncle; and crafted in gold were your settings and your engravings. On the day that you were created they were prepared."
Ezekiel 28:13

"You shall take two onyx stones, and engrave on them the names of the sons of Israel, six of their names on the one stone, and the names of the remaining six on the other stone, in the order of their birth. As a jeweler engraves signets, so shall you engrave the two stones with the names of the sons of Israel. You shall enclose them in settings of gold filigree. And you shall set the two stones on the shoulder pieces of the ephod, as stones of remembrance for the sons of Israel. And Aaron shall bear their names before the LORD on his two shoulders for remembrance."
Exodus 28:9-12

The foundations of the wall of the city were adorned with every kind of jewel. The first was jasper, the second sapphire, the third agate, the fourth emerald, the fifth onyx, the sixth carnelian, the seventh chrysolite, the eighth beryl, the ninth topaz, the tenth chrysoprase, the eleventh jacinth, the twelfth amethyst.
Revelation 21:19-20

- Or will the earth as we know it be _____?

Therefore, if anyone is in Christ, he is a new creation. The old has passed away; behold, the new has come.
2 Corinthians 5:17

For by him all things were created, in heaven and on earth, visible and invisible, whether thrones or dominions or rulers or authorities—all things were created through him and for him. And he is before all things, and in him all things hold together. And he is the head of the body, the church. He is the beginning, the firstborn from the dead, that in everything he might be preeminent. For in him all the fullness of God was pleased to dwell, and through him to reconcile to himself all things, whether on earth or in heaven, making peace by the blood of his cross.
Colossians 1:16-20

"No more let sins and sorrows grow
Nor thorns infest the ground;
He comes to make His blessings flow
Far as the curse is found."

Isaac Watts

*"This is my Father's world. O let me ne'er forget
That though the wrong seems oft so strong, God is the ruler yet.
This is my Father's world: the battle is not done:
Jesus who died shall be satisfied,
And earth and Heav'n be one."*

Maltbie Babcock

○ Correcting misconceptions …

"Repent therefore, and turn back, that your sins may be blotted out, that times of refreshing may come from the presence of the Lord, and that he may send the Christ appointed for you, Jesus, whom heaven must receive until the time for restoring all the things about which God spoke by the mouth of his holy prophets long ago."
Acts 3:19-21

■ Heaven is not non-earth, but _____ earth.

"New creation is the goal or purpose of God's redemptive-historical plan; new creation is the logical main point of Scripture."
Greg Beale

■ Heaven is not unfamiliar and otherworldly, but _____ and earthly.

For the creation waits with eager longing for the revealing of the sons of God. For the creation was subjected to futility, not willingly, but because of him who subjected it, in hope that the creation itself will be set free from its bondage to corruption and obtain the freedom of the glory of the children of God.
Romans 8:19-21

"The gospel is far greater than most of us imagine. It isn't just good news for us—it's good news for animals, plants, stars, and planets. It's good news for the sky above and the earth below."
Randy Alcorn

■ Heaven is not foreign, but _____.

"Heaven, as the eternal home of the divine Man and of all the redeemed members of the human race, must necessarily be thoroughly human in its structure, conditions, and activities. Its joys and activities must all be rational, moral, emotional, voluntary, and active. There must be the exercise of all the faculties, the gratification of all tastes, the development of all talent capacities, the realization of all ideals …. Heaven will prove the consummate flower and fruit of the whole creation and of all the history of the universe."
A.A. Hodge

- Heaven is not boring, but _____.

"If I find in myself a desire which no experience in this world can satisfy, the most probable explanation is that I was made for another world."
C.S. Lewis

- Heaven is not a place where we have nothing to do but float on the clouds, but a new earth where we have everything to do: a God to worship, a kingdom to rule, a universe to explore, work to accomplish, and friends to enjoy.

"Those hills," said Lucy, "the nice woody ones and the blue ones behind—aren't they very like the southern border of Narnia."

"Like!" cried Edmund after a moment's silence. "Why they're exactly like. Look, there's Mount Pire with his forked head, and there's the pass into Archenland and everything!"

"And yet they're not like," said Lucy. "They're different. They have more colours on them and they look further away than I remembered and they're more . . . more . . . oh, I don't know ... ."

"More like the real thing," said the Lord Digory softly.

Suddenly Farsight the Eagle spread his wings, soared thirty or forty feet up into the air, circled round and then alighted on the ground. "Kings and Queens," he cried, "we have all been blind. We are only beginning to see where we are. From up there I have seen it all—Ettinsmuir, Beaversdam, the Great River, and Cair Paravel still shining on the edge of the Eastern Sea. Narnia is not dead. This is Narnia."

"But how can it be?" said Peter. "For Aslan told us older ones that we should never return to Narnia, and here we are."

"Yes," said Eustace. "And we saw it all destroyed and the sun put out."

"And it's all so different," said Lucy.

"The Eagle is right," said the Lord Digory. "Listen, Peter. When Aslan said you could never go back to Narnia, he meant the Narnia you were thinking of. But that was not the real Narnia. That had a beginning and an end. It was only a shadow or a copy of the real Narnia, which has always been here and always will be here: just as our own world, England and all, is only a shadow or copy of something in Aslan's real world. You need not mourn over Narnia, Lucy. All of the old Narnia that mattered, all the dear creatures, have been drawn into the real Narnia through the Door. And of course it is different; as different as a real thing is from a shadow or as a waking life is from a dream." ...

The difference between the old Narnia and the new Narnia was like that. The new one is a deeper country: every rock and flower and blade of grass looked as if it meant more. I can't describe it any better than that: if you ever get there, you will know what I mean.

It was the Unicorn who summed up what everyone was feeling. He stamped his right forehoof on the ground and neighed and then cried: "I have come home at last! This is my real country! I belong here. This is the land I have been looking for all my life, though I never knew it till now. The reason why we loved the old Narnia is that it sometimes looked a little like this."
"The Last Battle," C.S. Lewis

Heaven Envisioned ...

Heaven is a place of full _____ with God.

And I heard a loud voice from the throne saying, "Behold, the dwelling place of God is with man. He will dwell with them, and they will be his people, and God himself will be with them as their God."
Revelation 21:3

"Let not your hearts be troubled. Believe in God; believe also in me. In my Father's house are many rooms. If it were not so, would I have told you that I go to prepare a place for you? And if I go and prepare a place for you, I will come again and will take you to myself, that where I am you may be also."
John 14:1-3

○ We will _____ _____ Him.

You make known to me the path of life; in your presence there is fullness of joy; at your right hand are pleasures forevermore.
Psalm 16:11

■ As priests in the temple.

The inner sanctuary he prepared in the innermost part of the house, to set there the ark of the covenant of the LORD. The inner sanctuary was twenty cubits long, twenty cubits wide, and twenty cubits high, and he overlaid it with pure gold. He also overlaid an altar of cedar.
1 Kings 6:19-20

And the one who spoke with me had a measuring rod of gold to measure the city and its gates and walls. The city lies foursquare, its length the same as its width. And he measured the city with his rod, 12,000 stadia. Its length and width and height are equal. He also measured its wall, 144 cubits by human measurement, which is also an angel's measurement. The wall was built of jasper, while the city was pure gold, like clear glass. The foundations of the wall of the city were adorned

with every kind of jewel. The first was jasper, the second sapphire, the third agate, the fourth emerald, the fifth onyx, the sixth carnelian, the seventh chrysolite, the eighth beryl, the ninth topaz, the tenth chrysoprase, the eleventh jacinth, the twelfth amethyst. And the twelve gates were twelve pearls, each of the gates made of a single pearl, and the street of the city was pure gold, like transparent glass. And I saw no temple in the city, for its temple is the Lord God the Almighty and the Lamb.
Revelation 21:15-22

- As a _____ with a husband.

Then I heard what seemed to be the voice of a great multitude, like the roar of many waters and like the sound of mighty peals of thunder, crying out, "Hallelujah! For the Lord our God the Almighty reigns. Let us rejoice and exult and give him the glory, for the marriage of the Lamb has come, and his Bride has made herself ready; it was granted her to clothe herself with fine linen, bright and pure"—for the fine linen is the righteous deeds of the saints.
Revelation 19:6-8

And I saw the holy city, new Jerusalem, coming down out of heaven from God, prepared as a bride adorned for her husband.
Revelation 21:2

- As children of a Father.

"Fear not, little flock, for it is your Father's good pleasure to give you the kingdom."
Luke 12:32

- As _____ of a King.

O LORD, our Lord, how majestic is your name in all the earth! You have set your glory above the heavens. Out of the mouth of babies and infants, you have established strength because of your foes, to still the enemy and the avenger. When I look at your heavens, the work of your fingers, the moon and the stars, which you have set in place, what is man that you are mindful of him, and the son of man that you care for him? Yet you have made him a little lower than the heavenly beings and crowned him with glory and honor. You have given him dominion over the works of your hands; you have put all things under his feet, all sheep and oxen, and also the beasts of the field, the birds of the heavens, and the fish of the sea, whatever passes along the paths of the seas. O LORD, our Lord, how majestic is your name in all the earth!
Psalm 8:1-9

The earth is the LORD's and the fullness thereof, the world and those who dwell therein ...
Psalm 24:1

*When you cry out, let your collection of idols deliver you! The wind will
carry them all off, a breath will take them away. But he who takes refuge
in me shall possess the land and shall inherit my holy mountain.*
Isaiah 57:13

*"Then the King will say to those on his right, 'Come, you who are blessed by my
Father, inherit the kingdom prepared for you from the foundation of the world.'"*
Matthew 25:34

*The Spirit himself bears witness with our spirit that we are children of God,
and if children, then heirs—heirs of God and fellow heirs with Christ, provided
we suffer with him in order that we may also be glorified with him.*
Romans 8:16-17

*And they sang a new song, saying, "Worthy are you to take the scroll and to
open its seals, for you were slain, and by your blood you ransomed people for
God from every tribe and language and people and nation, and you have made
them a kingdom and priests to our God, and they shall reign on the earth."*
Revelation 5:9-10

*Then the seventh angel blew his trumpet, and there were loud voices in heaven, saying,
"The kingdom of the world has become the kingdom of our Lord and of his Christ, and
he shall reign forever and ever." And the twenty-four elders who sit on their thrones
before God fell on their faces and worshiped God, saying, "We give thanks to you,
Lord God Almighty, who is and who was, for you have taken your great power and
begun to reign. The nations raged, but your wrath came, and the time for the dead to
be judged, and for rewarding your servants, the prophets and saints, and those who
fear your name, both small and great, and for destroying the destroyers of the earth."*
Revelation 11:15-18

*And night will be no more. They will need no light of lamp or sun, for the
Lord God will be their light, and they will reign forever and ever.*
Revelation 22:5

- As participants in a banquet.

*"You are those who have stayed with me in my trials, and I assign to you, as
my Father assigned to me, a kingdom, that you may eat and drink at my table
in my kingdom and sit on thrones judging the twelve tribes of Israel."*
Luke 22:28-30

*And the angel said to me, "Write this: Blessed are those who are invited to the marriage
supper of the Lamb." And he said to me, "These are the true words of God."*
Revelation 19:9

○ We will _____ Him.

Thus the LORD used to speak to Moses face to face, as a man speaks to
his friend. When Moses turned again into the camp, his assistant Joshua
the son of Nun, a young man, would not depart from the tent.
Exodus 33:11

Moses said, "Please show me your glory." And he said, "I will make all my goodness pass
before you and will proclaim before you my name 'The LORD.' And I will be gracious to
whom I will be gracious, and will show mercy on whom I will show mercy. But," he said
"you cannot see my face, for man shall not see me and live." And the LORD said, "Behold
there is a place by me where you shall stand on the rock, and while my glory passes by I
will put you in a cleft of the rock, and I will cover you with my hand until I have passed
Then I will take away my hand, and you shall see my back, but my face shall not be seen
Exodus 33:18-23

One thing have I asked of the LORD, that will I seek after: that I
may dwell in the house of the LORD all the days of my life, to gaze
upon the beauty of the LORD and to inquire in his temple.
Psalm 27:4

"For I know that my Redeemer lives, and at the last he will stand upon the earth. And
after my skin has been thus destroyed, yet in my flesh I shall see God, whom I shall see
for myself, and my eyes shall behold, and not another. My heart faints within me!"
Job 19:25-27

Jesus said to him, "Have I been with you so long, and you still do not know me, Philip?
Whoever has seen me has seen the Father. How can you say, 'Show us the Father'?"
John 14:9

They will see his face, and his name will be on their foreheads.
Revelation 22:4

"The seeing of God in the glorified body of Christ is the most perfect way of seeing God
with the bodily eyes that can be; for in seeing a real body that one of the persons of the
Trinity has assumed to be his body, and that he dwells in for ever as his own in which th
divine majesty and excellency appears as much as 'tis possible for it to appear in outward
form or shape."
Jonathan Edwards

"Not only will we see his face and live, but we will likely
wonder if we ever lived before we saw his face!"
Randy Alcorn

○ We will _____ Him.

fter this I heard what seemed to be the loud voice of a great multitude in heaven, crying
ut, "Hallelujah! Salvation and glory and power belong to our God, for his judgments
re true and just; for he has judged the great prostitute who corrupted the earth with her
imorality, and has avenged on her the blood of his servants." Once more they cried out,
Hallelujah! The smoke from her goes up forever and ever." And the twenty-four elders
id the four living creatures fell down and worshiped God who was seated on the throne,
iying, "Amen. Hallelujah!" And from the throne came a voice saying, "Praise our God,
all you his servants, you who fear him, small and great." Then I heard what seemed
to be the voice of a great multitude, like the roar of many waters and like the sound of
mighty peals of thunder, crying out, "Hallelujah! For the Lord our God the Almighty
reigns. Let us rejoice and exult and give him the glory, for the marriage of the Lamb
as come, and his Bride has made herself ready; it was granted her to clothe herself with
fine linen, bright and pure"— for the fine linen is the righteous deeds of the saints.
Revelation 19:1-8

No longer will there be anything accursed, but the throne of God and
of the Lamb will be in it, and his servants will worship him.
Revelation 22:3

- We will gather for corporate worship.

round the throne were twenty-four thrones, and seated on the thrones were twenty-four
elders, clothed in white garments, with golden crowns on their heads. From the throne
ime flashes of lightning, and rumblings and peals of thunder, and before the throne were
rning seven torches of fire, which are the seven spirits of God, and before the throne there
s as it were a sea of glass, like crystal. And around the throne, on each side of the throne,
: four living creatures, full of eyes in front and behind: the first living creature like a lion,
e second living creature like an ox, the third living creature with the face of a man, and
e fourth living creature like an eagle in flight. And the four living creatures, each of them
ith six wings, are full of eyes all around and within, and day and night they never cease
say, "Holy, holy, holy, is the Lord God Almighty, who was and is and is to come!" And
vhenever the living creatures give glory and honor and thanks to him who is seated on
e throne, who lives forever and ever, the twenty-four elders fall down before him who is
eated on the throne and worship him who lives forever and ever. They cast their crowns
fore the throne, saying, "Worthy are you, our Lord and God, to receive glory and honor
and power, for you created all things, and by your will they existed and were created."
Revelation 4:4-11

nd when he had taken the scroll, the four living creatures and the twenty-four elders fell
lown before the Lamb, each holding a harp, and golden bowls full of incense, which are
he prayers of the saints. And they sang a new song, saying, "Worthy are you to take the
roll and to open its seals, for you were slain, and by your blood you ransomed people for
God from every tribe and language and people and nation, and you have made them a
ingdom and priests to our God, and they shall reign on the earth." Then I looked, and I
eard around the throne and the living creatures and the elders the voice of many angels,

numbering myriads of myriads and thousands of thousands, saying with a loud voice
"Worthy is the Lamb who was slain, to receive power and wealth and wisdom and mig
and honor and glory and blessing!" And I heard every creature in heaven and on eart
and under the earth and in the sea, and all that is in them, saying, "To him who sits o
the throne and to the Lamb be blessing and honor and glory and might forever and eve
And the four living creatures said, "Amen!" and the elders fell down and worshiped.
Revelation 5:8-14

After this I looked, and behold, a great multitude that no one could number, from eve
nation, from all tribes and peoples and languages, standing before the throne and befo
the Lamb, clothed in white robes, with palm branches in their hands, and crying out w
a loud voice, "Salvation belongs to our God who sits on the throne, and to the Lamb!
And all the angels were standing around the throne and around the elders and the
four living creatures, and they fell on their faces before the throne and worshiped God
saying, "Amen! Blessing and glory and wisdom and thanksgiving and honor and powe
and might be to our God forever and ever! Amen." Then one of the elders addressed
me, saying, "Who are these, clothed in white robes, and from where have they come?"
said to him, "Sir, you know." And he said to me, "These are the ones coming out of th
great tribulation. They have washed their robes and made them white in the blood of
the Lamb. "Therefore they are before the throne of God, and serve him day and night
his temple; and he who sits on the throne will shelter them with his presence. They sha
hunger no more, neither thirst anymore; the sun shall not strike them, nor any scorchi
heat. For the Lamb in the midst of the throne will be their shepherd, and he will guid
them to springs of living water, and God will wipe away every tear from their eyes."
Revelation 7:9-17

- We will shout as we consider God's incomprehensible works.

Then the seventh angel blew his trumpet, and there were loud voices in heaven, saying
"The kingdom of the world has become the kingdom of our Lord and of his Christ, an
he shall reign forever and ever." And the twenty-four elders who sit on their thrones
before God fell on their faces and worshiped God, saying, "We give thanks to you,
Lord God Almighty, who is and who was, for you have taken your great power and
begun to reign. The nations raged, but your wrath came, and the time for the dead to
be judged, and for rewarding your servants, the prophets and saints, and those who
fear your name, both small and great, and for destroying the destroyers of the earth."
Revelation 11:15-18

- We will sing as we behold God's incomparable worth.

And I saw what appeared to be a sea of glass mingled with fire—and also those who
had conquered the beast and its image and the number of its name, standing beside
the sea of glass with harps of God in their hands. And they sing the song of Moses,
the servant of God, and the song of the Lamb, saying, "Great and amazing are
your deeds, O Lord God the Almighty! Just and true are your ways, O King of the

nations! Who will not fear, O Lord, and glorify your name? For you alone are holy.
All nations will come and worship you, for your righteous acts have been revealed."
Revelation 15:2-4

- We will live in continuous worship.

So, whether you eat or drink, or whatever you do, do all to the glory of God.
1 Corinthians 10:31

No legitimate activity of life—whether in marriage, family, business, play, friendship,
ucation, politics, etc.—escapes the claims of Christ's kingship .... Certainly those who
and reign with Christ forever will find the diversity and complexity of their worship of
d not less, but richer, in the life to come. Every legitimate activity of new creaturely life
will be included within the life of worship of God's people."
Cornelius Venema

o We will _____ Him.

"Therefore they are before the throne of God, and serve him day and night in his
temple; and he who sits on the throne will shelter them with his presence."
Revelation 7:15

For it will be like a man going on a journey, who called his servants and entrusted
o them his property. To one he gave five talents, to another two, to another one, to
ch according to his ability. Then he went away. He who had received the five talents
nt at once and traded with them, and he made five talents more. So also he who had
he two talents made two talents more. But he who had received the one talent went
nd dug in the ground and hid his master's money. Now after a long time the master
f those servants came and settled accounts with them. And he who had received the
ive talents came forward, bringing five talents more, saying, 'Master, you delivered
o me five talents; here I have made five talents more.' His master said to him, 'Well
ne, good and faithful servant. You have been faithful over a little; I will set you over
uch. Enter into the joy of your master.' And he also who had the two talents came
ward, saying, 'Master, you delivered to me two talents; here I have made two talents
ore.' His master said to him, 'Well done, good and faithful servant. You have been
faithful over a little; I will set you over much. Enter into the joy of your master.'

also who had received the one talent came forward, saying, 'Master, I knew you to be
ard man, reaping where you did not sow, and gathering where you scattered no seed,
I was afraid, and I went and hid your talent in the ground. Here you have what is
urs.' But his master answered him, 'You wicked and slothful servant! You knew that
eap where I have not sown and gather where I scattered no seed? Then you ought to
e invested my money with the bankers, and at my coming I should have received what
my own with interest. So take the talent from him and give it to him who has the ten
nts. For to everyone who has will more be given, and he will have an abundance. But

from the one who has not, even what he has will be taken away. And cast the worth
servant into the outer darkness. In that place there will be weeping and gnashing of te
Matthew 25:14-30

But Jesus answered them, "My Father is working until now, and I am working."
John 5:17

And to Adam he said, "Because you have listened to the voice of your wife and
have eaten of the tree of which I commanded you, 'You shall not eat of it,' cursed
is the ground because of you; in pain you shall eat of it all the days of your life;
thorns and thistles it shall bring forth for you; and you shall eat the plants of the
field. By the sweat of your face you shall eat bread, till you return to the ground,
for out of it you were taken; for you are dust, and to dust you shall return."
Genesis 3:17-19

No longer will there be anything accursed, but the throne of God and
of the Lamb will be in it, and his servants will worship him.
Revelation 22:3

"The eternal state is hardly inactivity for the redeemed but instead work—work that
is joyously freed from the frustration of a cursed earth. The new earth is not simply a
restoration of Eden but a glorious civilization with a city, and the glory of the nations
redeemed and brought into it. One can expect that the new earth would be abuzz
with culture—music, painting, literature, architecture, commerce, agriculture, and
everything that expresses the creativity of human beings as the image of God."
Russell Moore

○ We will be _____ _____ Him.

"Blessed are those servants whom the master finds awake when he comes. Truly, I say to you,
will dress himself for service and have them recline at table, and he will come and serve them
Luke 12:37

"For even the Son of Man came not to be served but to serve,
and to give his life as a ransom for many."
Mark 10:45

Peter said to him, "You shall never wash my feet." Jesus answered
him, "If I do not wash you, you have no share with me."
John 13:8

On this mountain the LORD of hosts will make for all peoples a feast of rich food,
a feast of well-aged wine, of rich food full of marrow, of aged wine well refined.
Isaiah 25:6

○ We will _____ with Him.

Then God said, "Let us make man in our image, after our likeness. And let them have dominion over the fish of the sea and over the birds of the heavens and over the livestock and over all the earth and over every creeping thing that creeps on the earth." So God created man in his own image, in the image of God he created him; male and female he created them. And God blessed them. And God said to them, "Be fruitful and multiply and fill the earth and subdue it, and have dominion over the fish of the sea and over the birds of the heavens and over every living thing that moves on the earth."
Genesis 1:26-28

"God's intention for humans was that we would occupy the whole Earth and reign over it. This dominion would produce God-exalting societies in which we would exercise the creativity, imagination, intellect, and skills befitting beings created in God's image, thereby manifesting his attributes."
Randy Alcorn

"And the kingdom and the dominion and the greatness of the kingdoms under the whole heaven shall be given to the people of the saints of the Most High; his kingdom shall be an everlasting kingdom, and all dominions shall serve and obey him."
Daniel 7:27

Jesus said to them, "Truly, I say to you, in the new world, when the Son of Man will sit on his glorious throne, you who have followed me will also sit on twelve thrones, judging the twelve tribes of Israel."
Matthew 19:28

"And he said to him, 'Well done, good servant! Because you have been faithful in a very little, you shall have authority over ten cities.'"
Luke 19:17

"You are those who have stayed with me in my trials, and I assign to you, as my Father assigned to me, a kingdom, that you may eat and drink at my table in my kingdom and sit on thrones judging the twelve tribes of Israel."
Luke 22:28-30

The saying is trustworthy, for: If we have died with him, we will also live with him; if we endure, we will also reign with him; if we deny him, he also will deny us; if we are faithless, he remains faithful—for he cannot deny himself.
2 Timothy 2:11-13

Henceforth there is laid up for me the crown of righteousness, which the Lord, the righteous judge, will award to me on that Day, and not only to me but also to all who have loved his appearing.
2 Timothy 4:8

"Do not fear what you are about to suffer. Behold, the devil is about to throw some of you into prison, that you may be tested, and for ten days you will have tribulation. Be faithful unto death, and I will give you the crown of life."
Revelation 2:10

"The one who conquers and who keeps my works until the end, to him I will give authority over the nations, and he will rule them with a rod of iron, as when earthen pots are broken in pieces, even as I myself have received authority from my Father."
Revelation 2:26-27

"I am coming soon. Hold fast what you have, so that no one may seize your crown."
Revelation 3:11

"The one who conquers, I will grant him to sit with me on my throne, as I also conquered and sat down with my Father on his throne."
Revelation 3:21

○ We will _____ in Him.

Thus the heavens and the earth were finished, and all the host of them. And on the seventh day God finished his work that he had done, and he rested on the seventh day from all his work that he had done. So God blessed the seventh day and made it holy, because on it God rested from all his work that he had done in creation.
Genesis 2:1-3

"Six days you shall labor, and do all your work, but the seventh day is a Sabbath to the LORD your God. On it you shall not do any work, you, or your son, or your daughter, your male servant, or your female servant, or your livestock, or the sojourner who is within your gates. For in six days the LORD made heaven and earth, the sea, and all that is in them, and rested on the seventh day. Therefore the LORD blessed the Sabbath day and made it holy."
Exodus 20:9-11

"For six years you shall sow your field, and for six years you shall prune your vineyard and gather in its fruits, but in the seventh year there shall be a Sabbath of solemn rest for the land, a Sabbath to the LORD. You shall not sow your field or prune your vineyard. You shall not reap what grows of itself in your harvest, or gather the grapes of your undressed vine. It shall be a year of solemn rest for the land."
Leviticus 25:3-5

So then, there remains a Sabbath rest for the people of God, for whoever has entered God's rest has also rested from his works as God did from his. Let us therefore strive to enter that rest, so that no one may fall by the same sort of disobedience.
Hebrews 4:9-11

"You know that David my father could not build a house for the name of the LORD his God because of the warfare with which his enemies surrounded him, until the LORD put them under the soles of his feet. But now the LORD my God has given me rest on every side. There is neither adversary nor misfortune."
1 Kings 5:3-4

And I heard a voice from heaven saying, "Write this: Blessed are the dead who die in the Lord from now on." "Blessed indeed," says the Spirit, "that they may rest from their labors, for their deeds follow them!"
Revelation 14:13

○ Based upon a biblical understanding of heaven as a place of reconciliation with God …
- To long for heaven is to long for God.
- To love heaven is to love God.
- To fill your heart and mind with truth about heaven is to fill your heart and mind with truth about God.
- To think unworthy thoughts of heaven is to think unworthy thoughts of _____.

o come to Thee is to come home from exile, to come to land out of the raging storm, to e to rest after long labor, to come to the goal of my desires and the summit of my wishes."
Charles Spurgeon

Heaven is a place of final _____ for our bodies.

There are heavenly bodies and earthly bodies, but the glory of the heavenly is of one kind, d the glory of the earthly is of another. There is one glory of the sun, and another glory of e moon, and another glory of the stars; for star differs from star in glory. So is it with the rrection of the dead. What is sown is perishable; what is raised is imperishable. It is sown in onor; it is raised in glory. It is sown in weakness; it is raised in power. It is sown a natural ody; it is raised a spiritual body. If there is a natural body, there is also a spiritual body.
1 Corinthians 15:40-44

○ Spiritually
- We will be completely free from _____.

But nothing unclean will ever enter it, nor anyone who does what is detestable or false, but only those who are written in the Lamb's book of life.
Revelation 21:27

ed are those who wash their robes, so that they may have the right to the tree of life and they may enter the city by the gates. Outside are the dogs and sorcerers and the sexually moral and murderers and idolaters, and everyone who loves and practices falsehood.
Revelation 22:14-15

- Robed in righteousness.

Then one of the elders addressed me, saying, "Who are these, clothed in white robes, and from where have they come?" I said to him, "Sir, you know." And he said to me, "These are the ones coming out of the great tribulation. They have washed their robes and made them white in the blood of the Lamb.
Revelation 7:13-14

"... it was granted her to clothe herself with fine linen, bright and pure"—for the fine linen is the righteous deeds of the saints.
Revelation 19:8

- Untouched by temptation.

... and the devil who had deceived them was thrown into the lake of fire and sulfur where the beast and the false prophet were, and they will be tormented day and night forever and ever.
Revelation 20:10

- We will be utterly free to _____.

"The freedom of heaven, then, is the freedom from sin; not that the believer just happens to be free from sin, but that he is so constituted or reconstituted that he cannot sin. He doesn't want to sin, and he does not want to want to sin."
Paul Helm

- Sin will literally be unthinkable to us.
- Sin will ultimately be undesirable to us.

For in this hope we were saved. Now hope that is seen is not hope. For who hopes for what he sees? But if we hope for what we do not see, we wait for it with patience.
Romans 8:24-25

○ Physically

"If the blueprints for our glorified bodies are in the DNA, then it would stand to reason that our bodies will be resurrected at the optimal stage of development determined by our DNA."
Hank Hanegraaff

- We will eat and drink.

On this mountain the LORD of hosts will make for all peoples a feast of rich food, a feast of well-aged wine, of rich food full of marrow, of aged wine well refined.
Isaiah 25:6

"I tell you, many will come from east and west and recline at table with Abraham, Isaac, and Jacob in the kingdom of heaven …"
Matthew 8:11

"I tell you I will not drink again of this fruit of the vine until that day when I drink it new with you in my Father's kingdom."
Matthew 26:29

"For I tell you that from now on I will not drink of the fruit of the vine until the kingdom of God comes."
Luke 22:18

"You are those who have stayed with me in my trials, and I assign to you, as my Father assigned to me, a kingdom, that you may eat and drink at my table in my kingdom and sit on thrones judging the twelve tribes of Israel."
Luke 22:28-30

As they were talking about these things, Jesus himself stood among them, and said to them, "Peace to you!" But they were startled and frightened and thought they saw a spirit. And he said to them, "Why are you troubled, and why do doubts arise in your hearts? See my hands and my feet, that it is I myself. Touch me, and see. For a spirit does not have flesh and bones as you see that I have." And when he had said this, he showed them his hands and his feet. And while they still disbelieved for joy and were marveling, he said to them, "Have you anything here to eat?" They gave him a piece of broiled fish …
Luke 24:36-42

- We will sing and shout.

After this I looked, and behold, a great multitude that no one could number, from every nation, from all tribes and peoples and languages, standing before the throne and before the Lamb, clothed in white robes, with palm branches in their hands, and crying out with a loud voice, "Salvation belongs to our God who sits on the throne, and to the Lamb!"
Revelation 7:9-10

- Our _____ will enable us to experience our surroundings.

And he carried me away in the Spirit to a great, high mountain, and showed me the holy city Jerusalem coming down out of heaven from God, having the glory of God, its radiance like a most rare jewel, like a jasper, clear as crystal.
Revelation 21:10-11

- Our _____ will allow us to achieve our aspirations.

Just as we have borne the image of the man of dust, we
shall also bear the image of the man of heaven.
1 Corinthians 15:49

- Our _____ will be preserved.

"For I know that my Redeemer lives, and at the last he will stand upon the earth. And
after my skin has been thus destroyed, yet in my flesh I shall see God, whom I shall see
for myself, and my eyes shall behold, and not another. My heart faints within me!"
Job 19:25-27

"But Abraham said, 'Child, remember that you in your lifetime
received your good things, and Lazarus in like manner bad things;
but now he is comforted here, and you are in anguish.'"
Luke 16:25

"I tell you I will not drink again of this fruit of the vine until that
day when I drink it new with you in my Father's kingdom."
Matthew 26:29

And if anyone's name was not found written in the book
of life, he was thrown into the lake of fire.
Revelation 20:15

"We can banish all fear of being absorbed into the 'All' which Buddhism holds before us,
reincarnated in some other life form as in the post-mortem prospect of Hinduism .... The
self with which we were endowed by the Creator in his gift of life to us, the self whose wor
was secured forever in the self-substitution of God for us on the cross, that self will endur
into eternity. Death cannot destroy us."
Bruce Milne

- Our humanity will be _____.

And as he was praying, the appearance of his face was
altered, and his clothing became dazzling white.
Luke 9:29

Beloved, we are God's children now, and what we will be has not yet appeared;
but we know that when he appears we shall be like him, because we shall see him
as he is. And everyone who thus hopes in him purifies himself as he is pure.
1 John 3:2-3

"Then the righteous will shine like the sun in the kingdom of their Father."
Matthew 13:43a

- Our bodies will be pleasing to the Lord.
- Our bodies will be pleasing to ourselves.
- Our bodies will be pleasing to others.
- Mentally
  - Our knowledge of God …

Love never ends. As for prophecies, they will pass away; as for tongues, they will cease; as for knowledge, it will pass away. For we know in part and we prophesy in part, but when the perfect comes, the partial will pass away. When I was a child, I spoke like a child, I thought like a child, I reasoned like a child. When I became a man, I gave up childish ways. For now we see in a mirror dimly, but then face to face. Now I know in part; then I shall know fully, even as I have been fully known.
1 Corinthians 13:8-12

"1 Corinthians 13:12 does not say that we will be omniscient or know everything (Paul could have said we will know all things, ta panta, if he had wished to do so), but rightly translated, simply says that we will know in a fuller or more intensive way, 'even as we have been known,' that is, without any error or misconceptions in our knowledge."
Wayne Grudem

- Will always be true.
- Will never be _____.

Great is the LORD, and greatly to be praised, and his greatness is unsearchable.
Psalm 145:3

But God, being rich in mercy, because of the great love with which he loved us, even when we were dead in our trespasses, made us alive together with Christ—by grace you have been saved—and raised us up with him and seated us with him in the heavenly places in Christ Jesus, so that in the coming ages he might show the immeasurable riches of his grace in kindness toward us in Christ Jesus.
Ephesians 2:4-7

"When we enjoy God, we enjoy him in his eternity without any flux …. Time is fluid, but eternity is stable; and after many ages, the joys will be as savory and satisfying as if they had been but that moment first tasted by our hungry appetites. When the glory of the Lord shall rise upon you, it shall be so far from ever setting, that after millions of years are expired, as numerous as the sands on the seashore, the sun, in the light of whose countenance you shall live, shall be as bright as at the first appearance; he will be so far from ceasing to flow, that he will flow as strong, as full, as at the first communication of himself in glory to the creature. God is always vigorous and flourishing; a pure act of life, sparkling new and fresh rays of life and light to the creature, flourishing with a perpetual spring, and contenting the most capacious desire;

forming your interest, pleasure, and satisfaction; with an infinite variety, without any change or succession; he will have variety to increase delights, and eternity to perpetuate them; this will be the fruit of the enjoyment of an infinite and eternal God.
"Discourse on the Eternity of God", Stephen Charnock

- If in pride we want to be equal to God in knowledge, this will depress us.
- If in humility we want to enjoy God in heaven, this will delight us.
■ Our knowledge of the world …
  - Will continually expand.
  - As we perpetually _____.
○ Emotionally

Delight yourself in the LORD, and he will give you the desires of your heart.
Psalm 37:4

■ Our feelings will be entirely enjoyable.

"Blessed are you who are hungry now, for you shall be satisfied. Blessed are you who weep now, for you shall laugh. Blessed are you when people hate you and when they exclude you and revile you and spurn your name as evil, on account of the Son of Man! Rejoice in that day, and leap for joy, for behold, your reward is great in heaven; for so their fathers did to the prophets."
Luke 6:21-23

"He will wipe away every tear from their eyes, and death shall be no more, neither shall there be mourning, nor crying, nor pain anymore, for the former things have passed away."
Revelation 21:4

■ Our cravings will be completely _____.

Jesus said to them, "I am the bread of life; whoever comes to me shall not hunger, and whoever believes in me shall never thirst."
John 6:35

- Hunger and thirst will not be ultimately quieted.

"They shall hunger no more, neither thirst anymore; the sun shall not strike them, nor any scorching heat. For the Lamb in the midst of the throne will be their shepherd, and he will guide them to springs of living water, and God will wipe away every tear from their eyes."
Revelation 7:16-17

- Hunger and thirst will be unfailingly quenched.

And he said to me, "It is done! I am the Alpha and the Omega, the beginning and the end. To the thirsty I will give from the spring of the water of life without payment."
Revelation 21:6

- Our desires will be totally fulfilled.

> *"When Christ calls me Home I shall go with the gladness*
> *of a boy bounding away from school."*
> *Adoniram Judson*

- The goal of Buddhism: The elimination of all desire.
- The goal of Christianity: The _____ of all desire.

The Spirit and the Bride say, "Come." And let the one who hears say, "Come." And let the one who is thirsty come; let the one who desires take the water of life without price.
Revelation 22:17

- Our wants will be fully _____.

> *"One of the greatest things about Heaven is that we'll no longer have to battle our desires. They'll always be pure, attending to their proper objects. We'll enjoy food without gluttony and eating disorders. We'll express admiration and affection without lust, fornication, or betrayal. Those simply won't exist."*
> *Randy Alcorn*

> *"I've a feeling we've got to the country where everything is allowed."*
> *Lucy, "The Last Battle," C.S. Lewis*

> *"Love God and do as you please."*
> *Augustine*

Heaven is a place of future _____ with the church.

But you have come to Mount Zion and to the city of the living God, the heavenly Jerusalem, and to innumerable angels in festal gathering, and to the assembly of the firstborn who are enrolled in heaven, and to God, the judge of all, and to the spirits of the righteous made perfect, and to Jesus, the mediator of a new covenant, and to the sprinkled blood that speaks a better word than the blood of Abel.
Hebrews 12:22-24

o We will _____ one another.

And after six days Jesus took with him Peter and James, and John his brother, and led them up a high mountain by themselves. And he was transfigured before them, and his face shone like the sun, and his clothes became white as light. And behold,

there appeared to them Moses and Elijah, talking with him. And Peter said to Jesus, "Lord, it is good that we are here. If you wish, I will make three tents here, one for you and one for Moses and one for Elijah." He was still speaking when, behold, a bright cloud overshadowed them, and a voice from the cloud said, "This is my beloved Son, with whom I am well pleased; listen to him." When the disciples heard this, they fell on their faces and were terrified. But Jesus came and touched them, saying, "Rise, and have no fear." And when they lifted up their eyes, they saw no one but Jesus only.
Matthew 17:1-8

"I tell you, many will come from east and west and recline at table with Abraham, Isaac, and Jacob in the kingdom of heaven …"
Matthew 8:11

For since we believe that Jesus died and rose again, even so, through Jesus, God will bring with him those who have fallen asleep. For this we declare to you by a word from the Lord, that we who are alive, who are left until the coming of the Lord, will not precede those who have fallen asleep. For the Lord himself will descend from heaven with a cry of command, with the voice of an archangel, and with the sound of the trumpet of God. And the dead in Christ will rise first. Then we who are alive, who are left, will be caught up together with them in the clouds to meet the Lord in the air, and so we will always be with the Lord. Therefore encourage one another with these words.
1 Thessalonians 4:14-18

"There would be no point in these words of consolation if they did not imply the mutual recognition of saints. The hope with which he cheers wearied Christians is the hope of meeting their beloved friends again …. But in the moment that we who are saved shall meet our several friends in heaven, we shall at once know them, and they will at once know us."
J.C. Ryle

"Shall we know one another in Heaven? Shall we love and remember? I do not think anyone need wonder about this or doubt for a single moment. We are never told we shall, because, I expect, it was not necessary to say anything about this which our own hearts tell us. We do not need words. For if we think for a minute, we know. Would you be yourself if you did not love and remember? We are told that we shall be like our Lord Jesus. Surely this does not mean in holiness only, but in everything; and does not He know and love and remember? He would not be Himself if He did not, and we should be ourselves if we did not."
Amy Carmichael

○ We will _____ one another.

But when the Pharisees heard that he had silenced the Sadducees, they gathered together. And one of them, a lawyer, asked him a question to test him. "Teacher, which is the great commandment in the Law?" And he said to him, "You shall love the Lord your God with all your heart and with all your soul and with all your mind. This is the

great and first commandment. And a second is like it: You shall love your neighbor as yourself. On these two commandments depend all the Law and the Prophets."
Matthew 22:34-40

"By this all people will know that you are my disciples, if you have love for one another."
John 13:35

By this we know love, that he laid down his life for us, and we ought to lay down our lives for the brothers. But if anyone has the world's goods and sees his brother in need, yet closes his heart against him, how does God's love abide in him? Little children, let us not love in word or talk but in deed and in truth.
1 John 3:16-18

○ We will be a family before our Father.

Jesus said, "Truly, I say to you, there is no one who has left house or brothers or sisters or mother or father or children or lands, for my sake and for the gospel, who will not receive a hundredfold now in this time, houses and brothers and sisters and mothers and children and lands, with persecutions, and in the age to come eternal life."
Mark 10:29-30

○ We will be a bride with our Savior.
- ■ Will there be marriage?
  - • No, in the sense of the earthly _____.

"For in the resurrection they neither marry nor are given in marriage, but are like angels in heaven."
Matthew 22:30

"For when they rise from the dead, they neither marry nor are given in marriage, but are like angels in heaven."
Mark 12:25

And Jesus said to them, "The sons of this age marry and are given in marriage, but those who are considered worthy to attain to that age and to the resurrection from the dead neither marry nor are given in marriage, for they cannot die anymore, because they are equal to angels and are sons of God, being sons of the resurrection."
Luke 20:34-36

  - • Yes, in the sense of the eternal _____.

"Therefore a man shall leave his father and mother and hold fast to his wife, and the two shall become one flesh." This mystery is profound, and I am saying that it refers to Christ and the church.
Ephesians 5:31-32

- Will there be sex?
  - Yes, in the sense of gender _____.

Then God said, "Let us make man in our image, after our likeness. And let them have dominion over the fish of the sea and over the birds of the heavens and over the livestock and over all the earth and over every creeping thing that creeps on the earth." So God created man in his own image, in the image of God he created him; male and female he created them. And God blessed them. And God said to them, "Be fruitful and multiply and fill the earth and subdue it, and have dominion over the fish of the sea and over the birds of the heavens and over every living thing that moves on the earth."
Genesis 1:26-28

Then the LORD God said, "It is not good that the man should be alone; I will make him a helper fit for him." Now out of the ground the LORD God had formed every beast of the field and every bird of the heavens and brought them to the man to see what he would call them. And whatever the man called every living creature, that was its name. The man gave names to all livestock and to the birds of the heavens and to every beast of the field. But for Adam there was not found a helper fit for him. So the LORD God caused a deep sleep to fall upon the man, and while he slept took one of his ribs and closed up its place with flesh. And the rib that the LORD God had taken from the man he made into a woman and brought her to the man. Then the man said, "This at last is bone of my bones and flesh of my flesh; she shall be called Woman, because she was taken out of Man."
Genesis 2:18-23

  - No, in the sense of marital _____.

Now concerning the matters about which you wrote: "It is good for a man not to have sexual relations with a woman." But because of the temptation to sexual immorality, each man should have his own wife and each woman her own husband. The husband should give to his wife her conjugal rights, and likewise the wife to her husband. For the wife does not have authority over her own body, but the husband does. Likewise the husband does not have authority over his own body, but the wife does. Do not deprive one another, except perhaps by agreement for a limited time, that you may devote yourselves to prayer; but then come together again, so that Satan may not tempt you because of your lack of self-control. Now as a concession, not a command, I say this. I wish that all were as I myself am. But each has his own gift from God, one of one kind and one of another. To the unmarried and the widows I say that it is good for them to remain single as I am. But if they cannot exercise self-control, they should marry. For it is better to marry than to burn with passion.
1 Corinthians 7:1-9

"I think our present outlook might be like that of a small boy who, on being told that the sexual act was the highest bodily pleasure should immediately ask whether you ate chocolates at the same time. On receiving the answer, 'No,' he might regard absence of chocolates as the chief characteristic of sexuality. In vain would you tell him that the reason why lovers in their carnal raptures don't bother about chocolates is that they have

something better to think of. The boy knows chocolate: he does not know the positive thing that excludes it. We are in the same position. We know the sexual life; we do not know, except in glimpses, the other thing which, in Heaven, will leave no room for it."

C.S. Lewis

o We will be a people from every nation.

Now there were dwelling in Jerusalem Jews, devout men from every nation under heaven. And at this sound the multitude came together, and they were bewildered, because each one was hearing them speak in his own language. And they were amazed and astonished, saying, "Are not all these who are speaking Galileans? And how is it that we hear, each of us in his own native language? Parthians and Medes and Elamites and residents of Mesopotamia, Judea and Cappadocia, Pontus and Asia, Phrygia and Pamphylia, Egypt and the parts of Libya belonging to Cyrene, and visitors from Rome, both Jews and proselytes, Cretans and Arabians—we hear them telling in our own tongues the mighty works of God." And all were amazed and perplexed, saying to one another, "What does this mean?" But others mocking said, "They are filled with new wine."

Acts 2:5-13

After this I looked, and behold, a great multitude that no one could number, from every nation, from all tribes and peoples and languages, standing before the throne and before the Lamb, clothed in white robes, with palm branches in their hands, and crying out with a loud voice, "Salvation belongs to our God who sits on the throne, and to the Lamb!"

Revelation 7:9-10

o We will be an ancestry from every _____.

"Every Christian friend that goes before us from this world is a ransomed spirit waiting to welcome us in heaven. There will be the infant of days that we have lost below, through grace to be found above. There the Christian father, and mother, and wife, and child, and friend, with whom we shall renew the holy fellowship of the satins, which was interrupted by death here, but shall be commenced again in the upper sanctuary, and then shall never end. There we shall have companionship with the patriarchs and fathers and saints of the Old and New Testaments, and those of whom the world was not worthy .... And there, above all, we shall enjoy and dwell with God the Father, whom we have loved with all our hearts on earth; and with Jesus Christ, our beloved Savior, who has always been to us the chief among ten thousands, and altogether lovely; and with the Holy Spirit, our Sanctifier, and Guide, and Comforter; and shall be filled with all the fullness of the Godhead forever!"

Jonathan Edwards

o What about infants who have died?
  ▪ Revere: God is _____, righteous, and good.

"Far be it from you to do such a thing, to put the righteous to death with the wicked, so that the righteous fare as the wicked! Far be that from you! Shall not the Judge of all the earth do what is just?"
Genesis 18:25

"See that you do not despise one of these little ones. For I tell you that in heaven their angels always see the face of my Father who is in heaven. What do you think? If a man has a hundred sheep, and one of them has gone astray, does he not leave the ninety-nine on the mountains and go in search of the one that went astray? And if he finds it, truly, I say to you, he rejoices over it more than over the ninety-nine that never went astray. So it is not the will of my Father who is in heaven that one of these little ones should perish."
Matthew 18:10-14

The Lord is not slow to fulfill his promise as some count slowness, but is patient toward you, not wishing that any should perish, but that all should reach repentance.
2 Peter 3:9

- Recognize: The Bible expresses _____ that believers will see young children after death.

But when David saw that his servants were whispering together, David understood that the child was dead. And David said to his servants, "Is the child dead?" They said, "He is dead." Then David arose from the earth and washed and anointed himself and changed his clothes. And he went into the house of the LORD and worshiped. He then went to his own house. And when he asked, they set food before him, and he ate. Then his servants said to him, "What is this thing that you have done? You fasted and wept for the child while he was alive; but when the child died, you arose and ate food." He said, "While the child was still alive, I fasted and wept, for I said, 'Who knows whether the LORD will be gracious to me, that the child may live?' But now he is dead. Why should I fast? Can I bring him back again? I shall go to him, but he will not return to me."
2 Samuel 12:19-23

- Reflect: The Bible holds young children to a different _____ of accountability before God.

For the wrath of God is revealed from heaven against all ungodliness and unrighteousness of men, who by their unrighteousness suppress the truth. For what can be known about God is plain to them, because God has shown it to them. For his invisible attributes, namely, his eternal power and divine nature, have been clearly perceived, ever since the creation of the world, in the things that have been made. So they are without excuse. For although they knew God, they did not honor him as God or give thanks to him, but they became futile in their thinking, and their foolish hearts were darkened.
Romans 1:18-21

For when Gentiles, who do not have the law, by nature do what the law requires,
they are a law to themselves, even though they do not have the law. They show
that the work of the law is written on their hearts, while their conscience also bears
witness, and their conflicting thoughts accuse or even excuse them on that day
when, according to my gospel, God judges the secrets of men by Christ Jesus.
Romans 2:14-16

"And the LORD heard your words and was angered, and he swore, 'Not one of these
men of this evil generation shall see the good land that I swore to give to your fathers,
except Caleb the son of Jephunneh. He shall see it, and to him and to his children I
will give the land on which he has trodden, because he has wholly followed the LORD!'
Even with me the LORD was angry on your account and said, 'You also shall not
go in there. Joshua the son of Nun, who stands before you, he shall enter. Encourage
him, for he shall cause Israel to inherit it. And as for your little ones, who you said
would become a prey, and your children, who today have no knowledge of good or
evil, they shall go in there. And to them I will give it, and they shall possess it.'"
Deuteronomy 1:34-39

- Remember: The only way for sinful mankind (including children born with a sinful nature) to be saved is by the sacrifice of _____ on the cross.

Therefore, just as sin came into the world through one man, and death through
sin, and so death spread to all men because all sinned—for sin indeed was in the
world before the law was given, but sin is not counted where there is no law. Yet
death reigned from Adam to Moses, even over those whose sinning was not like the
transgression of Adam, who was a type of the one who was to come. But the free
gift is not like the trespass. For if many died through one man's trespass, much more
have the grace of God and the free gift by the grace of that one man Jesus Christ
abounded for many. And the free gift is not like the result of that one man's sin. For
the judgment following one trespass brought condemnation, but the free gift following
many trespasses brought justification. For if, because of one man's trespass, death
reigned through that one man, much more will those who receive the abundance of
grace and the free gift of righteousness reign in life through the one man Jesus Christ.
Therefore, as one trespass led to condemnation for all men, so one act of righteousness
leads to justification and life for all men. For as by the one man's disobedience the
many were made sinners, so by the one man's obedience the many will be made
righteous. Now the law came in to increase the trespass, but where sin increased,
grace abounded all the more, so that, as sin reigned in death, grace also might reign
through righteousness leading to eternal life through Jesus Christ our Lord.
Romans 5:12-21

This is good, and it is pleasing in the sight of God our Savior, who desires
all people to be saved and to come to the knowledge of the truth. For there is
one God, and there is one mediator between God and men, the man Christ

Jesus, who gave himself as a ransom for all, which is the testimony given at the proper time. For this I was appointed a preacher and an apostle (I am telling the truth, I am not lying), a teacher of the Gentiles in faith and truth.
1 Timothy 2:3-7

○ What about loved ones who are in hell?

And they sing the song of Moses, the servant of God, and the song of the Lamb, saying, "Great and amazing are your deeds, O Lord God the Almighty! Just and true are your ways, O King of the nations! Who will not fear, O Lord, and glorify your name? For you alone are holy. All nations will come and worship you, for your righteous acts have been revealed."
Revelation 15:3-4

"God the Father (who now pleads with mankind to accept the reconciliation that Christ's death secured for all) and God the Son (our appointed Judge, who wept over Jerusalem) will in a final judgment express wrath and administer justice against rebellious humans. God's holy righteousness will hereby be revealed; God will be doing the right thing, vindicating himself at last against all who have defied him …. (Read through Matt. 25; John 5:22-29; Rom. 2:15-16, 12:19; 2 Thess. 1:7-9; Rev. 18:1-19:3, 20:11-35, and you will see that clearly.) God will judge justly, and all angels, saints, and martyrs will praise him for it. So it seems inescapable that we shall, with them, approve the judgment of persons—rebels—whom we have known and loved."
J.I. Packer

• Heaven is a place of complete restoration of creation.
    ○ A place of _____ reality.

And the LORD God planted a garden in Eden, in the east, and there he put the man whom he had formed. And out of the ground the LORD God made to spring up every tree that is pleasant to the sight and good for food. The tree of life was in the midst of the garden, and the tree of the knowledge of good and evil.
Genesis 2:8-9

Then the angel showed me the river of the water of life, bright as crystal, flowing from the throne of God and of the Lamb through the middle of the street of the city; also, on either side of the river, the tree of life with its twelve kinds of fruit, yielding its fruit each month. The leaves of the tree were for the healing of the nations.
Revelation 22:1-2

    ○ A place of visual _____.

And he carried me away in the Spirit to a great, high mountain, and showed me the holy city Jerusalem coming down out of heaven from God, having the glory of God, its radiance like a most rare jewel, like a jasper, clear as crystal.
Revelation 21:10-11

The wall was built of jasper, while the city was pure gold, like clear glass. The foundations of the wall of the city were adorned with every kind of jewel. The first was jasper, the second sapphire, the third agate, the fourth emerald, the fifth onyx, the sixth carnelian, the seventh chrysolite, the eighth beryl, the ninth topaz, the tenth chrysoprase, the eleventh jacinth, the twelfth amethyst. And the twelve gates were twelve pearls, each of the gates made of a single pearl, and the street of the city was pure gold, like transparent glass.
Revelation 21:18-21

"Look at God's track record in creating natural wonders in this universe. On Mars, the volcano Olympus Mons rises 79,000 feet, nearly three times higher than Mount Everest. The base of Olympus Mons is 370 miles across and would cover the entire state of Nebraska. The Valles Marineris is a vast canyon that stretches one-sixth of the way around Mars. It's 2,800 miles long, 370 miles wide, and 4.5 miles deep. Hundreds of our Grand Canyons could fit inside it. [And] the New Earth may have far more spectacular features than these."
Randy Alcorn

○ A place of natural harmony.

No longer will there be anything accursed, but the throne of God and of the Lamb will be in it, and his servants will worship him.
Revelation 22:3

○ A place of continual worship.

The heavens declare the glory of God, and the sky above proclaims his handiwork. Day to day pours out speech, and night to night reveals knowledge. There is no speech, nor are there words, whose voice is not heard.
Psalm 19:1-3

○ What about animals?
  ▪ Animals were created _____ by God.

And God blessed them. And God said to them, "Be fruitful and multiply and fill the earth and subdue it, and have dominion over the fish of the sea and over the birds of the heavens and over every living thing that moves on the earth." And God said, "Behold, I have given you every plant yielding seed that is on the face of all the earth, and every

tree with seed in its fruit. You shall have them for food. And to every beast of the earth and to every bird of the heavens and to everything that creeps on the earth, everything that has the breath of life, I have given every green plant for food." And it was so.
Genesis 1:28-30

Now out of the ground the LORD God had formed every beast of the field and every bird of the heavens and brought them to the man to see what he would call them. And whatever the man called every living creature, that was its name. The man gave names to all livestock and to the birds of the heavens and to every beast of the field.
Genesis 2:19-20a

"Do you give the horse his might? Do you clothe his neck with a mane? Do you make him leap like the locust? His majestic snorting is terrifying. He paws in the valley and exults in his strength; he goes out to meet the weapons. He laughs at fear and is not dismayed; he does not turn back from the sword. Upon him rattle the quiver, the flashing spear, and the javelin. With fierceness and rage he swallows the ground; he cannot stand still at the sound of the trumpet. When the trumpet sounds, he says 'Aha!' He smells the battle from afar, the thunder of the captains, and the shouting. "Is it by your understanding that the hawk soars and spreads his wings toward the south? Is it at your command that the eagle mounts up and makes his nest on high? On the rock he dwells and makes his home, on the rocky crag and stronghold. From there he spies out the prey; his eyes behold it from far away. His young ones suck up blood, and where the slain are, there is he."
Job 39:19-30

O LORD, how manifold are your works! In wisdom have you made them all; the earth is full of your creatures. Here is the sea, great and wide, which teems with creatures innumerable, living things both small and great. There go the ships, and Leviathan, which you formed to play in it. These all look to you, to give them their food in due season. When you give it to them, they gather it up; when you open your hand, they are filled with good things. When you hide your face, they are dismayed; when you take away their breath, they die and return to their dust. When you send forth your Spirit, they are created, and you renew the face of the ground.
Psalm 104:24-30

Let them praise the name of the LORD! For he commanded and they were created. And he established them forever and ever; he gave a decree, and it shall not pass away. Praise the LORD from the earth, you great sea creatures and all deeps, fire and hail, snow and mist, stormy wind fulfilling his word! Mountains and all hills, fruit trees and all cedars! Beasts and all livestock, creeping things and flying birds!
Psalm 148:5-10

- Animals were placed under the authority of man.

When I look at your heavens, the work of your fingers, the moon and the stars, which you have set in place, what is man that you are mindful of him, and the son of man that you care for him? Yet you have made him a little lower than the heavenly beings and crowned him with glory and honor. You have given him dominion over the works of your hands; you have put all things under his feet, all sheep and oxen, and also the beasts of the field, the birds of the heavens, and the fish of the sea, whatever passes along the paths of the seas.
Psalm 8:3-8

- Animals were _____ by the fall of man.

And the LORD God made for Adam and for his wife garments of skins and clothed them.
Genesis 3:21

For the creation was subjected to futility, not willingly, but because of him who subjected it, in hope that the creation itself will be set free from its bondage to corruption and obtain the freedom of the glory of the children of God. For we know that the whole creation has been groaning together in the pains of childbirth until now.
Romans 8:20-22

- Animals were spared in the flood of the old earth.

"For behold, I will bring a flood of waters upon the earth to destroy all flesh in which is the breath of life under heaven. Everything that is on the earth shall die. But I will establish my covenant with you, and you shall come into the ark, you, your sons, your wife, and your sons' wives with you. And of every living thing of all flesh, you shall bring two of every sort into the ark to keep them alive with you. They shall be male and female. Of the birds according to their kinds, and of the animals according to their kinds, of every creeping thing of the ground, according to its kind, two of every sort shall come in to you to keep them alive. Also take with you every sort of food that is eaten, and store it up. It shall serve as food for you and for them." Noah did this; he did all that God commanded him.
Genesis 6:17-22

"Behold, I establish my covenant with you and your offspring after you, and with every living creature that is with you, the birds, the livestock, and every beast of the earth with you, as many as came out of the ark; it is for every beast of the earth. I establish my covenant with you, that never again shall all flesh be cut off by the waters of the flood, and never again shall there be a flood to destroy the earth." And God said, "This is the sign of the covenant that I make between me and you and every living creature that is with you, for all future generations: I have set my bow in the cloud, and it shall be a sign of the covenant between me and the earth. When I bring clouds over the earth and the bow is seen in the clouds, I will remember my covenant that is between me and you and every living creature of all flesh. And the waters shall never again become a flood to destroy all flesh. When the bow is in the

clouds, I will see it and remember the everlasting covenant between God and every living creature of all flesh that is on the earth." God said to Noah, "This is the sign of the covenant that I have established between me and all flesh that is on the earth."
Genesis 9:9-17

- Animals will be included in the _____ of the new earth.

The wolf shall dwell with the lamb, and the leopard shall lie down with the young goat, and the calf and the lion and the fattened calf together; and a little child shall lead them. The cow and the bear shall graze; their young shall lie down together; and the lion shall eat straw like the ox. The nursing child shall play over the hole of the cobra, and the weaned child shall put his hand on the adder's den. They shall not hurt or destroy in all my holy mountain; for the earth shall be full of the knowledge of the LORD as the waters cover the sea.
Isaiah 11:6-9

- A new earth with no human or animal predation.

"The wolf and the lamb shall graze together; the lion shall eat straw like the ox, and dust shall be the serpent's food. They shall not hurt or destroy in all my holy mountain," says the LORD.
Isaiah 65:25

- Consequently a new earth where we will likely eat a lot of _____.

And God said, "Behold, I have given you every plant yielding seed that is on the face of all the earth, and every tree with seed in its fruit. You shall have them for food. And to every beast of the earth and to every bird of the heavens and to everything that creeps on the earth, everything that has the breath of life, I have given every green plant for food." And it was so.
Genesis 1:29-30

And God blessed Noah and his sons and said to them, "Be fruitful and multiply and fill the earth. The fear of you and the dread of you shall be upon every beast of the earth and upon every bird of the heavens, upon everything that creeps on the ground and all the fish of the sea. Into your hand they are delivered. Every moving thing that lives shall be food for you. And as I gave you the green plants, I give you everything."
Genesis 9:1-3

○ What about the sun, moon, and stars?

The sun shall be no more your light by day, nor for brightness shall the moon give you light; but the LORD will be your everlasting light, and your God will be your

*glory. Your sun shall no more go down, nor your moon withdraw itself; for the
LORD will be your everlasting light, and your days of mourning shall be ended.*
Isaiah 60:19-20

*And the city has no need of sun or moon to shine on it, for the glory of
God gives it light, and its lamp is the Lamb. By its light will the nations
walk, and the kings of the earth will bring their glory into it, and its gates
will never be shut by day—and there will be no night there.*
Revelation 21:23-25

*And night will be no more. They will need no light of lamp or sun, for the
Lord God will be their light, and they will reign forever and ever.*
Revelation 22:5

*And God said, "Let there be light," and there was light. And God saw that the light was
good. And God separated the light from the darkness. God called the light Day, and the
darkness he called Night. And there was evening and there was morning, the first day.*
Genesis 1:3-5

○ What about the sea?

*Then I saw a new heaven and a new earth, for the first heaven and
the first earth had passed away, and the sea was no more.*
Revelation 21:1

*Then you shall see and be radiant; your heart shall thrill and exult, because the
abundance of the sea shall be turned to you, the wealth of the nations shall come to you.
A multitude of camels shall cover you, the young camels of Midian and Ephah; all
those from Sheba shall come. They shall bring gold and frankincense, and shall bring
good news, the praises of the LORD. All the flocks of Kedar shall be gathered to you;
the rams of Nebaioth shall minister to you; they shall come up with acceptance on my
altar, and I will beautify my beautiful house. Who are these that fly like a cloud, and
like doves to their windows? For the coastlands shall hope for me, the ships of Tarshish
first, to bring your children from afar, their silver and gold with them, for the name of the
LORD your God, and for the Holy One of Israel, because he has made you beautiful.*
Isaiah 60:5-9

○ What about weather?

*"Under the whole heaven he lets it go, and his lightning to the corners of the earth.
After it his voice roars; he thunders with his majestic voice, and he does not restrain the
lightnings when his voice is heard. God thunders wondrously with his voice; he does great
things that we cannot comprehend. For to the snow he says, 'Fall on the earth,' likewise
to the downpour, his mighty downpour. He seals up the hand of every man, that all men
whom he made may know it. Then the beasts go into their lairs, and remain in their*

dens. From its chamber comes the whirlwind, and cold from the scattering winds. By the breath of God ice is given, and the broad waters are frozen fast. He loads the thick cloud with moisture; the clouds scatter his lightning. They turn around and around by his guidance, to accomplish all that he commands them on the face of the habitable world. Whether for correction or for his land or for love, he causes it to happen."
Job 37:3-13

"When we live on the New Earth, could we go hiking in a snowstorm without fear of trauma or death? Could we jump off a cliff into a river three hundred feet below? Could we stand in an open field in flashing lightning and roaring thunder and experience the exhilaration of God's powerful hand?"
Randy Alcorn

- Heaven is a place of comprehensive _____ of culture.
  - ○ Music and the arts …

And they sang a new song, saying, "Worthy are you to take the scroll and to open its seals, for you were slain, and by your blood you ransomed people for God from every tribe and language and people and nation, and you have made them a kingdom and priests to our God, and they shall reign on the earth."
Revelation 5:9-10

- ○ Writing and storytelling …

One generation shall commend your works to another, and shall declare your mighty acts. On the glorious splendor of your majesty, and on your wondrous works, I will meditate. They shall speak of the might of your awesome deeds, and I will declare your greatness. They shall pour forth the fame of your abundant goodness and shall sing aloud of your righteousness. The LORD is gracious and merciful, slow to anger and abounding in steadfast love. The LORD is good to all, and his mercy is over all that he has made. All your works shall give thanks to you, O LORD, and all your saints shall bless you! They shall speak of the glory of your kingdom and tell of your power, to make known to the children of man your mighty deeds, and the glorious splendor of your kingdom. Your kingdom is an everlasting kingdom, and your dominion endures throughout all generations.
Psalm 145:4-13a

Now there are also many other things that Jesus did. Were every one of them to be written, I suppose that the world itself could not contain the books that would be written.
John 21:25

"We remember the great delight with which he recounted the course, the counsels, the perils and escapes of the prophets, and the learning with which he discoursed on all the ages of the Church, thereby showing that he was inflamed by no ordinary passion for these wonderful men. Now he embraces them and rejoices to hear them

speak and to speak to them in turn. Now they hail him gladly as a companion,
and thank God with him for having gathered and preserved the Church."
Philip Melanchthon, on Martin Luther

○ Drama and entertainment …

"And there was greeting and kissing and handshaking and old jokes revived (you've no idea how
good an old joke sounds after you take it out again after a rest of five or six hundred years)."
C.S. Lewis, on the great reunion in the New Narnia

○ Inventing and building …

And he carried me away in the Spirit to a great, high mountain, and showed me the holy
city Jerusalem coming down out of heaven from God, having the glory of God, its radiance
like a most rare jewel, like a jasper, clear as crystal. It had a great, high wall, with twelve
gates, and at the gates twelve angels, and on the gates the names of the twelve tribes of the
sons of Israel were inscribed—on the east three gates, on the north three gates, on the south
three gates, and on the west three gates. And the wall of the city had twelve foundations,
and on them were the twelve names of the twelve apostles of the Lamb. And the one who
spoke with me had a measuring rod of gold to measure the city and its gates and walls.
The city lies foursquare, its length the same as its width. And he measured the city with
his rod, 12,000 stadia. Its length and width and height are equal. He also measured its
wall, 144 cubits by human measurement, which is also an angel's measurement. The
wall was built of jasper, while the city was pure gold, like clear glass. The foundations
of the wall of the city were adorned with every kind of jewel. The first was jasper, the
second sapphire, the third agate, the fourth emerald, the fifth onyx, the sixth carnelian,
the seventh chrysolite, the eighth beryl, the ninth topaz, the tenth chrysoprase, the eleventh
jacinth, the twelfth amethyst. And the twelve gates were twelve pearls, each of the gates
made of a single pearl, and the street of the city was pure gold, like transparent glass.
Revelation 21:10-21

○ Trade and business …

By its light will the nations walk, and the kings of the earth will bring their glory
into it, and its gates will never be shut by day—and there will be no night there.
Revelation 21:24-25

○ Sports and recreation …

Do you not know that in a race all the runners run, but only one receives the prize?
So run that you may obtain it. Every athlete exercises self-control in all things.
They do it to receive a perishable wreath, but we an imperishable. So I do not run
aimlessly; I do not box as one beating the air. But I discipline my body and keep
it under control, lest after preaching to others I myself should be disqualified.
1 Corinthians 9:24-27

Not that I have already obtained this or am already perfect, but I press on to make it my own, because Christ Jesus has made me his own. Brothers, I do not consider that I have made it my own. But one thing I do: forgetting what lies behind and straining forward to what lies ahead, I press on toward the goal for the prize of the upward call of God in Christ Jesus.
Philippians 3:12-14

I have fought the good fight, I have finished the race, I have kept the faith. Henceforth there is laid up for me the crown of righteousness, which the Lord, the righteous judge, will award to me on that Day, and not only to me but also to all who have loved his appearing.
2 Timothy 4:7-8

"He made me fast, and when I run I feel God's pleasure …. To give up running would be to hold him in contempt."
Eric Liddell

○ Travel and exploration …

"Skydiving without a parachute? Maybe, maybe not. Scuba diving without an air tank? I hope so. Will we be able to tolerate diving to depths of hundreds of feet without special equipment? We know that our resurrection bodies will be superior. Won't it be fantastic to test their limits and to invent new technologies that extend our ability to explore and enjoy God in the mighty realms he makes? Those who know God and believe his promise of bodily resurrection can dream great dreams. One day we will live those dreams."
Randy Alcorn

Heaven Anticipated …

• We long for a new earth …
  ○ Where we will _____ God's glory continually.

   So, whether you eat or drink, or whatever you do, do all to the glory of God.
   1 Corinthians 10:31

  ○ As we _____ God's gifts eternally.

   He who did not spare his own Son but gave him up for us all, how will he not also with him graciously give us all things?
   Romans 8:32

   Every good gift and every perfect gift is from above, coming down from the Father of lights with whom there is no variation or shadow due to change.
   James 1:17

   "God is the highest good of the reasonable creature, and the enjoyment of him is the only happiness with which our souls can be satisfied. To go to heaven fully to enjoy God,

is infinitely better than the most pleasant accommodations here. Fathers and mothers, husbands, wives, children, or the company of earthly friends, are but shadows. But the enjoyment of God is the substance. These are but scattered beams, but God is the sun. These are but streams, but God is the fountain. These are but drops, but God is the ocean."
Jonathan Edwards

"Hearts on earth may say in the course of a joyful experience, 'I don't want this ever to end.' But invariably it does. The hearts of those in heaven say, 'I want this to go on forever.' And it will. There is no better news than this."
J.I. Packer

We live on this earth …
  o With a commitment to _____.

Since all these things are thus to be dissolved, what sort of people ought you to be in lives of holiness and godliness, waiting for and hastening the coming of the day of God, because of which the heavens will be set on fire and dissolved, and the heavenly bodies will melt as they burn! But according to his promise we are waiting for new heavens and a new earth in which righteousness dwells.
2 Peter 3:11-13

  ▪ In our purity.

And we all, with unveiled face, beholding the glory of the Lord, are being transformed into the same image from one degree of glory to another. For this comes from the Lord who is the Spirit.
2 Corinthians 3:18

By faith Moses, when he was grown up, refused to be called the son of Pharaoh's daughter, choosing rather to be mistreated with the people of God than to enjoy the fleeting pleasures of sin. He considered the reproach of Christ greater wealth than the treasures of Egypt, for he was looking to the reward.
Hebrews 11:24-26

  ▪ With our possessions.

"Do not lay up for yourselves treasures on earth, where moth and rust destroy and where thieves break in and steal, but lay up for yourselves treasures in heaven, where neither moth nor rust destroys and where thieves do not break in and steal. For where your treasure is, there your heart will be also."
Matthew 6:19-21

"When we realize the pleasure that awaits us in God's presence, we can forgo lesser pleasures now. When we realize the possessions that await us in Heaven, we will gladly give away possessions on Earth to store up treasures in Heaven."
Randy Alcorn

But recall the former days when, after you were enlightened, you endured a hard struggle with sufferings, sometimes being publicly exposed to reproach and affliction, and sometimes being partners with those so treated. For you had compassion on those in prison, and you joyfully accepted the plundering of your property, since you knew that you yourselves had a better possession and an abiding one. Therefore do not throw away your confidence, which has a great reward. For you have need of endurance, so that when you have done the will of God you may receive what is promised. For, "Yet a little while, and the coming one will come and will not delay; but my righteous one shall live by faith, and if he shrinks back, my soul has no pleasure in him." But we are not of those who shrink back and are destroyed, but of those who have faith and preserve their souls.
Hebrews 10:32-39

■ For one purpose.

"And now, behold, I am going to Jerusalem, constrained by the Spirit, not knowing what will happen to me there, except that the Holy Spirit testifies to me in every city that imprisonment and afflictions await me. But I do not account my life of any value nor as precious to myself, if only I may finish my course and the ministry that I received from the Lord Jesus, to testify to the gospel of the grace of God."
Acts 20:22-24

This is evidence of the righteous judgment of God, that you may be considered worthy of the kingdom of God, for which you are also suffering—since indeed God considers it just to repay with affliction those who afflict you, and to grant relief to you who are afflicted as well as to us, when the Lord Jesus is revealed from heaven with his mighty angels in flaming fire, inflicting vengeance on those who do not know God and on those who do not obey the gospel of our Lord Jesus. They will suffer the punishment of eternal destruction, away from the presence of the Lord and from the glory of his might, when he comes on that day to be glorified in his saints, and to be marveled at among all who have believed, because our testimony to you was believed. To this end we always pray for you, that our God may make you worthy of his calling and may fulfill every resolve for good and every work of faith by his power, so that the name of our Lord Jesus may be glorified in you, and you in him, according to the grace of our God and the Lord Jesus Christ.
2 Thessalonians 1:5-12

"I must keep alive in myself the desire for my true country, which I shall not find till after death; I must never let it get snowed under or turned aside; I must make it the main object of life to press on to that other country and to help others do the same."
C.S. Lewis

○ With confidence amidst _____.

Now faith is the assurance of things hoped for, the conviction of things not seen. For by it the people of old received their commendation.
Hebrews 11:1-2

These all died in faith, not having received the things promised, but having seen them and greeted them from afar, and having acknowledged that they were strangers and exiles on the earth. For people who speak thus make it clear that they are seeking a homeland. If they had been thinking of that land from which they had gone out, they would have had opportunity to return. But as it is, they desire a better country, that is, a heavenly one. Therefore God is not ashamed to be called their God, for he has prepared for them a city.
Hebrews 11:13-16

And what more shall I say? For time would fail me to tell of Gideon, Barak, Samson, Jephthah, of David and Samuel and the prophets—who through faith conquered kingdoms, enforced justice, obtained promises, stopped the mouths of lions, quenched the power of fire, escaped the edge of the sword, were made strong out of weakness, became mighty in war, put foreign armies to flight. Women received back their dead by resurrection. Some were tortured, refusing to accept release, so that they might rise again to a better life. Others suffered mocking and flogging, and even chains and imprisonment. They were stoned, they were sawn in two, they were killed with the sword. They went about in skins of sheep and goats, destitute, afflicted, mistreated—of whom the world was not worthy—wandering about in deserts and mountains, and in dens and caves of the earth. And all these, though commended through their faith, did not receive what was promised, since God had provided something better for us, that apart from us they should not be made perfect.
Hebrews 11:32-40

"The sands of time are sinking, the dawn of heaven breaks,
The summer morn I've sighed for, the fair sweet morn awakes;
Dark, dark hath been the midnight, but dayspring is at hand,
And glory, glory dwelleth in Emmanuel's land.

"The king there in his beauty without a veil is seen;
It were a well-spent journey though sev'n deaths lay between:
The Lamb with his fair army doth on Mount Zion stand,
And glory, glory dwelleth in Emmanuel's land.

"O Christ, he is the fountain, the deep sweet well of love!
The streams on earth I've tasted, more deep I'll drink above:
There to an ocean fullness his mercy doth expand,
And glory, glory dwelleth in Emmanuel's land.

"The bride eyes not her garment, but her dear bridegroom's face;
I will not gaze at glory, but on my King of grace;
Not at the crown he giveth, but on his pierced hand:
The lamb is all the glory of Emmanuel's land."

Anne R. Cousin

THREE CONTROVERSIAL QUESTIONS IN REVELATION

- It is _____ to disagree about these questions.
- It is _____ to divide over these questions.

"Everything in God's Word is important. Yet good Christians have different views on the millennium. A month ago, and during this whole series, I would have said, 'I'm an amillennialist.' But I've actually changed my mind as I studied this passage. So how much trust are you going to put in me tonight? Right? I'm not very stable on this issue. You know, that's a good thing to be reminded of, that our confidence is not in a preacher, but in God's Word. It's in the truth of God's Word. That's what matters; not my opinion towards something. I think we also learn from this to be charitable towards different views. Each person must be fully convinced in his own mind, at least if you can be. But we must distinguish between central issues of the faith and issues which aren't central. Some people have a hard time doing that. Everything for them is of equal importance in the Bible. But that's not true. There are some things that are non-negotiable in our faith. The Trinity is non-negotiable. The authority of Scripture is non-negotiable. The substitutionary atonement, justification by faith alone, the deity of Christ, and, of course, I could mention other things. But there are less clear matters in the Bible as well; things like when the rapture will take place and what we're looking at today regarding the millennium. We must beware of being divisive, and schismatic, and inflexible on matters that are less important. That really shows, I think, a character flaw in us—something that God wants to work on in us. At the same time, we need to be aware of being namby-pamby. That's another problem ... not to hold strong convictions. We want to speak the truth of the gospel in love. That's what's crucial. We need balance. I need balance that comes from the Holy Spirit. We all need that. We need the Holy Spirit to be our teacher."
Tom Schreiner

1. What does this book mean and why do we have it?

The revelation of Jesus Christ, which God gave him to show to his servants the things that must soon take place. He made it known by sending his angel to his servant John, who bore witness to the word of God and to the testimony of Jesus Christ, even to all that he saw. Blessed is the one who reads aloud the words of this prophecy, and blessed are those who hear, and who keep what is written in it, for the time is near. John to the seven churches that are in Asia: Grace to you and peace from him who is and who was and who is to come, and from the seven spirits who are before his throne, and from Jesus Christ the faithful witness, the firstborn of the dead, and the ruler of kings on earth. To him who loves us and has freed us from our sins by his blood and made us a kingdom, priests to his God and Father, to him be glory and dominion forever and ever. Amen. Behold, he is coming with the clouds, and every eye will see him, even those who pierced him, and all tribes of the earth will wail on account of him. Even so. Amen. "I am the Alpha and the Omega," says the Lord God, "who is and who was and who is to come, the Almighty."
Revelation 1:1-8

Four historic interpretations:

- o Preterist: They were fulfilled in the _____ few centuries of Christianity.
- o Historicist: They have been and are being fulfilled in the course of _____ Christian history.
- o Futurist: They are largely _____ (chapters 4-22 are still awaiting fulfillment in the future).
- o Idealist: They are fulfilled _____ throughout the history of the church.

- Three different genres:
  - o A series of apocalyptic _____ ...
    - Predominant use of symbols and numbers.
  - o Filled with _____ pronouncements ...
    - The kingdom of God has come and will soon be consummated.
  - o Written as a congregational _____.
    - From God in Christ through an angel to His servant for the church.
- Two significant contexts:
  - o Specific _____ context.
  - o Overall _____ context.
- One essential reminder:
  - o This book was not written to promote hopeless speculation about the future; this book was written to fuel hopeful _____ in the present.

Blessed is the one who reads aloud the words of this prophecy, and blessed are those who hear, and who keep what is written in it, for the time is near.
Revelation 1:3

"And behold, I am coming soon. Blessed is the one who keeps the words of the prophecy of this book."
Revelation 22:7

2. What is the millennium and when will it happen?

Then I saw an angel coming down from heaven, holding in his hand the key to the bottomless pit and a great chain. And he seized the dragon, that ancient serpent, who is the devil and Satan, and bound him for a thousand years, and threw him into the pit, and shut it and sealed it over him, so that he might not deceive the nations any longer, until the thousand years were ended. After that he must be released for a little while. Then I saw thrones, and seated on them were those to whom the authority to judge was committed. Also I saw the souls of those who had been beheaded for the testimony of Jesus and for the word of God, and those who had not worshiped the beast or its image and had not received its mark on their foreheads or their hands. They came to life and reigned with Christ for a thousand years. The rest of the dead did not come to life until the thousand years were ended. This is the first resurrection. Blessed and holy is the one who shares in the first resurrection! Over such the second death has no power, but they will be priests of God and of Christ, and they will reign with him for a thousand

years. And when the thousand years are ended, Satan will be released from his prison and will come out to deceive the nations that are at the four corners of the earth, Gog and Magog, to gather them for battle; their number is like the sand of the sea. And they marched up over the broad plain of the earth and surrounded the camp of the saints and the beloved city, but fire came down from heaven and consumed them, and the devil who had deceived them was thrown into the lake of fire and sulfur where the beast and the false prophet were, and they will be tormented day and night forever and ever.
Revelation 20:1-10

"The millennium is a thousand years of peace that Christians like to fight about."
Anonymous

Three Major Questions ...

- When?
  - Is the Book of Revelation arranged _____ or cyclically?

Then I saw heaven opened, and behold, a white horse! The one sitting on it is called Faithful and True, and in righteousness he judges and makes war. His eyes are like a flame of fire, and on his head are many diadems, and he has a name written that no one knows but himself. He is clothed in a robe dipped in blood, and the name by which he is called is The Word of God. And the armies of heaven, arrayed in fine linen, white and pure, were following him on white horses. From his mouth comes a sharp sword with which to strike down the nations, and he will rule them with a rod of iron. He will tread the winepress of the fury of the wrath of God the Almighty. On his robe and on his thigh he has a name written, King of kings and Lord of lords. Then I saw an angel standing in the sun, and with a loud voice he called to all the birds that fly directly overhead, "Come, gather for the great supper of God, to eat the flesh of kings, the flesh of captains, the flesh of mighty men, the flesh of horses and their riders, and the flesh of all men, both free and slave, both small and great." And I saw the beast and the kings of the earth with their armies gathered to make war against him who was sitting on the horse and against his army. And the beast was captured, and with it the false prophet who in its presence had done the signs by which he deceived those who had received the mark of the beast and those who worshiped its image. These two were thrown alive into the lake of fire that burns with sulfur. And the rest were slain by the sword that came from the mouth of him who was sitting on the horse, and all the birds were gorged with their flesh.
Revelation 19:11-21

And I saw, coming out of the mouth of the dragon and out of the mouth of the beast and out of the mouth of the false prophet, three unclean spirits like frogs. For they are demonic spirits, performing signs, who go abroad to the kings of the whole world, to assemble them for battle on the great day of God the Almighty.

("Behold, I am coming like a thief! Blessed is the one who stays awake, keeping his garments on, that he may not go about naked and be seen exposed!") And they assembled them at the place that in Hebrew is called Armageddon.
Revelation 16:13-16

And I saw the beast and the kings of the earth with their armies gathered to make war against him who was sitting on the horse and against his army.
Revelation 19:19

o Is the millennium before Christ returns or after Christ returns?
o Is the millennium present (happening now) or future (still to come)?
How long?
o Is the millennium _____ 1,000 years?
o Or is the millennium simply a planned, perfect, limited time?
What and where?
o Will the millennium involve a _____ resurrection of Christians to reign on earth during the millennium?
o Will the millennium involve a spiritual resurrection of Christians to reign in heaven during the millennium?

Three Major Views ...

Premillennialism: Jesus will return _____ the millennium.
o After a time of great tribulation, Jesus will return to establish a millennial kingdom on earth.

And the Spirit of the LORD shall rest upon him, the Spirit of wisdom and understanding, the Spirit of counsel and might, the Spirit of knowledge and the fear of the LORD. And his delight shall be in the fear of the LORD. He shall not judge by what his eyes see, or decide disputes by what his ears hear, but with righteousness he shall judge the poor, and decide with equity for the meek of the earth; and he shall strike the earth with the rod of his mouth, and with the breath of his lips he shall kill the wicked. Righteousness shall be the belt of his waist, and faithfulness the belt of his loins. The wolf shall dwell with the lamb, and the leopard shall lie down with the young goat, and the calf and the lion and the fattened calf together; and a little child shall lead them. The cow and the bear shall graze; their young shall lie down together; and the lion shall eat straw like the ox. The nursing child shall play over the hole of the cobra, and the weaned child shall put his hand on the adder's den. They shall not hurt or destroy in all my holy mountain; for the earth shall be full of the knowledge of the LORD as the waters cover the sea. In that day the root of Jesse, who shall stand as a signal for the peoples—of him shall the nations inquire, and his resting place shall be glorious. In that day the Lord will extend his hand yet a second time to recover the remnant that remains of his people, from Assyria, from Egypt, from Pathros, from Cush, from Elam, from Shinar, from Hamath, and from the coastlands of the sea.
Isaiah 11:2-11

No more shall there be in it an infant who lives but a few days, or an old man who does not fill out his days, for the young man shall die a hundred years old, and the sinner a hundred years old shall be accursed.
Isaiah 65:20

- Jesus will _____ on earth.

On that day there shall be no light, cold, or frost. And there shall be a unique day, which known to the LORD, neither day nor night, but at evening time there shall be light. On th day living waters shall flow out from Jerusalem, half of them to the eastern sea and half c them to the western sea. It shall continue in summer as in winter. And the LORD will b king over all the earth. On that day the LORD will be one and his name one. The whole land shall be turned into a plain from Geba to Rimmon south of Jerusalem. But Jerusale shall remain aloft on its site from the Gate of Benjamin to the place of the former gate, t the Corner Gate, and from the Tower of Hananel to the king's winepresses. And it shall l inhabited, for there shall never again be a decree of utter destruction. Jerusalem shall dwe in security. And this shall be the plague with which the LORD will strike all the peoples that wage war against Jerusalem: their flesh will rot while they are still standing on their feet, their eyes will rot in their sockets, and their tongues will rot in their mouths. And o that day a great panic from the LORD shall fall on them, so that each will seize the hand another, and the hand of the one will be raised against the hand of the other. Even Judah will fight at Jerusalem. And the wealth of all the surrounding nations shall be collected, gold, silver, and garments in great abundance. And a plague like this plague shall fall or the horses, the mules, the camels, the donkeys, and whatever beasts may be in those camp

Then everyone who survives of all the nations that have come against Jerusalem shall go up year after year to worship the King, the LORD of hosts, and to keep the Feast of Booth And if any of the families of the earth do not go up to Jerusalem to worship the King, th LORD of hosts, there will be no rain on them. And if the family of Egypt does not go up and present themselves, then on them there shall be no rain; there shall be the plague wit which the LORD afflicts the nations that do not go up to keep the Feast of Booths. This shall be the punishment to Egypt and the punishment to all the nations that do not go up to keep the Feast of Booths. And on that day there shall be inscribed on the bells of the horses, "Holy to the LORD." And the pots in the house of the LORD shall be as the bowls before the altar. And every pot in Jerusalem and Judah shall be holy to the LORD of hosts so that all who sacrifice may come and take of them and boil the meat of the sacrifice in them. And there shall no longer be a trader in the house of the LORD of hosts on that day
Zechariah 14:6-21

But each in his own order: Christ the firstfruits, then at his coming those who belong to Christ. Then comes the end, when he delivers the kingdom to God the Father after destroying every rule and every authority and power. For he must reign until he has put all his enemies under his feet.
1 Corinthians 15:23-25

*From his mouth comes a sharp sword with which to strike down the
nations, and he will rule them with a rod of iron. He will tread the
winepress of the fury of the wrath of God the Almighty.*
Revelation 19:15

- Satan will be _____ in hell.

*Then I saw an angel coming down from heaven, holding in his hand the key to the
bottomless pit and a great chain. And he seized the dragon, that ancient serpent, who is
the devil and Satan, and bound him for a thousand years, and threw him into the pit,
and shut it and sealed it over him, so that he might not deceive the nations any longer,
until the thousand years were ended. After that he must be released for a little while.*
Revelation 20:1-3

*In their case the god of this world has blinded the minds of the unbelievers, to keep them
from seeing the light of the gospel of the glory of Christ, who is the image of God.*
2 Corinthians 4:4

*For we do not wrestle against flesh and blood, but against the rulers,
against the authorities, against the cosmic powers over this present
darkness, against the spiritual forces of evil in the heavenly places.*
Ephesians 6:12

We know that we are from God, and the whole world lies in the power of the evil one.
1 John 5:19

- Christians will _____ with Christ.

*"And he said to him, 'Well done, good servant! Because you have been faithful in a very
little, you shall have authority over ten cities.' And the second came, saying, 'Lord, your
mina has made five minas.' And he said to him, 'And you are to be over five cities.'"*
Luke 19:17-19

*Do you not know that we are to judge angels? How much
more, then, matters pertaining to this life!*
1 Corinthians 6:3

*"The one who conquers and who keeps my works until the end, to him I will give
authority over the nations, and he will rule them with a rod of iron, as when earthen
pots are broken in pieces, even as I myself have received authority from my Father."*
Revelation 2:26-27

○ At the end of the millennium (a literal or figurative 1,000 years), Satan will
be _____.

And when the thousand years are ended, Satan will be released from his prison and will come out to deceive the nations that are at the four corners of the earth, Gog and Magog, to gather them for battle; their number is like the sand of the sea. And they marched up over the broad plain of the earth and surrounded the camp of the saints and the beloved city, but fire came down from heaven and consumed them, and the devil who had deceived them was thrown into the lake of fire and sulfur where the beast and the false prophet were, and they will be tormented day and night forever and ever.
Revelation 20:7-10

- Rebels will battle against Christ.
- Rebels will be defeated by Christ.
- All unbelievers who have died will be resurrected to judgment.

Then I saw a great white throne and him who was seated on it. From his presence earth and sky fled away, and no place was found for them. And I saw the dead, great and small, standing before the throne, and books were opened. Then another book was opened, which is the book of life. And the dead were judged by what was written in the books, according to what they had done. And the sea gave up the dead who were in it, Death and Hades gave up the dead who were in them, and they were judged, each one of them, according to what they had done. Then Death and Hades were thrown into the lake of fire. This is the second death, the lake of fire. And if anyone's name was not found written in the book of life, he was thrown into the lake of fire.
Revelation 20:11-15

o The eternal state will _____.

Then I saw a new heaven and a new earth, for the first heaven and the first earth had passed away, and the sea was no more.
Revelation 21:1

- Postmillennialism: Jesus will return _____ the millennium.
  o During the millennium (a literal or figurative 1,000 years), the gospel will spread throughout the world and many will become Christians, thus ushering in an age of peace and righteousness on earth.

Give the king your justice, O God, and your righteousness to the royal son! May he judge your people with righteousness, and your poor with justice! Let the mountains bear prosperity for the people, and the hills, in righteousness! May he defend the cause of the poor of the people, give deliverance to the children of the needy, and crush the oppressor!
Psalm 72:1-4

"Turn to me and be saved, all the ends of the earth! For I am God, and there is no other. By myself I have sworn; from my mouth has gone out in righteousness a word that shall not return: 'To me every knee shall bow, every tongue shall swear allegiance.'

*Only in the LORD, it shall be said of me, are righteousness and strength;
to him shall come and be ashamed all who were incensed against him. In
the LORD all the offspring of Israel shall be justified and shall glory."*
Isaiah 45:22-25

*"And in that day I will answer, declares the LORD, I will answer the heavens,
and they shall answer the earth, and the earth shall answer the grain, the
wine, and the oil, and they shall answer Jezreel, and I will sow her for myself
in the land. And I will have mercy on No Mercy, and I will say to Not My
People, 'You are my people'; and he shall say, 'You are my God.'"*
Hosea 2:21-23

*He put another parable before them, saying, "The kingdom of heaven is like a
grain of mustard seed that a man took and sowed in his field. It is the smallest
of all seeds, but when it has grown it is larger than all the garden plants and
becomes a tree, so that the birds of the air come and make nests in its branches."
He told them another parable. "The kingdom of heaven is like leaven that a
woman took and hid in three measures of flour, till it was all leavened."*
Matthew 13:31-33

*And this gospel of the kingdom will be proclaimed throughout the whole
world as a testimony to all nations, and then the end will come.*
Matthew 24:14

*And Jesus came and said to them, "All authority in heaven and on earth has been given
to me. Go therefore and make disciples of all nations, baptizing them in the name of
the Father and of the Son and of the Holy Spirit, teaching them to observe all that I
have commanded you. And behold, I am with you always, to the end of the age."*
Matthew 28:18-20

- At the end of the millennium, Jesus will return.
  - He will quell final rebellion.
  - He will enact final resurrection.
- The eternal state will begin.
- Amillennialism: The millennium is the present _____ age, and there is
no other future millennium to come (before or after Jesus' return).
  - As a result of the death and resurrection of Christ, Satan is _____
    in the present church age.

*"But if it is by the Spirit of God that I cast out demons, then the kingdom of God
has come upon you. Or how can someone enter a strong man's house and plunder his
goods, unless he first binds the strong man? Then indeed he may plunder his house."*
Matthew 12:28-29

And you, who were dead in your trespasses and the uncircumcision of your flesh, God made alive together with him, having forgiven us all our trespasses, by canceling the record of debt that stood against us with its legal demands. This he set aside, nailing it to the cross. He disarmed the rulers and authorities and put them to open shame, by triumphing over them in him.
Colossians 2:13-15

Since therefore the children share in flesh and blood, he himself likewise partook of the same things, that through death he might destroy the one who has the power of death, that is, the devil, and deliver all those who through fear of death were subject to lifelong slavery.
Hebrews 2:14-15

- The gospel is going forward to the nations.

And Jesus came and said to them, "All authority in heaven and on earth has been given to me. Go therefore and make disciples of all nations, baptizing them in the name of the Father and of the Son and of the Holy Spirit, teaching them to observe all that I have commanded you. And behold, I am with you always, to the end of the age."
Matthew 28:18-20

Then he opened their minds to understand the Scriptures, and said to them, "Thus it is written, that the Christ should suffer and on the third day rise from the dead, and that repentance and forgiveness of sins should be proclaimed in his name to all nations, beginning from Jerusalem. You are witnesses of these things. And behold, I am sending the promise of my Father upon you. But stay in the city until you are clothed with power from on high."
Luke 24:45-49

"But you will receive power when the Holy Spirit has come upon you, and you will be my witnesses in Jerusalem and in all Judea and Samaria, and to the end of the earth."
Acts 1:8

For I tell you that Christ became a servant to the circumcised to show God's truthfulness, order to confirm the promises given to the patriarchs, and in order that the Gentiles might glorify God for his mercy. As it is written, "Therefore I will praise you among the Gentiles and sing to your name." And again it is said, "Rejoice, O Gentiles, with his people." And again, "Praise the Lord, all you Gentiles, and let all the peoples extol him." And again Isaiah says, "The root of Jesse will come, even he who arises to rule the Gentiles; in him will the Gentiles hope." May the God of hope fill you with all joy and peace in believing so that by the power of the Holy Spirit you may abound in hope. I myself am satisfied about you, my brothers, that you yourselves are full of goodness, filled with all knowledge and able to instruct one another. But on some points I have written to you very boldly by way of reminder, because of the grace given me by God to be a minister of Christ Jesus to the Gentiles in the priestly service of the gospel of God, so that the offering of the Gentiles may be acceptable, sanctified by the Holy Spirit. In Christ Jesus, then, I have reason to

be proud of my work for God. For I will not venture to speak of anything except what Christ has accomplished through me to bring the Gentiles to obedience—by word and deed, by the power of signs and wonders, by the power of the Spirit of God—so that from Jerusalem and all the way around to Illyricum I have fulfilled the ministry of the gospel of Christ; and thus I make it my ambition to preach the gospel, not where Christ has already been named, lest I build on someone else's foundation, but as it is written, "Those who have never been told of him will see, and those who have never heard will understand."
Romans 15:8-21

After this I looked, and behold, a great multitude that no one could number, from every nation, from all tribes and peoples and languages, standing before the throne and before the Lamb, clothed in white robes, with palm branches in their hands, and crying out with a loud voice, "Salvation belongs to our God who sits on the throne, and to the Lamb!"
Revelation 7:9-10

- The church is experiencing persecution by the nations.

"Then they will deliver you up to tribulation and put you to death, and you will be hated by all nations for my name's sake. And then many will fall away and betray one another and hate one another. And many false prophets will arise and lead many astray. And because lawlessness will be increased, the love of many will grow cold. But the one who endures to the end will be saved. And this gospel of the kingdom will be proclaimed throughout the whole world as a testimony to all nations, and then the end will come."
Matthew 24:9-14

Then they left the presence of the council, rejoicing that they were counted worthy to suffer dishonor for the name. And every day, in the temple and from house to house, they did not cease teaching and preaching that the Christ is Jesus.
Acts 5:41-42

Indeed, all who desire to live a godly life in Christ Jesus will be persecuted ...
2 Timothy 3:12

"'I know your tribulation and your poverty (but you are rich) and the slander of those who say that they are Jews and are not, but are a synagogue of Satan. Do not fear what you are about to suffer. Behold, the devil is about to throw some of you into prison, that you may be tested, and for ten days you will have tribulation. Be faithful unto death, and I will give you the crown of life.'"
Revelation 2:9-10

They cried out with a loud voice, "O Sovereign Lord, holy and true, how long before you will judge and avenge our blood on those who dwell on the earth?" Then they were each given a white robe and told to rest a little longer, until the number of their fellow servants and their brothers should be complete, who were to be killed as they themselves had been.
Revelation 6:10-11

○ During the church age, Christians _____ with Christ.

But God, being rich in mercy, because of the great love with which he loved us, even when we were dead in our trespasses, made us alive together with Christ—by grace you have been saved—and raised us up with him and seated us with him in the heavenly places in Christ Jesus, so that in the coming ages he might show the immeasurable riches of his grace in kindness toward us in Christ Jesus.
Ephesians 2:4-7

- While they are alive on earth.

Who shall separate us from the love of Christ? Shall tribulation, or distress, or persecution or famine, or nakedness, or danger, or sword? As it is written, "For your sake we are being killed all the day long; we are regarded as sheep to be slaughtered." No, in all these things we are more than conquerors through him who loved us. For I am sure that neither death nor life, nor angels nor rulers, nor things present nor things to come, nor powers ...
Romans 8:35-38

- When they die and go to the intermediate heaven.

Then I saw thrones, and seated on them were those to whom the authority to judge was committed. Also I saw the souls of those who had been beheaded for the testimony of Jesus and for the word of God, and those who had not worshiped the beast or its image and had not received its mark on their foreheads or their hands. They came to life and reigned with Christ for a thousand years. The rest of the dead did not come to life until the thousand years were ended. This is the first resurrection. Blessed and holy is the one who shares in the first resurrection! Over such the second death has no power, but they will be priests of God and of Christ, and they will reign with him for a thousand years.
Revelation 20:4-6

○ At the end of the church age, Jesus will _____ to usher in the eternal state.

"At that time shall arise Michael, the great prince who has charge of your people. And there shall be a time of trouble, such as never has been since there was a nation till that time. But at that time your people shall be delivered, everyone whose name shall be found written in the book. And many of those who sleep in the dust of the earth shall awake, some to everlasting life, and some to shame and everlasting contempt."
Daniel 12:1-2

"Do not marvel at this, for an hour is coming when all who are in the tombs will hear his voice and come out, those who have done good to the resurrection of life, and those who have done evil to the resurrection of judgment."
John 5:28-29

"But this I confess to you, that according to the Way, which they call a sect, I worship the God of our fathers, believing everything laid down by the Law and written in the Prophets, having a hope in God, which these men themselves accept, that there will be a resurrection of both the just and the unjust."
Acts 24:14-15

For the Lord himself will descend from heaven with a cry of command, with the voice of an archangel, and with the sound of the trumpet of God. And the dead in Christ will rise first. Then we who are alive, who are left, will be caught up together with them in the clouds to meet the Lord in the air, and so we will always be with the Lord. Therefore encourage one another with these words.
1 Thessalonians 4:16-18

3. What is the tribulation and who will experience it?

"For then there will be great tribulation, such as has not been from the beginning of the world until now, no, and never will be. And if those days had not been cut short, no human being would be saved. But for the sake of the elect those days will be cut short. Then if anyone says to you, 'Look, here is the Christ!' or 'There he is!' do not believe it. For false christs and false prophets will arise and perform great signs and wonders, so as to lead astray, if possible, even the elect. See, I have told you beforehand. So, if they say to you, 'Look, he is in the wilderness,' do not go out. If they say, 'Look, he is in the inner rooms,' do not believe it. For as the lightning comes from the east and shines as far as the west, so will be the coming of the Son of Man. Wherever the corpse is, there the vultures will gather. Immediately after the tribulation of those days the sun will be darkened, and the moon will not give its light, and the stars will fall from heaven, and the powers of the heavens will be shaken. Then will appear in heaven the sign of the Son of Man, and then all the tribes of the earth will mourn, and they will see the Son of Man coming on the clouds of heaven with power and great glory. And he will send out his angels with a loud trumpet call, and they will gather his elect from the four winds, from one end of heaven to the other."
Matthew 24:21-31

Then one of the elders addressed me, saying, "Who are these, clothed in white robes, and from where have they come?" I said to him, "Sir, you know." And he said to me, "These are the ones coming out of the great tribulation. They have washed their robes and made them white in the blood of the Lamb.
Revelation 7:13-14

The tribulation is an _____ time of trial and trouble on the earth that will precede the millennial reign of Christ.

"Then they will deliver you up to tribulation and put you to death, and you will be hated by all nations for my name's sake. And then many will fall away and betray one another and hate one another. And many false prophets will

arise and lead many astray. And because lawlessness will be increased, the love of many will grow cold. But the one who endures to the end will be saved."
Matthew 24:9-13

○ Particularly horrifying time.

> *"For in those days there will be such tribulation as has not been from the beginning of the creation that God created until now, and never will be."*
> *Mark 13:19*

○ Potentially _____ years.

"He shall speak words against the Most High, and shall wear out the saints of the Most High, and shall think to change the times and the law; and they shall be given into his hand for a time, times, and half a time. But the court shall sit in judgment, and his dominion shall be taken away, to be consumed and destroyed to the end."
Daniel 7:25-26

"Seventy weeks are decreed about your people and your holy city, to finish the transgression, to put an end to sin, and to atone for iniquity, to bring in everlasting righteousness, to seal both vision and prophet, and to anoint a most holy place. Know therefore and understand that from the going out of the word to restore and build Jerusalem to the coming of an anointed one, a prince, there shall be seven weeks. Then for sixty-two weeks it shall be built again with squares and moat, but in a troubled time. And after the sixty-two weeks, an anointed one shall be cut off and shall have nothing. And the people of the prince who is to come shall destroy the city and the sanctuary. Its end shall come with a flood, and to the end there shall be war. Desolations are decreed. And he shall make a strong covenant with many for one week, and for half of the week he shall put an end to sacrifice and offering. And on the wing of abominations shall come one who makes desolate, until the decreed end is poured out on the desolator."
Daniel 9:24-27

And I heard the man clothed in linen, who was above the waters of the stream; he raised his right hand and his left hand toward heaven and swore by him who lives forever that it would be for a time, times, and half a time, and that when the shattering of the power of the holy people comes to an end all these things would be finished.
Daniel 12:7

Then I was given a measuring rod like a staff, and I was told, "Rise and measure the temple of God and the altar and those who worship there, but do not measure the court outside the temple; leave that out, for it is given over to the nations, and they will trample the holy city for forty-two months. And I will grant authority to my two witnesses, and they will prophesy for 1,260 days, clothed in sackcloth." These are the two olive trees and the two lampstands that stand before the Lord of the earth. And if anyone would harm them, fire pours from their mouth and consumes their foes.

If anyone would harm them, this is how he is doomed to be killed. They have the power to shut the sky, that no rain may fall during the days of their prophesying, and they have power over the waters to turn them into blood and to strike the earth with every kind of plague, as often as they desire. And when they have finished their testimony, the beast that rises from the bottomless pit will make war on them and conquer them and kill them, and their dead bodies will lie in the street of the great city that symbolically is called Sodom and Egypt, where their Lord was crucified. For three and a half days some from the peoples and tribes and languages and nations will gaze at their dead bodies and refuse to let them be placed in a tomb, and those who dwell on the earth will rejoice over them and make merry and exchange presents, because these two prophets had been a torment to those who dwell on the earth.
Revelation 11:1-10

She gave birth to a male child, one who is to rule all the nations with a rod of iron, but her child was caught up to God and to his throne, and the woman fled into the wilderness, where she has a place prepared by God, in which she is to be nourished for 1,260 days.
Revelation 12:5-6

But the woman was given the two wings of the great eagle so that she might fly from the serpent into the wilderness, to the place where she is to be nourished for a time, and times, and half a time.
Revelation 12:14

And the beast was given a mouth uttering haughty and blasphemous words, and it was allowed to exercise authority for forty-two months. It opened its mouth to utter blasphemies against God, blaspheming his name and his dwelling, that is, those who dwell in heaven. Also it was allowed to make war on the saints and to conquer them. And authority was given it over every tribe and people and language and nation ...
Revelation 13:5-7

Post-tribulational premillennialism ...
- The church will _____ the tribulation.

"I have said these things to you, that in me you may have peace. In the world you will have tribulation. But take heart; I have overcome the world."
John 16:33

... and if children, then heirs—heirs of God and fellow heirs with Christ, provided we suffer with him in order that we may also be glorified with him.
Romans 8:17

For it was fitting that he, for whom and by whom all things exist, in bringing many sons to glory, should make the founder of their salvation perfect through suffering.
Hebrews 2:10

For to this you have been called, because Christ also suffered for you,
leaving you an example, so that you might follow in his steps.
1 Peter 2:21

If you are insulted for the name of Christ, you are blessed,
because the Spirit of glory and of God rests upon you.
1 Peter 4:14

■ Believers will experience the wrath of Satan.

"Do not fear what you are about to suffer. Behold, the devil is about to throw
some of you into prison, that you may be tested, and for ten days you will have
tribulation. Be faithful unto death, and I will give you the crown of life."
Revelation 2:10

Then one of the elders addressed me, saying, "Who are these, clothed in white
robes, and from where have they come?" I said to him, "Sir, you know." And
he said to me, "These are the ones coming out of the great tribulation. They
have washed their robes and made them white in the blood of the Lamb."
Revelation 7:13-14

○ Christ will return _____ the tribulation to inaugurate
the millennium.

"Immediately after the tribulation of those days the sun will be darkened, and
the moon will not give its light, and the stars will fall from heaven, and the
powers of the heavens will be shaken. Then will appear in heaven the sign
of the Son of Man, and then all the tribes of the earth will mourn, and they
will see the Son of Man coming on the clouds of heaven with power and great
glory. And he will send out his angels with a loud trumpet call, and they will
gather his elect from the four winds, from one end of heaven to the other."
Matthew 24:29-31

For the Lord himself will descend from heaven with a cry of
command, with the voice of an archangel, and with the sound of
the trumpet of God. And the dead in Christ will rise first.
1 Thessalonians 4:16

Behold! I tell you a mystery. We shall not all sleep, but we shall all be changed,
in a moment, in the twinkling of an eye, at the last trumpet. For the trumpet will
sound, and the dead will be raised imperishable, and we shall be changed.
1 Corinthians 15:51-52

Then I saw heaven opened, and behold, a white horse! The one sitting on it is called Faithful and True, and in righteousness he judges and makes war.
Revelation 19:11

- Believers will not experience the wrath of God.

Since, therefore, we have now been justified by his blood, much more shall we be saved by him from the wrath of God.
Romans 5:9

This is evidence of the righteous judgment of God, that you may be considered worthy of the kingdom of God, for which you are also suffering—since indeed God considers it just to repay with affliction those who afflict you, and to grant relief to you who are afflicted as well as to us, when the Lord Jesus is revealed from heaven with his mighty angels in flaming fire, inflicting vengeance on those who do not know God and on those who do not obey the gospel of our Lord Jesus. They will suffer the punishment of eternal destruction, away from the presence of the Lord and from the glory of his might, when he comes on that day to be glorified in his saints, and to be marveled at among all who have believed, because our testimony to you was believed.
2 Thessalonians 1:5-10

Pre-tribulational premillennialism …
  ○ The church will be _____ before the tribulation.

For this we declare to you by a word from the Lord, that we who are alive, who are left until the coming of the Lord, will not precede those who have fallen asleep. For the Lord himself will descend from heaven with a cry of command, with the voice of an archangel, and with the sound of the trumpet of God. And the dead in Christ will rise first. Then we who are alive, who are left, will be caught up together with them in the clouds to meet the Lord in the air, and so we will always be with the Lord. Therefore encourage one another with these words.
1 Thessalonians 4:15-18

"Because you have kept my word about patient endurance, I will keep you from the hour of trial that is coming on the whole world, to try those who dwell on the earth."
Revelation 3:10

  ○ Various _____ (including those pertaining to Israel) will be fulfilled during the tribulation.

Now concerning the times and the seasons, brothers, you have no need to have anything written to you. For you yourselves are fully aware that the day of the Lord will come like a thief in the night.
1 Thessalonians 5:1-2

Lest you be wise in your own sight, I do not want you to be unaware of this mystery, brothers: a partial hardening has come upon Israel, until the fullness of the Gentiles has come in. And in this way all Israel will be saved, as it is written, "The Deliverer will come from Zion, he will banish ungodliness from Jacob"; "and this will be my covenant with them when I take away their sins." As regards the gospel, they are enemies for your sake. But as regards election, they are beloved for the sake of their forefathers. For the gifts and the calling of God are irrevocable. For just as you were at one time disobedient to God but now have received mercy because of their disobedience, so they too have now been disobedient in order that by the mercy shown to you they also may now receive mercy. For God has consigned all to disobedience, that he may have mercy on all.
Romans 11:25-32

○ Christ will return again _____ the tribulation to inaugurate the millennium.

On that day his feet shall stand on the Mount of Olives that lies before Jerusalem on the east, and the Mount of Olives shall be split in two from east to west by a very wide valley, so that one half of the Mount shall move northward, and the other half southward. And you shall flee to the valley of my mountains, for the valley of the mountains shall reach to Azal. And you shall flee as you fled from the earthquake in the days of Uzziah king of Judah. Then the LORD my God will come, and all the holy ones with him.
Zechariah 14:4-5

SEVEN CRITICAL CONCLUSIONS FROM REVELATION

1. God is _____.

*"I am the Alpha and the Omega," says the Lord God, "who is
and who was and who is to come, the Almighty."*
Revelation 1:8

*Now I watched when the Lamb opened one of the seven seals, and I heard one of the
four living creatures say with a voice like thunder, "Come!" And I looked, and behold, a
white horse! And its rider had a bow, and a crown was given to him, and he came out
conquering, and to conquer. When he opened the second seal, I heard the second living
creature say, "Come!" And out came another horse, bright red. Its rider was permitted
to take peace from the earth, so that people should slay one another, and he was given a
great sword. When he opened the third seal, I heard the third living creature say, "Come!"
And I looked, and behold, a black horse! And its rider had a pair of scales in his hand.
And I heard what seemed to be a voice in the midst of the four living creatures, saying,
"A quart of wheat for a denarius, and three quarts of barley for a denarius, and do not
harm the oil and wine!" When he opened the fourth seal, I heard the voice of the fourth
living creature say, "Come!" And I looked, and behold, a pale horse! And its rider's name
was Death, and Hades followed him. And they were given authority over a fourth of
the earth, to kill with sword and with famine and with pestilence and by wild beasts of
the earth. When he opened the fifth seal, I saw under the altar the souls of those who
had been slain for the word of God and for the witness they had borne. They cried out
with a loud voice, "O Sovereign Lord, holy and true, how long before you will judge
and avenge our blood on those who dwell on the earth?" Then they were each given a
white robe and told to rest a little longer, until the number of their fellow servants and
their brothers should be complete, who were to be killed as they themselves had been.*
Revelation 6:1-11

*Then I saw another angel ascending from the rising of the sun, with
the seal of the living God, and he called with a loud voice to the four
angels who had been given power to harm earth and sea ...*
Revelation 7:2

*When the Lamb opened the seventh seal, there was silence in heaven for
about half an hour. Then I saw the seven angels who stand before God, and
seven trumpets were given to them. And another angel came and stood at
the altar with a golden censer, and he was given much incense to offer with
the prayers of all the saints on the golden altar before the throne ...*
Revelation 8:1-3

And the fifth angel blew his trumpet, and I saw a star fallen from heaven to earth, and he was given the key to the shaft of the bottomless pit. He opened the shaft of the bottomless pit, and from the shaft rose smoke like the smoke of a great furnace, and the sun and the air were darkened with the smoke from the shaft. Then from the smoke came locusts on the earth, and they were given power like the power of scorpions of the earth. They were told not to harm the grass of the earth or any green plant or any tree, but only those people who do not have the seal of God on their foreheads. They were allowed to torment them for five months, but not to kill them, and their torment was like the torment of a scorpion when it stings someone.
Revelation 9:1-5

And the beast was given a mouth uttering haughty and blasphemous words, and it was allowed to exercise authority for forty-two months. It opened its mouth to utter blasphemies against God, blaspheming his name and his dwelling, that is, those who dwell in heaven. Also it was allowed to make war on the saints and to conquer them. And authority was given it over every tribe and people and language and nation,
Revelation 13:5-7

It performs great signs, even making fire come down from heaven to earth in front of people, and by the signs that it is allowed to work in the presence of the beast it deceives those who dwell on earth, telling them to make an image for the beast that was wounded by the sword and yet lived. And it was allowed to give breath to the image of the beast, so that the image of the beast might even speak and might cause those who would not worship the image of the beast to be slain.
Revelation 13:13-15

… for God has put it into their hearts to carry out his purpose by being of one mind and handing over their royal power to the beast, until the words of God are fulfilled.
Revelation 17:17

2. Satan is _____.

- He is limited.
- He is doomed.

"Therefore, rejoice, O heavens and you who dwell in them! But woe to you, O earth and sea, for the devil has come down to you in great wrath, because he knows that his time is short!"
Revelation 12:12

3. _____ _____ _____.

- His gospel will advance through the church.

After this I looked, and behold, a great multitude that no one could number, from every nation, from all tribes and peoples and languages, standing before the throne and before the Lamb, clothed in white robes, with palm branches in their hands, and crying out with a loud voice, "Salvation belongs to our God who sits on the throne, and to the Lamb!"
Revelation 7:9-10

His Son will return for the church.

"I am the Alpha and the Omega," says the Lord God, "who is and who was and who is to come, the Almighty."
Revelation 1:8

Then the seventh angel blew his trumpet, and there were loud voices in heaven, saying, "The kingdom of the world has become the kingdom of our Lord and of his Christ, and he shall reign forever and ever." And the twenty-four elders who sit on their thrones before God fell on their faces and worshiped God, saying, "We give thanks to you, Lord God Almighty, who is and who was, for you have taken your great power and begun to reign."
Revelation 11:15-17

His greatness will be exalted across the earth.

And I heard every creature in heaven and on earth and under the earth and in the sea, and all that is in them, saying, "To him who sits on the throne and to the Lamb be blessing and honor and glory and might forever and ever!" And the four living creatures said, "Amen!" and the elders fell down and worshiped.
Revelation 5:13-14

4. We must see the world in all its _____.

Then one of the seven angels who had the seven bowls came and said to me, "Come, I will show you the judgment of the great prostitute who is seated on many waters, with whom the kings of the earth have committed sexual immorality, and with the wine of whose sexual immorality the dwellers on earth have become drunk." And he carried me away in the Spirit into a wilderness, and I saw a woman sitting on a scarlet beast that was full of blasphemous names, and it had seven heads and ten horns. The woman was arrayed in purple and scarlet, and adorned with gold and jewels and pearls, holding in her hand a golden cup full of abominations and the impurities of her sexual immorality. And on her forehead was written a name of mystery: "Babylon the great, mother of prostitutes and of earth's abominations." And I saw the woman, drunk with the blood of the saints, the blood of the martyrs of Jesus. When I saw her, I marveled greatly. But the angel said to me, "Why do you marvel? I will tell you the mystery of the woman, and of the beast with seven heads and ten horns that carries her. The beast that you saw was, and is not, and is about to rise from the bottomless pit and go to destruction.

And the dwellers on earth whose names have not been written in the book of life from the foundation of the world will marvel to see the beast, because it was and is not and is to come. This calls for a mind with wisdom: the seven heads are seven mountains on which the woman is seated; they are also seven kings, five of whom have fallen, one is, the other has not yet come, and when he does come he must remain only a little while. As for the beast that was and is not, it is an eighth but it belongs to the seven, and it goes to destruction. And the ten horns that you saw are ten kings who have not yet received royal power, but they are to receive authority as kings for one hour, together with the beast. These are of one mind, and they hand over their power and authority to the beast.
Revelation 17:1-13

It exercises all the authority of the first beast in its presence, and makes the earth and its inhabitants worship the first beast, whose mortal wound was healed. It performs great signs, even making fire come down from heaven to earth in front of people, and by the signs that it is allowed to work in the presence of the beast it deceives those who dwell on earth, telling them to make an image for the beast that was wounded by the sword and yet lived. And it was allowed to give breath to the image of the beast, so that the image of the beast might even speak and might cause those who would not worship the image of the beast to be slain. Also it causes all, both small and great, both rich and poor, both free and slave, to be marked on the right hand or the forehead, so that no one can buy or sell unless he has the mark, that is, the name of the beast or the number of its name. This calls for wisdom: let the one who has understanding calculate the number of the beast, for it is the number of a man, and his number is 666.
Revelation 13:12-18

- The beast: Do not put your hope in government.
- The false prophet: Do not put your hope in religion.
- The prostitute: Do not put your hope in material affluence and social acceptance.
- This world is full of deceptive _____.

> *"Today, the greatest challenge facing American evangelicals is not persecution from the world, but seduction by the world."*
> C.J. Mahaney

> *"I believe that one reason why the church of God at this present moment has so little influence over the world is because the world has so much influence over the church. Put your finger on any prosperous page in the Church's history, and [you] will find a little marginal note: 'In this age [people] could readily see where the Church began and where the world ended.'*
> Charles Spurgeon

- ○ Sensual pleasures.
- ○ Material possessions.
- ○ The promise of satisfaction.
- ○ The hope of security.
- ○ The insatiable lust for power.
- ○ The subtle lure of pride.

- This world is headed to a definite _____.

And they threw dust on their heads as they wept and mourned, crying out, "Alas, alas, for the great city where all who had ships at sea grew rich by her wealth! For in a single hour she has been laid waste. Rejoice over her, O heaven, and you saints and apostles and prophets, for God has given judgment for you against her!" Then a mighty angel took up a stone like a great millstone and threw it into the sea, saying, "So will Babylon the great city be thrown down with violence, and will be found no more; and the sound of harpists and musicians, of flute players and trumpeters, will be heard in you no more, and a craftsman of any craft will be found in you no more, and the sound of the mill will be heard in you no more, and the light of a lamp will shine in you no more, and the voice of bridegroom and bride will be heard in you no more, for your merchants were the great ones of the earth, and all nations were deceived by your sorcery. And in her was found the blood of prophets and of saints, and of all who have been slain on earth."
Revelation 18:19-24

- ○ This world will pass away completely.
- ○ This world will pass away suddenly.
- ○ This world will pass away eternally.

When he opened the sixth seal, I looked, and behold, there was a great earthquake, and the sun became black as sackcloth, the full moon became like blood, and the stars of the sky fell to the earth as the fig tree sheds its winter fruit when shaken by a gale. The sky vanished like a scroll that is being rolled up, and every mountain and island was removed from its place. Then the kings of the earth and the great ones and the generals and the rich and the powerful, and everyone, slave and free, hid themselves in the caves and among the rocks of the mountains, calling to the mountains and rocks, "Fall on us and hide us from the face of him who is seated on the throne, and from the wrath of the Lamb, for the great day of their wrath has come, and who can stand?"
Revelation 6:12-17

"Try to visualize what John saw, taking the picture as a whole: heaven itself curling up like a piece of paper, rolling up like a scroll; the sun, it's light blotted out so that it resembles a black sack used in mourning; the big, full moon, a huge, awe-inspiring bloody ball; the stars, turned out of their orbits and plunging to the earth in great showers; the earth itself quaking violently so that every house crashes to the ground; and every mountain and island suddenly disappearing. What a picture of dread and despair, of confusion and consternation—for the wicked!"
William Hendriksen

- Clearly, love for the world and love for God _____ coexist.

> Then I heard another voice from heaven saying, "Come out of her, my people,
> lest you take part in her sins, lest you share in her plagues; for her sins are
> heaped high as heaven, and God has remembered her iniquities."
> *Revelation 18:4-5*

○ Love for the world pushes out love for God.
○ Love for God pushes out love for the world.

> "We are half-hearted creatures, fooling about with drink and sex and
> ambition when infinite joy is offered to us, like an ignorant child who goes
> on making mud pies in the slum because he cannot imagine what is meant
> by the offer of a holiday at the sea. We are far too easily pleased."
> *C.S. Lewis*

5. We must see the Christ in all His _____.

> The revelation of Jesus Christ, which God gave him to show to his servants the things
> that must soon take place. He made it known by sending his angel to his servant John,
> who bore witness to the word of God and to the testimony of Jesus Christ, even to all
> that he saw. Blessed is the one who reads aloud the words of this prophecy, and blessed
> are those who hear, and who keep what is written in it, for the time is near. John to
> the seven churches that are in Asia: Grace to you and peace from him who is and who
> was and who is to come, and from the seven spirits who are before his throne, and from
> Jesus Christ the faithful witness, the firstborn of the dead, and the ruler of kings on
> earth. To him who loves us and has freed us from our sins by his blood and made us a
> kingdom, priests to his God and Father, to him be glory and dominion forever and ever.
> Amen. Behold, he is coming with the clouds, and every eye will see him, even those who
> pierced him, and all tribes of the earth will wail on account of him. Even so. Amen.
> *Revelation 1:1-7*

> "We need to see Jesus—to meet his blazing eyes of heart-searching holiness, to
> wake up at the trumpet blast of his voice, to respond to his jealous demand for
> exclusive and passionate loyalty. Shocked insensible by the impact of his splendor,
> we need then to hear his words of compassionate comfort, quelling our fears and
> quaking our hopes. Every congregation, whatever its struggle at its post on the
> battlefront, needs to fix its eyes on Jesus, the pioneer and perfecter of faith."
> *Dennis Johnson*

• He is fully human and fully _____.

> "I am the Alpha and the Omega," says the Lord God, "who is
> and who was and who is to come, the Almighty."
> *Revelation 1:8*

And he said to me, "It is done! I am the Alpha and the Omega, the beginning and the end. To the thirsty I will give from the spring of the water of life without payment."
Revelation 21:6

"I am the Alpha and the Omega, the first and the last, the beginning and the end."
Revelation 22:13

- He is the fulfillment of prophecy and the final high priest.

Then I turned to see the voice that was speaking to me, and on turning I saw seven golden lampstands, and in the midst of the lampstands one like a son of man, clothed with a long robe and with a golden sash around his chest.
Revelation 1:12-13

"I, Jesus, have sent my angel to testify to you about these things for the churches. I am the root and the descendant of David, the bright morning star."
Revelation 22:16

- He is infinitely old and infinitely _____.

The hairs of his head were white, like white wool, like snow. His eyes were like a flame of fire …
Revelation 1:14

- His purity has no error and His power knows no equal.

… his feet were like burnished bronze, refined in a furnace, and his voice was like the roar of many waters.
Revelation 1:15

- His voice resounds with authority and His _____ radiates with light.

In his right hand he held seven stars, from his mouth came a sharp two-edged sword, and his face was like the sun shining in full strength.
Revelation 1:16

- He had the first word in creation, and He will have the last word in creation.

When I saw him, I fell at his feet as though dead. But he laid his right hand on me, saying, "Fear not, I am the first and the last …"
Revelation 1:17

- He was dead for a time, but He is _____ for all time.

> *"... and the living one. I died, and behold I am alive forevermore,*
> *and I have the keys of Death and Hades."*
> Revelation 1:18

- He is the conquering Lion and the slaughtered Lamb.

> *And one of the elders said to me, "Weep no more; behold, the Lion of the tribe*
> *of Judah, the Root of David, has conquered, so that he can open the scroll and its*
> *seven seals." And between the throne and the four living creatures and among the*
> *elders I saw a Lamb standing, as though it had been slain, with seven horns and*
> *with seven eyes, which are the seven spirits of God sent out into all the earth.*
> Revelation 5:5-6

- His worth is undisputed, His work is unforgettable, and His worship is universal.

And he went and took the scroll from the right hand of him who was seated on the throne.
And when he had taken the scroll, the four living creatures and the twenty-four elders fell
down before the Lamb, each holding a harp, and golden bowls full of incense, which are
the prayers of the saints. And they sang a new song, saying, "Worthy are you to take the
scroll and to open its seals, for you were slain, and by your blood you ransomed people for
God from every tribe and language and people and nation, and you have made them a
kingdom and priests to our God, and they shall reign on the earth." Then I looked, and I
heard around the throne and the living creatures and the elders the voice of many angels,
numbering myriads of myriads and thousands of thousands, saying with a loud voice,
"Worthy is the Lamb who was slain, to receive power and wealth and wisdom and might
and honor and glory and blessing!" And I heard every creature in heaven and on earth
and under the earth and in the sea, and all that is in them, saying, "To him who sits on
the throne and to the Lamb be blessing and honor and glory and might forever and ever!"
And the four living creatures said, "Amen!" and the elders fell down and worshiped.
Revelation 5:7-14

- His birth declared the death of the ancient serpent, His death defanged the
  adversary, and His resurrection demolished every accusation against the church.

And a great sign appeared in heaven: a woman clothed with the sun, with the moon under
her feet, and on her head a crown of twelve stars. She was pregnant and was crying out in
birth pains and the agony of giving birth. And another sign appeared in heaven: behold,
a great red dragon, with seven heads and ten horns, and on his heads seven diadems.
His tail swept down a third of the stars of heaven and cast them to the earth. And the
dragon stood before the woman who was about to give birth, so that when she bore her
child he might devour it. She gave birth to a male child, one who is to rule all the nations
with a rod of iron, but her child was caught up to God and to his throne, and the woman
fled into the wilderness, where she has a place prepared by God, in which she is to be
nourished for 1,260 days. Now war arose in heaven, Michael and his angels fighting
against the dragon. And the dragon and his angels fought back, but he was defeated, and

there was no longer any place for them in heaven. And the great dragon was thrown down, that ancient serpent, who is called the devil and Satan, the deceiver of the whole world—he was thrown down to the earth, and his angels were thrown down with him. And I heard a loud voice in heaven, saying, "Now the salvation and the power and the kingdom of our God and the authority of his Christ have come, for the accuser of our brothers has been thrown down, who accuses them day and night before our God."
Revelation 12:1-10

• He is _____ and true.

… and from Jesus Christ the faithful witness, the firstborn of the dead, and the ruler of kings on earth. To him who loves us and has freed us from our sins by his blood …
Revelation 1:5

"And to the angel of the church in Laodicea write: 'The words of the Amen, the faithful and true witness, the beginning of God's creation.'"
Revelation 3:14

And he said to me, "These words are trustworthy and true. And the Lord, the God of the spirits of the prophets, has sent his angel to show his servants what must soon take place."
Revelation 22:6

• He is the righteous Judge and Messianic Warrior.

Then I saw heaven opened, and behold, a white horse! The one sitting on it is called Faithful and True, and in righteousness he judges and makes war.
Revelation 19:11

• Many crowns adorn His head, and much mystery surrounds His name.

His eyes are like a flame of fire, and on his head are many diadems, and he has a name written that no one knows but himself.
Revelation 19:12

• He _____ God's enemies and He reveals God's Word.

He is clothed in a robe dipped in blood, and the name by which he is called is The Word of God. And the armies of heaven, arrayed in fine linen, white and pure, were following him on white horses.
Revelation 19:13-14

• He rules the nations of this world and He brings God's wrath upon this world.

*From his mouth comes a sharp sword with which to strike down the
nations, and he will rule them with a rod of iron. He will tread the
winepress of the fury of the wrath of God the Almighty.*
Revelation 19:15

• He is King of kings and Lord of lords.

*From his mouth comes a sharp sword with which to strike down the
nations, and he will rule them with a rod of iron. He will tread the
winepress of the fury of the wrath of God the Almighty.*
Revelation 19:15

• His grace is free and His joy is _____.

*The Spirit and the Bride say, "Come." And let the one who hears say, "Come." And let
the one who is thirsty come; let the one who desires take the water of life without price.*
Revelation 22:17

• He is the Savior who came once, and He is the Sovereign who is coming back soon.

*"And behold, I am coming soon. Blessed is the one who
keeps the words of the prophecy of this book."*
Revelation 22:7

*And he said to me, "Do not seal up the words of the
prophecy of this book, for the time is near."*
Revelation 22:10

*"Behold, I am coming soon, bringing my recompense with
me, to repay each one for what he has done."*
Revelation 22:12

He who testifies to these things says, "Surely I am coming soon." Amen. Come, Lord Jesus!
Revelation 22:20

• No one and nothing _____ to Him.

*"When you think of Jesus Christ, do you see him in all the ways that Revelation's
images portray him? When you think that you have hidden your sins well from
others, do you remember his eyes like flames? When fear grips your heart – fear
for yourself, your family, or Christ's church – do you fight that fear with the picture
of the rider on the white horse, against whom the devil's worst, last weapons are
impotent? When you are confused, not knowing whom to trust or which path to
take, do you hear the voice of the faithful witness ringing in your ears, 'These words
are faithful and true,' and do you turn expectantly to his words to find your way?*

When the accuser, though disbarred from heaven, renews his prosecution against your conscience, do you stand with John in awestruck wonder, gazing at the slain Lamb who poured out his blood to wash you clean and robe you in his own fine linen, bright and clean, to make you—yes, you!—God's precious treasure."
Dennis Johnson

6. We must see the church in all her _____.

"'He who has an ear, let him hear what the Spirit says to the churches.'"
Revelation 3:22

• We are His body.

"If one really wants to a see a theology for the church in action, one might walk into an old church graveyard at night. Walk about and see the headstones weathered and ground down by the elements. Contemplate the fact that beneath your feet are men and women who once had youthful skin and quick steps and hectic calendars but who are now piles of forgotten bones. Thank about the fact that the scattered teeth in the earth below you once sang hymns of hope—maybe 'When the Roll Is Called Up Yonder I'll Be There' or 'When We All Get to Heaven.' They are silent now. But while you are there, think about what every generation of Christians has held against the threat of sword and guillotine and chemical weaponry. This stillness will one day be interrupted by a shout from the eastern sky, a joyful call with a distinctly northern Galilean accent. And that's when life really gets interesting."
Russell Moore

• We are His _____.

"Let us rejoice and exult and give him the glory, for the marriage of the Lamb has come, and his Bride has made herself ready; it was granted her to clothe herself with fine linen, bright and pure"—for the fine linen is the righteous deeds of the saints.
Revelation 19:7-8

7. We must see our lives in proper _____.

• Fight against _____.

It is these who have not defiled themselves with women, for they are virgins. It is these who follow the Lamb wherever he goes. These have been redeemed from mankind as firstfruits for God and the Lamb, and in their mouth no lie was found, for they are blameless.
Revelation 14:4-5

  ○ Resist compromise.

"But I have a few things against you: you have some there who hold the teaching of Balaam, who taught Balak to put a stumbling block before the sons of Israel, so that they might eat food sacrificed to idols and practice sexual immorality. So also you have some who hold the teaching of the Nicolaitans. Therefore repent. If not, I will come to you soon and war against them with the sword of my mouth."
Revelation 2:14-16

"But I have this against you, that you tolerate that woman Jezebel, who calls herself a prophetess and is teaching and seducing my servants to practice sexual immorality and to eat food sacrificed to idols."
Revelation 2:20

○ Refuse complacency.

"But I have this against you, that you have abandoned the love you had at first. Remember therefore from where you have fallen; repent, and do the works you did at first. If not, I will come to you and remove your lampstand from its place, unless you repent."
Revelation 2:4-5

"And to the angel of the church in Sardis write: 'The words of him who has the seven spirits of God and the seven stars. I know your works. You have the reputation of being alive, but you are dead. Wake up, and strengthen what remains and is about to die, for I have not found your works complete in the sight of my God. Remember, then, what you received and heard. Keep it, and repent. If you will not wake up, I will come like a thief, and you will not know at what hour I will come against you.'"
Revelation 3:1-3

"And to the angel of the church in Laodicea write: 'The words of the Amen, the faithful and true witness, the beginning of God's creation. I know your works: you are neither cold nor hot. Would that you were either cold or hot! So, because you are lukewarm, and neither hot nor cold, I will spit you out of my mouth. For you say, I am rich, I have prospered, and I need nothing, not realizing that you are wretched, pitiable, poor, blind, and naked. I counsel you to buy from me gold refined by fire, so that you may be rich, and white garments so that you may clothe yourself and the shame of your nakedness may not be seen, and salve to anoint your eyes, so that you may see. Those whom I love, I reprove and discipline, so be zealous and repent.'"
Revelation 3:14-19

"The essence of lukewarmness is the statement, 'I need nothing.' The lukewarm are spiritually self-satisfied. To find out whether you are among that number, don't look into your head to see if you think that you are needy; rather, look at your prayer life. Do you seek the Lord earnestly and often in secret for deeper knowledge of Christ, for greater earnestness in prayer, for more boldness in witness, for sweeter

joy in the Holy Spirit, for deeper sorrow for sin, for warmer compassion for the
lost, for more divine power to love? Or is the coolness and perfunctoriness of your
prayer life Exhibit A that you are spiritually self-satisfied and lukewarm?"
John Piper

○ God promises blessing for the _____.

Blessed is the one who reads aloud the words of this prophecy, and blessed are those
who hear, and who keep what is written in it, for the time is near. Revelation 1:3

"And behold, I am coming soon. Blessed is the one who
keeps the words of the prophecy of this book."
Revelation 22:7

Blessed are those who wash their robes, so that they may have the right
to the tree of life and that they may enter the city by the gates.
Revelation 22:14

○ God promises judgment for those who _____ _____.

"Remember therefore from where you have fallen; repent, and do the works you did at first.
If not, I will come to you and remove your lampstand from its place, unless you repent."
Revelation 2:5

"Therefore repent. If not, I will come to you soon and war
against them with the sword of my mouth."
Revelation 2:16

"Behold, I will throw her onto a sickbed, and those who commit adultery with
her I will throw into great tribulation, unless they repent of her works ..."
Revelation 2:22

"Remember, then, what you received and heard. Keep it, and repent. If you will not wake
up, I will come like a thief, and you will not know at what hour I will come against you."
Revelation 3:3

"So, because you are lukewarm, and neither hot nor cold, I will spit you out of my mouth."
Revelation 3:16

- God gives warnings to Christians about falling away to keep Christians from falling away.

They went out from us, but they were not of us; for if they had been of us, they would have
continued with us. But they went out, that it might become plain that they all are not of us.
1 John 2:19

- By grace through faith, true followers of Christ _____ persevere to the end.

> Blessed be the God and Father of our Lord Jesus Christ! According to his great mercy, he has caused us to be born again to a living hope through the resurrection of Jesus Christ from the dead, to an inheritance that is imperishable, undefiled, and unfading, kept in heaven for you, who by God's power are being guarded through faith for a salvation ready to be revealed in the last time.
> 1 Peter 1:3-5

> "My sheep hear my voice, and I know them, and they follow me. I give them eternal life, and they will never perish, and no one will snatch them out of my hand. My Father, who has given them to me, is greater than all, and no one is able to snatch them out of the Father's hand."
> John 10:27-29

> In him you also, when you heard the word of truth, the gospel of your salvation, and believed in him, were sealed with the promised Holy Spirit, who is the guarantee of our inheritance until we acquire possession of it, to the praise of his glory.
> Ephesians 1:13-14

- By grace through faith, true followers of Christ _____ to persevere to the end.

> "But the one who endures to the end will be saved."
> Matthew 24:13

> For we have come to share in Christ, if indeed we hold our original confidence firm to the end.
> Hebrews 3:14

> For you have need of endurance, so that when you have done the will of God you may receive what is promised.
> Hebrews 10:36

• Endure amidst _____.

> If anyone has an ear, let him hear: If anyone is to be taken captive, to captivity he goes; if anyone is to be slain with the sword, with the sword must he be slain. Here is a call for the endurance and faith of the saints.
> Revelation 13:9-10

○ Do not be surprised by it.

*I, John, your brother and partner in the tribulation and the kingdom
and the patient endurance that are in Jesus, was on the island called
Patmos on account of the word of God and the testimony of Jesus.*
Revelation 1:9

*"If we close our eyes to Revelation's harshly realistic portrait of the church's life as one
of suffering and martyrdom, we will be caught off guard when pain, social rejection,
or even violent opposition break in upon our lives. Is it our intentional deafness to
Revelation's call to expect and endure suffering that leaves so many comfortable Western
churches and Christians ill-prepared to stand fast when life gets hard? Does this
explain their disappointment with God when he does not deliver the tranquil life they
expected and instead calls them to endure hardship – walking by faith, not sight?"*
Dennis Johnson

○ Do not be _____ in it.

*"'He who has an ear, let him hear what the Spirit says to the churches. To the one
who conquers I will grant to eat of the tree of life, which is in the paradise of God.'"*
Revelation 2:7

*"'He who has an ear, let him hear what the Spirit says to the churches.
The one who conquers will not be hurt by the second death.'"*
Revelation 2:11

*"'He who has an ear, let him hear what the Spirit says to the churches. To the one who
conquers I will give some of the hidden manna, and I will give him a white stone, with
a new name written on the stone that no one knows except the one who receives it.'"*
Revelation 2:17

*"'The one who conquers and who keeps my works until the end,
to him I will give authority over the nations ...'"*
Revelation 2:26

*"The one who conquers will be clothed thus in white garments, and I will never blot his
name out of the book of life. I will confess his name before my Father and before his angels."*
Revelation 3:5

*"The one who conquers, I will make him a pillar in the temple of my
God. Never shall he go out of it, and I will write on him the name of
my God, and the name of the city of my God, the new Jerusalem, which
comes down from my God out of heaven, and my own new name."*
Revelation 3:12

*"The one who conquers, I will grant him to sit with me on my throne, as
I also conquered and sat down with my Father on his throne."*
Revelation 3:21

- _____ the gospel of Christ.
  - Let's _____ passionately.

*Then I saw the seven angels who stand before God, and seven trumpets were given to them
And another angel came and stood at the altar with a golden censer, and he was given
much incense to offer with the prayers of all the saints on the golden altar before the throne
and the smoke of the incense, with the prayers of the saints, rose before God from the hand
of the angel. Then the angel took the censer and filled it with fire from the altar and threw
it on the earth, and there were peals of thunder, rumblings, flashes of lightning, and an
earthquake. Now the seven angels who had the seven trumpets prepared to blow them.*
Revelation 8:2-6

- Our cries go up.
- His kingdom comes down.

*"What are the real master-powers behind the world and what are the deeper
secrets of our destiny? Here is the astonishing answer: the prayers of the saints and
the fire of God. That means that more potent, more powerful than all the dark
and mighty powers let loose in [this] world, more powerful than anything else, is
the power of prayer set ablaze by the fire of God and cast upon the earth."*
John Piper

- Let's _____ sacrificially.
- Let's _____ confidently.
  - To everyone we know.
  - To the ends of the earth.
- Let's _____ willingly.

*I, John, your brother and partner in the tribulation and the kingdom
and the patient endurance that are in Jesus, was on the island called
Patmos on account of the word of God and the testimony of Jesus.*
Revelation 1:9

*When he opened the fifth seal, I saw under the altar the souls of those who
had been slain for the word of God and for the witness they had borne.*
Revelation 6:9

*Then the dragon became furious with the woman and went off to make war
on the rest of her offspring, on those who keep the commandments of God
and hold to the testimony of Jesus. And he stood on the sand of the sea.*
Revelation 12:17

Then I saw thrones, and seated on them were those to whom the authority to judge was committed. Also I saw the souls of those who had been beheaded for the testimony of Jesus and for the word of God, and those who had not worshiped the beast or its image and had not received its mark on their foreheads or their hands. They came to life and reigned with Christ for a thousand years.

Revelation 20:4

_____ the coming of Christ.

This is now the second letter that I am writing to you, beloved. In both of them I am stirring up your sincere mind by way of reminder, that you should remember the predictions of the holy prophets and the commandment of the Lord and Savior through your apostles, knowing this first of all, that scoffers will come in the last days with scoffing, following their own sinful desires. They will say, "Where is the promise of his coming? For ever since the fathers fell asleep, all things are continuing as they were from the beginning of creation." For they deliberately overlook this fact, that the heavens existed long ago, and the earth was formed out of water and through water by the word of God, and that by means of these the world that then existed was deluged with water and perished. But by the same word the heavens and earth that now exist are stored up for fire, being kept until the day of judgment and destruction of the ungodly.

But do not overlook this one fact, beloved, that with the Lord one day is as a thousand years, and a thousand years as one day. The Lord is not slow to fulfill his promise as some count slowness, but is patient toward you, not wishing that any should perish, but that all should reach repentance. But the day of the Lord will come like a thief, and then the heavens will pass away with a roar, and the heavenly bodies will be burned up and dissolved, and the earth and the works that are done on it will be exposed. Since all these things are thus to be dissolved, what sort of people ought you to be in lives of holiness and godliness, waiting for and hastening the coming of the day of God, because of which the heavens will be set on fire and dissolved, and the heavenly bodies will melt as they burn! But according to his promise we are waiting for new heavens and a new earth in which righteousness dwells.

Therefore, beloved, since you are waiting for these, be diligent to be found by him without spot or blemish, and at peace. And count the patience of our Lord as salvation, just as our beloved brother Paul also wrote to you according to the wisdom given him, as he does in all his letters when he speaks in them of these matters. There are some things in them that are hard to understand, which the ignorant and unstable twist to their own destruction, as they do the other Scriptures. You therefore, beloved, knowing this beforehand, take care that you are not carried away with the error of lawless people and lose your own stability. But grow in the grace and knowledge of our Lord and Savior Jesus Christ. To him be the glory both now and to the day of eternity. Amen.

2 Peter 3:1-18

o God, give us unwavering _____ in this world …

"Believing that further delay would be sinful, some of God's insignificants and nobodie in particular, but trusting in our Omnipotent God, have decided on certain simple line according to the Book of God, to make a definite attempt to render the evangelization of the world an accomplished fact …. Too long have we been waiting for one another to begin! The time for waiting is past! The hour of God has struck! In God's holy name let us arise and build! We will not build on the sand, but on the bedrock sayings of Christ, and the gates and minions of hell shall not prevail against us. Should such men as we fear? Before the whole world, aye, before the sleepy, lukewarm, faithless, namby-pamby Christian world, we will dare to trust our God, we will venture our all for Him, we will live and we will die for Him, and we will do it with His joy unspeakable singing aloud in our hearts. We will a thousand times sooner die trusting only in our God than live trusting in man. And when we come to this position the battle is already won, and the end of the glorious campaign in sight. We will have the real Holiness of God, not the sickly stuff of talk and dainty words and pretty thoughts; we will have [real] Holiness, one of daring faith and works for Jesus Christ."
C.T. Studd

o With unshakeable _____ in the world to come.

"The things that began to happen after that were so great and beautiful that I cannot write them. And for us this is the end of all the stories, and we can most truly say that they all lived happily ever after. But for them it was only the beginning of the real story. All their life in this world and all their adventures in Narnia had only been the cover and the title page: now at last they were beginning Chapter One of the Great Story which no one on earth has read: which goes on forever: in which every chapter is better than the one before."
"The Last Battle," C.S. Lewis

He who testifies to these things says, "Surely I am coming soon." Amen.
Come, Lord Jesus! The grace of the Lord Jesus be with all. Amen.
Revelation 22:20-21

Recommended Reading

If you are interested in exploring specific topics from our Secret Church gathering further, the following resources are recommended. Many of these resources were foundational for the truths we explored in our study. Please note, however, that though these books are recommended, Dr. Platt does not necessarily agree with everything written in every one of them. We urge you to read and learn from these books, but at the same time, to filter them through the truth of God's Word.

GENERAL THEOLOGY
- Wayne Grudem, *Systematic Theology*
- Danny Akin, ed., *Theology for the Church*
- Millard Erickson, *Christian Theology*

GENERAL ESCHATOLOGY
- Millard Erickson, *A Basic Guide to Eschatology*
- Robert Clouse, ed., *The Meaning of the Millennium: Four Views*
- Stan Gundry and Darrell Bock, eds., *Three Views of the Millennium and Beyond*
- Stan Gundry and Gleason Archer, eds., *Three Views on the Rapture*
- Anthony Hoekema, *The Bible and the Future*
- George Ladd, *The Blessed Hope*
- Hank Hanegraff, *Resurrection*

HEAVEN
- Randy Alcorn, *Heaven*
- John MacArthur, *The Glory of Heaven*
- Paul Enns, *Heaven Revealed*

HELL
- Francis Chan, *Erasing Hell*
- Ajith Fernando, *Crucial Questions About Hell*
- Christopher Morgan and Robert Peterson, *Hell Under Fire*

REVELATION
- Grant Osborne, *Baker Exegetical Commentary on the New Testament: Revelation*
- Dennis Johnson, *Triumph of the Lamb*
- William Hendriksen, *More Than Conquerors*
- George Ladd, *A Commentary on the Revelation of John*

Pray for the Hui

China, the world's most populated country of more than 1.3 billion people and over 500 indigenous ethnic groups, is quickly emerging as one of the great global powers of our time. With a growing economy and a leading role in global finance, China is pivotal in shaping our world in the 21st century. But like every strong nation, they are not exempt from wrongs. China's record with privacy issues, unsustainable growth, materialism, human rights, and the suppression of minority groups continues to present challenges for the global community as China rises to power.

Suppression and strict administrative control of the five officially recognized religious groups (Buddhism, Daoism, Islam, Protestant, Catholic) have characterized Communist rule. During The Cultural Revolution of the 1960s and 1970s, all religious activities were forced underground, giving birth to the house church movement. As restrictions eased in 1978, the growth of the church in China happened so fast and with such strength that even severe persecution and cruelties only encouraged the church and gospel to flourish.

Operation World states, "More Christians are detained in China than in any other country, but many regard the persecution of house churches as an issue of political control rather than of religious freedom" (OW p. 215). God refines and strengthens His church through persecution, and today there are estimated to be over 75 million Evangelical Christians in China. Moreover, a significant number of missionaries are now being sent from China. Although persecution still continues, the government has begun to recognize such growth and to engage leaders of the underground church. While this new reality is encouraging, one of the greatest challenges now is that most of the church growth has been among the majority Han with significantly less growth among minority peoples.

As we gather, we want to focus our attention on these minority peoples, specifically Chinese Muslims. More than 24 million Muslims live across China, 13 million of whom identify themselves ethnically as Hui, Salar or Dongxiang. Chinese Muslims trace their roots back to Muslim traders, soldiers and officials who came to China along the Silk Road between the 7th and 14th centuries. Over the centuries they settled and intermarried with the Han Chinese. Today, most Chinese Muslims make their homeland in Northwest China; however, Hui families are scattered all over China and live in every province.

Since the 1800s, Christians have intentionally planted their lives among the Hui, yet today there are still fewer than a thousand followers of Christ. Among the Hui, persecution looks different than the political pressure the underground church has experienced in the rest of China. The few Hui believers that do exist experience pressure and persecution primarily from their families and communities. This is especially complex because Hui identity is tied to being Muslim. In this culture, to be Hui is to be Muslim and to be Muslim is to be Hui. Because of such strong Islamic identity, many new Hui believers experience isolation, rejection and in a few circumstances even death as a result of becoming a Christian.

With so few Christians, most Hui believers are fearful to share the gospel with their friends and family. Therefore, they are either forced to join the Han church—extracting them from their original culture—or forced to live in isolation within their own culture. As a result, church planting among Chinese Muslims is difficult and complex, and the workers are few. Together we have the privilege to pray for the few Hui believers living in China and for God's Spirit to move among this people group and open their eyes and hearts to salvation through Christ.

How to Pray for the Hui

- Praise God for what he is doing among the Hui. Although there are still very few believers among the Hui, there is renewed interest from both Han Chinese and Christians from around the world to share the gospel and help establish Hui churches where they do not exist.

- Hui identity is deeply tied to Muslim identity. To be Hui is to the Muslim, so technically one cannot be both Hui and Christian. Most Hui who become Christians assimilate into Chinese churches and lose their Hui identity. Extraction from their community only leaves that community with no followers of Christ to share with their friends and family. Pray for a movement to Christ that allows Hui to follow Jesus and retain their cultural distinctives so the establishment of healthy multiplying Hui churches might become a reality.

- The Bible and other Christian resources are being adapted to Hui terminology. Pray for the gospel to be appropriately expressed without losing the change of allegiance demanded by following Christ.

- Pray for the Han Chinese Christians to be sensitive and humble as they are mobilized to share with their Muslim neighbors. Past and present episodes of enmity generate attitudes of suspicion and mistrust from Hui towards the majority Han. Outreach therefore demands Han Christians to have great cultural sensitivity and humility when engaging and sharing the gospel with Hui. Pray for Han Christians to follow Christ's example when they share.

- Pray for the few Hui Christians who face pressures from their families to return to their Muslim religion. Pray for boldness and sensitivity for the believers who have been ostracized from the community and sometimes from their families. Pray they will remain faithful to share the gospel despite the cost.

- Ask God to increasingly establish faithful followers of Jesus among the Hui so that they might be examples of godliness and bearers of hope in difficult situations.

- Ask the Lord to establish and raise up strong local churches among the Hui and use Hui believers to share the gospel and make disciples among other Muslim people groups and all nations.

For more stories, information and ways to pray for the Hui visit www.pray4hui.com

The Church at Brook Hills

you are a guest of The Church at Brook Hills tonight, we would like to extend a ecial welcome to you. If you are not a part of a local church in the Birmingham ea, we invite you to join us for one of our Worship Gatherings. Below is our regular unday schedule. Each of the worship gatherings on Sunday are identical (i.e., the me worship gathering at 9:00am, 11:00am and 6:00pm).

UNDAY SCHEDULE

8:00am	Adult Small Groups
9:00am	Small Groups for all ages
	Worship Gathering
11:00am	Small Groups for all ages
	Worship Gathering
6:00pm	Worship Gathering

MALL GROUPS

ook Hills Small Groups gather weekly to make disciples in the context of ationships with one another. These groups meet at various times throughout the ek, and there is a group meeting just about anytime on any day throughout the y. Some meet on the church campus on Sundays and others meet in homes or area thering places during the week—so we're pretty confident there's one near you at a ae and day that will fit your schedule and/or family.

r a complete listing of Small Group opportunities, you can visit us online at ookHills.org/local or stop by the Welcome Desk in the lobby at Brook Hills for istance in connecting with a Small Group.

r more information about The Church at Brook Hills visit our website, BrookHills.org.

About The Teacher

Dr. David Platt is deeply devoted to Christ and His Word. David's first love in ministry is disciple-making – the simple, biblical model of teaching God's Word, mentoring others and sharing faith. He has traveled extensively to teach the Bible alongside church leaders throughout the United States and around the world. Atlanta natives, he and his wife Heather, made their home in New Orleans, until they were displaced by flooding following Hurricane Katrina, in 2005. In 2006 David became the Pastor of The Church at Brook Hills in Birmingham, Alabama.

A life-long learner, David has earned two undergraduate and three advanced degrees. He holds a Bachelor of Arts (B.A.) and Bachelor of Arts in Journalism (A.B.J.) from the University of Georgia, and a Master of Divinity (M.Div.), Master of Theology (Th.M) and Doctor of Philosophy (Ph.D) from New Orleans Baptist Theological Seminary. He has previously served at New Orleans Baptist Theological Seminary as Dean of Chapel and Assistant Professor of Expository Preaching and Apologetics and as Staff Evangelist at Edgewater Baptist Church in New Orleans. David has written several books, *Radical – Taking Back Your Faith from the American Dream*, *Radical Together – Unleashing the People of God for the Purpose of God* and most recently, *Follow Me: A Call to Die, A Call to Live*. He recently founded Radical (Radical.net), a ministry devoted to platforming and disseminating disciple-making resources, so that the gospel might be made known to the ends of the earth.

David and his wife, Heather, live in Birmingham with their children.

About Radical

Radical exists to serve the church in accomplishing the mission of Christ.

We long to see the church making disciples who make disciples who make disciples throughout the world – from our neighbors across the street to the unreached people groups across the globe – all for the glory of God.

Radical is a parachurch ministry that serves alongside the local church, providing multi-lingual biblical resources birthed in the context of a local church that we hope will support disciple-making in other local churches around the world.

Radical serves these churches by providing resources in multiple languages, organizing events, like Secret Church, and facilitating opportunities through multiple venues that all aim to encourage followers of Christ in the global purpose God has designed for us as His people. Many of our resources come from the ministry of David Platt, who serves as one of the pastors of The Church at Brook Hills in Birmingham, Alabama.

To learn more about Radical visit our website, Radical.net.

Additional Resources

PAST SECRET CHURCH RESOURCES
Past Secret Church resources (DVDs, CDs and Study Guides) are available for purchase at The Church at Brook Hills and online at Radical (Radical.net).

ONLINE RESOURCES
Secret Church resources, including audio and video recordings of the teaching sessions, downloadable study guides and links to additional information about the persecuted church, are available on the Secret Church web site (SecretChurch.org) and through the Radical website (Radical.net).

TRANSLATED RESOURCES
Secret Church resources and other message series have been translated into multiple languages. Audio recordings, transcripts, and study guides can be downloaded from the Radical website in the Resource Library (Radical.net). Current languages include Arabic, Spanish, Mandarin, Hindi, Indonesian, Russian, Farsi, French, Vietnamese, Thai, and Amharic. New resources and languages are continually being added.

BOOKS BY DAVID PLATT
David Platt is the author of several books: *Radical: Taking Back Your Faith from the American Dream*, *Radical Together: Unleashing the People of God for the Purpose of God* and most recently, *Follow Me: A Call to Die, A Call to Live*. These books are available online at Radical (Radical.net).

If you would like additional information about the books, visit RadicalTheBook.com and FollowMeBook.org. All proceeds from book sales go toward promoting the glory of Christ in all nations.

ADDITIONAL RESOURCES
Additional resources such as sermons, Small Group Guides, Family Worship Guides and more are available on the Radical website (Radical.net). Free, downloadable discipleship resources can be found at MultiplyMovement.com.

blished by LifeWay Press®, Nashville, Tennessee
inted in the United States of America

NOTES